CARY GRANT

The Light Touch

CARY GRANT

The Light Touch

LIONEL GODFREY

ST. MARTIN'S PRESS ● NEW YORK

Library of Congress Cataloging in Publication Data

Godfrey, Lionel.
  Cary Grant.

    1. Grant, Cary, 1904-   2. Moving-picture
actors and actresses—United States—Biography.
PN2287.G675G58   791.43′028′0924 [B]   81-8780
ISBN 0-312-12309-4   AACR2

10 9 8 7 6 5 4 3 2 1

First Edition

Contents

List of Illustrations

CREDITS

Ernest Kingdon, 1, 8, 17; G.H. Calvert, 3; S. Dawson Taylor, 5; R. St Clair Winter, 6; MGM, 9, 10, 24; RKO, 11, 12, 14, 15, 18, 19, 20; Columbia, 13; Warner Brothers, 16; United Artists, 21; Popper Photos, 22, 34, 35, 36, 37, 39, 40, 41; Paramount, 26, 32; Universal-Rank, 25, 33; Jack Garland Collection, 38, 44, 45; Bristol United Press, 43, 46; the remainder supplied by the author.

Acknowledgements

For their valuable assistance from both sides of the Atlantic, I should like to express my gratitude to the following:
Bob Bennett, Vera R. Bryant, Reg Buston, G.H. Calvert MA, Alice Davis, Doris H. Davis (née Guest), Nona Deakin, R.J.A. Dewdney, Geraldine Doughton, Georgia J. Douglas, G.B. Farnsworth and the staff of Bristol United Press Limited, Jack Garland, John Greenfield, L.E. Grogan, David Gunningham, Dora G. Hanney (née Morley), Peggy D. Hedges (née Sharp), Stella K. Hershan, Michael Hobbs, Mrs W.M. Howell, Eric W. Hutton, Mrs Samuel T. Katz, Ralph B. Jones, Elizabeth Joy, Eve Kellett, Pete Kent of *Movie Disc*, Ernest and May Kingdon, Marie Kingdon, Stan Kirkby, Kathleen Knight, Leonard C. Leslie, Madge Newton, Lillian Pearce, Captain E.L. Plunkett, Mrs G. Schofield, Mary Shenton, Guy Smith and his colleagues of BBC Radio Bristol, Joan Stone, S. Dawson Taylor, Eddie Tinker, Geraldine Ward (Mrs Dale L. Ward), Gertie Wilkins, Mary E. Williams, BA (Bristol City Archivist), Reece Winstone, FRPS, Robert St Clair Winter.

My special appreciation to Deborah Kerr for her generous co-operation.

LIONEL GODFREY

To
Jerry Warriner, Walter Burns, C.K. Dexter Haven, Leopold Dilg,
Jim Blandings, Noah Praetorius, John Robie, Roger O. Thornhill,
Peter Joshua and, of course, Devlin
multum in parvo

CARY GRANT

The Light Touch

Introduction

We live in the first great age of advertising and universal education — the one, our century's self-deluding expression of incurable and unjustified optimism, the other, a potent medium for the propagation of myths. The two combine most closely through their shared faiths in self-improvement and success by means of hard work. (Or, better yet, without the hard work.) "We grew up founding our dreams on the infinite promise of American advertising," wrote Zelda Fitzgerald. "I *still* believe that one can learn to play the piano by mail and that mud will give you a perfect complexion."

Perhaps we are no longer so naïve as to think that any infant may grow up to be the President of the United States, but we nevertheless dote on those children of our times who flatter our largely unscathed optimism. We love the great leap forward, the overnight success, the breath-taking reach that culminates in the bold, triumphant grasp. Because they are the embodiment of our faith, the vicarious realization of our dreams, we take for our legends and idols the 'ordinary' folk who turn into the beautiful people.

For the very young, these are frequently the rock stars who find fame and riches long before they have discovered talent and maturity, especially those shooting-stars that sometimes come and go leaving their admirers gasping at the ephemerality of it all.

For the somewhat older among us, though, movie stars remain the popular heroes and heroines who best demonstrate the century's conviction that almost anybody can do almost anything. There are outstanding exemplars and archetypes for us to respect and admire, their lustre undimmed even by death.

The untutored Swedish shopgirl who became Greta Garbo. The Tasmanian drifter and ne'er-do-well who vaulted to strutting fame as Errol Flynn. The unlikely, uncouth chrysalis from which emerged James Dean. The ambitious beauty who clawed her way from waitress to chorus-line to Broadway to stardom as Joan Crawford. The acrobat and floor-walker in the lingerie department of Marshall Fields' who became Burt Lancaster. The descendant of pure German stock, former school drop-out, mechanic, lumberjack and oil-rigger who surfaced as the all-American Clark Gable, artisan 'king' of a mythical kingdom. Norma Jean, whose messy, random life served only to enhance, by contrast, her luminous screen presence and who was apotheosized into simply Marilyn.

Or the unhappy child called Archie Leach who grew up to be the buoyant and suave Cary Grant.

Cary Grant ... Now *there* was a living endorsement of those ideas implicit in modern advertising and education. He was so personable, so talented, so easy to like, and he declared: "I know I'm sticking my neck out in saying this, and the ill-fortuned won't agree with me. But I do believe people can do practically anything they set out to do − if they apply themselves diligently and learn."

Should we not, then, reserve our special affection for one who pulled himself up by his own bootstraps? To do so is tempting − the more so as Archie Leach's self-improvement harmonizes with our notions of justice, of rewards proportionate to striving, and it aids us to shrug off such imponderables as luck and such less-imponderables as the thousands of aspirant Cary Grants who didn't make it.

Besides, nobody ever deserved success more than Cary Grant.

But one of his greatest gifts was to make it look easy. And it wasn't. Not really so easy. For most people, as Zelda Fitzgerald found out, it never is. Even if we overlook good fortune, it's not enough to be determined. You have to have talent.

Grant had it. It was always there, but he worked at it and developed it. Just how great it was is a matter for argument. "His range," carped one commentator, "must be the most limited of all the great matinée idols." Another offered the considered statement: "He is the best and most important actor in the history of the cinema."

Cary Grant has been retired these fifteen years, no doubt irrevocably. But as it always does with the great ones, the debate continues.

To that debate there are certain objective, factual and therefore undismissible foot-notes. In the days when motion pictures were made with and around stars, the preliminary attraction being the name above the title, twenty-eight Cary Grant movies played at Radio City Music Hall for a total of 113 weeks − a record that it would take a momentous reversal of social trends, at least, to eclipse.

In 1970, four years after he had retired with *Walk, Don't Run*, his seventy-second film, the US Academy of Motion Picture Arts and Sciences, in a gesture at once opaque and transparent, made him a special award for 'sheer brilliance'. On the one hand, the Academy's decision was inscrutable, since no specific picture was mentioned, Grant having previously failed to win a prize despite nominations in 1941 (*Penny Serenade*) and 1944 (*None But the Lonely Heart*). On the other hand, the Academy, notorious for its arbitrary and unpredictable selection, has evolved something of a tradition in making amends for ghastly oversights, and Cary Grant had certainly been owed some sort of formal recognition by his peers.

Despite these statistics, his achievement may be minimized; but it cannot be forgotten. Though he has not made a film since 1966, his pictures are watched avidly when they are re-shown on television or at revivals, and he is remembered not merely with affection but also with the special respect inspired by one unique in his field.

"Unique in his field ..." The phrase sounds pat and cautious; it has memorial overtones. But the field, as we shall see, was bigger than a baseball diamond, less circumscribed than a Greek amphitheatre, much wider than the bounds of any Hollywood typecasting.

1

A Bristol Childhood

Dumped down without warning in the modern centre of Bristol, a visitor would have no idea which British town or city he found himself in. In common with many other places, whether they were blitzed in the Second World War or not, Bristol has undergone wholesale redevelopment since that event, and much of its central area has the anonymity and characterlessness for which postwar planning has become notorious. The stranger would stare at the façades of Woolworths, Marks and Spencers and Boots the Chemists, at once familiar and ubiquitously uniform, to be found in almost every small and large town in England; he would inspect the gauntly paved traffic-free precincts and wonder whether he was in Manchester, Coventry or a suburb of London; he would eye the skyline and, unless he were an expert in church architecture, find few clues with which to orientate himself.

If, however, the hypothetical stranger were to walk for two minutes in any direction, he would encounter features that, even if they did not immediately identify the city as Bristol for him, would at least indicate a town with a distinct flavour and a colourful antiquity. Its streets and buildings have a quirkiness and eccentricity that would be hard to rival elsewhere – even in the British Isles, the home of such qualities. Ancient public houses, quaint alleys and steep flights of stone steps provide a whiff of history. Park Street rises sharply from the quay and floating harbour, where the SS *Britain*, Brunel's iron ship of 1838, is moored. At the top end of Park Street is the university, opened in 1925 by King George V and modern by local standards; near the bottom end is the twelfth-century cathedral. The city is noted for its early nineteenth- and eighteenth-century terraces, as well as for fine examples of Victorian industrial architecture.

The big new hotels that dominate the older areas do so as interlopers and, by contrast, remind us that Bristol has a long, famous history, both as a city and as a seaport on the River Avon seven miles from the Bristol Channel. Since the Middle Ages, Bristol has imported wine from Bordeaux and Spain. Trade with the Americas flourished in the seventeenth and eighteenth centuries. With more than a modicum of justification, some have called the city "the birthplace of America". In 1497, John Cabot and his son, having sailed from Bristol, discovered the mainland of America, and Bristol was also the home of William Penn, the founder and developer of Pennsylvania. More than twenty communities in the United States, it is estimated, are named for the English city.

There were other famous sons of Bristol who had their chapters, large or small, in history. But for all the significance of the Penns and the Cabots, none other has been so popular or has meant so much to ordinary people the world over as Cary Grant — film star, matinée idol, tireless bon vivant, heart-throb of five decades. Historians may deplore the fact, puritans gnash their teeth at it. But it is the truth for thousands of folk who never heard of Penn or Cabot or who believe that Bristol Cream must be a dairy product.

Bristol is the home of Cary Grant.

Or was.

And if this city really was the birthplace of America, what more fitting than that one of America's legendary motion picture stars should have been born and bred in Bristol?

In 1974, his friends made plans to celebrate Grant's seventieth birthday, but they were disappointed when he declined to co-operate, giving as his reason his own uncertainty about his exact age. His birth records, he said, had been destroyed in Bristol during the Second World War. Such documents are kept centrally, however, at the General Register Office in London, and the truth, which may be verified at that source, is exactly as it is presented in the reference books. He was born as Archibald Alexander Leach on 18th January 1904, though his entry of birth gives the second name in its contracted form of Alec.

His father was Elias Leach, a tailor's presser by trade, and his mother was Elsie Kingdon Leach. Almost without exception, her family-name of Kingdon has since appeared in print as 'Kingdom', and even the registrar managed, after altering his first mis-spelling, to write 'Kingsdon' on the birth certificate.

The family lived at 15 Hughenden Road, Horfield — a sturdily built, terraced house in one of the maze of side streets off the main

Gloucester Road leading out of Bristol. By modern standards, the stone house was poorly heated by small coal fires in small fireplaces, and Archie Leach was born in the early hours of one of the coldest mornings in the year. As Cary Grant, he was to live literally and figuratively in near-perpetual sunshine and to be famous for his permanent tan — a striking contrast to his chilly start and the comparative privation of his early years.

Archie was born into an unhappy home, but not one without love and caring. As there had been an earlier child, a boy, who had died in infancy, his arrival was greeted with all the more joy. Archie was healthy, and he was to grow up with no major ailments. Elsie Leach, his mother, was delicate and shy, but she possessed a deceptive strength in her will to survive — strength that she would soon need in her rather sad life. Before her marriage, Elsie was the youngest left at home, where she looked after her parents. She had four brothers — Bill, Dave, Charles and Tom, who went to Alberta in Canada. Archie Leach inherited much from his mother, the most obvious physical trait being his cleft-chin. "His great assets were his humour and his movements — both Kingdon assets. The voice, the intonation of the voice, goes right through the Kingdon family. His father was rather a quiet-speaking man."[1]

Photographs show Elias James Leach to have been a handsome fellow, his features somewhat melancholy in repose, with an elaborate moustache. Outwardly, though, he was cheerful enough and something of a ladies' man. In later years, his son half guessed at and half remembered the frustrations of his father's predictable and unexciting existence. For there was little material progress to be made as a tailor's presser, and for most of his life Elias worked for the same firm, Todd's Clothing Factory off Portland Square in much the same capacity, earning enough to keep his family decently clothed and the ever-hungry Archie well fed, but with little left over for life's luxuries. Elias lived in that state aptly called by Thoreau "quiet desperation", and during the first decade of his son's boyhood, the uneasy relationship between husband and wife deteriorated.

Both of them came from large families, and the young Archie met many relatives, nearly all of whom he was to forget, at least temporarily, when changed circumstances kept him away from Bristol for a long time. But all that was years ahead, and at the beginning of the century, Archie was a normal, lively boy, if not particularly happy. Just a minute away from his home in Hughenden Road was a park —

the first of many places where he flexed tiny muscles and fast growing limbs in what was to be an athletic boyhood, much of it spent outdoors.

As Bob Bennett, later a companion of Archie in the Boy Scouts, said recently: "In those days, people changed houses more frequently. There were a lot of houses to let. People never thought of buying a house."[2] By the time Archie was ten, the Leaches had rented a number of homes. The first move was a few years after his birth, to a more spacious house with, greatly to the boy's taste, a long garden in which Elias erected a swing. Or *was* that swing in the Leach's garden? The grown-up Cary Grant said so, but memory plays tricks. Dora Morley, a neighbour at Berkeley Road, Bishopston, had slightly contradictory recollections: "Archie liked to come into our garden and use our swing. I had a photo for years of him − I on the swing − which my mother took with her large box-camera on a stand. We always had to say 'pop' when she took the brass cap off ... Archie's mother was so nice and always singing about the house. I often used to pop down to the shops for her and do shopping, and she would give me sixpence."[3]

This was indeed the happiest period for the three Leaches. When he was four-and-a-half, Archie had gone to his first school, Bishop Road Junior School in Bishopston. England was not then the tight bureaucracy it has since become, and though five was the official starting age for primary education, children were frequently accepted earlier if schools had places for them. Elsie Leach had convinced herself that her son was bright beyond his years, and she was always ambitious for him − mainly, and perhaps predictably, in artistic and intellectual pursuits. Thus the young Archie was to be encouraged in both elocution and music, which were to play a significant part in his later life. (Ernest Kingdon, a cousin, has a revealing memory of an early Cary Grant visit to Bristol: "The second time, his mother was staying in Whiteladies Road in a flat, and I was there when he walked in, and that was the first time I knew he played the piano. I was playing the piano, which she always had, because *she intended him to be a pianist in the first place* [author's italics]. He had these lessons ... He's a very accomplished pianist. I remember I was playing the St Louis Blues. He said, 'I'll show you how to play it.' And he sat down and played it his way."[4]) In those days, though, and throughout Archie's youth, there were few signs of such talents maturing, the accent being more on physical accomplishment. When he first went to school, his great discovery was football, in which he was an agile goalkeeper who enjoyed both his prowess and the praise it sometimes earned from his team-mates.

Archie began to grow up quite rapidly – not least physically. (He was to stop growing at six feet two inches.) He could run errands for his mother and polish his own shoes. Like most other little boys of the period, he collected stamps for a while. Sometimes, after school, he would appear at Todd's Clothing Factory, where Mr A.E.C. Ivory was manager. One of his daughters still remembers Archie. She would occasionally be taken into Bristol for shopping by her mother, and after those excursions they would call at Todd's in the late afternoon and wait for Mr Ivory and then go home together. Whilst at the factory, she would meet Archie Leach (a year older than she), and they would both sit on the counter waiting for the factory to close, when Archie would be taken home by his father.[5]

At least once, though, Elias would try to better himself – by moving to another clothing firm in Southampton eighty miles away. The venture was ill-fated. He returned to Bristol after only a few months, and his reasons for going to Southampton in the first place, though they may only be guessed at, were doubtless not unconnected with marital problems.

Meanwhile, Archie and Elsie Leach had moved into 5 Seymour Avenue, Horfield, which Elias occupied from 1911 to 1915. Two young women, cousins of Archie, accompanied mother and son when they made the move, the new house being larger than the previous one. Archie was seven by this time, and though his progress at school was erratic, there was evidence that he had real ability, even if he often failed to realize its potential. He was given piano lessons by an easily irritated teacher, and he became fascinated by the cinema, especially the weekly serials, to which he rapidly became addicted, reliving the adventures with his playmates and yearning for the next week's episode. By the time he was nine, he had begun to study in earnest for a scholarship to a better school, but he was neither a model pupil nor a model son. Daydreaming about the films he had seen or speculating over the outcome of a favourite serial caused him to neglect his homework. As for any domestic misbehaviour, it might well have been attributed to tension within the home.

The progress of the marriage had never been smooth, and it became rougher as Archie approached his ninth year. Some of the friction inevitably revolved about him. When he was little, Elias would put the boy on a table to recite at parties, sometimes getting him out of bed at night for the purpose. Elsie did not take kindly to such stunts. On one occasion, "she tried to pull Archie off the table, and Elias pushed her away."[6]

A climax was approaching in the home at Seymour Avenue. Before it arrived, "Elsie had been through a very bad time ... Elias held parties and brought friends in. She objected to it."[7] Such conflict indicated deepening incompatibility, from whatever cause. Perhaps Elsie and Elias should never have married. Perhaps experience and events had soured a union of theoretically well-matched partners.

It might have seemed as though the open clashes and, possibly worse, the suppressed tension and hostility could go on indefinitely. But they could not.

Elias came home tired at the end of the day's work and had taken to going to bed early. The unease in the house was palpable. One afternoon, Archie returned from school to find that his mother was gone – though it took some time for the fact to sink in.

He was not to see her again for over twenty years.

2

Blemished Youth

For a nine-year-old, the unprecedented and unexpected development was all but incomprehensible. Nor was Archie encouraged to understand too readily. When he asked where his mother was, he was told she had gone away to a seaside resort not too far distant. The explanation seemed odd, but he accepted it: adults did all sorts of things that they did not feel called upon to justify to a small boy. As the weeks elapsed, however, and without his consciously reaching any conclusion, he accepted the permanence of Elsie Leach's absence and gradually became accustomed to returning from school to an empty house. He had not been struck a mortal blow; rather, he drifted around with vague feelings of loss, aware – if with a bearable sadness – that there was an emptiness at the centre of his life. Years went by, and his memories of his mother dimmed – not to be refreshed over two decades by the sight of her or the sound of her voice, let alone her presence beneath the same roof. Understandably, he moved closer, psychologically, to his father, who, for the adult Cary Grant, provided the most vivid parental recollections of his boyhood. With juvenile resilience, Archie Leach survived his loss, though it did not leave him unmarked, and in some ways it was worse than the clean severance of a bereavement.

Much later, he learned the truth. Elsie Leach had suffered a nervous breakdown and had been taken to a mental institution at Fishponds.

That she could not resume a normal existence for more than twenty years, that she should never be reunited with her husband (for good or ill), that she should be deprived of visits from or the sight of her son for over two decades may seem staggering to us in the 'eighties – like the ingredients of a Gothic novel, its events played out creepily to the accompaniment of gaslight. Today, no doubt, an Elsie Leach would be institutionalized, if at all, for a short time; a prescription for valium would deaden her misery; psychotherapists and marriage counsellors would move in; before long, she would be returned to a normal life.

But the early years of the century *were* the time of gaslight. Surrounded by ignorance and dread, mental illness carried an enormous stigma. There was certainly no general acceptance that it could afflict anyone, would probably afflict most people at some time during their lives and was very often curable. (The last truth was not always accepted by members of the medical profession themselves.) Not uncommonly, patients were shut away unnecessarily, sometimes for lengthy periods.

Archie was a young boy, and he could not be expected to know about such matters. Even if he had been told that his mother had had a nervous breakdown, he would not automatically have asked when she would return or, if the answer was vague or negative, *why* she was being kept in hospital.

Elsie Leach proved that she had resilience of her own that saw her through those years. "We used to go and visit her," Ernest Kingdon said, his short, declarative sentences illustrating her spirit. "She used to write beautiful letters asking why she could not be released ... She had her dancing-shoes sent to her because they had dances at the institute."[1]

Though with inevitable qualifications, life went on for Elsie, as it did for her husband and son. The female cousins moved away, and Elias and Archie went to live with Elias' mother in Picton Street, Montpelier, nearer to the centre of Bristol – in theory, so that someone would be in the house to look after the boy when he returned from school. In fact, however, Archie pretty much tended to himself and saw little of his grandmother, since she, on the one hand, and he and his father, on the other, occupied separate parts of the house. Saturday and Sunday breakfasts and lunches were the main times when all three of them gathered for a family meal; at other times, Archie foraged for himself in the kitchen.

'School' was now Fairfield Secondary, which, after having won a scholarship, Archie entered on 2nd September, 1915, the start of the new academic year. He had a so-called 'free place', and his school number was 993.

As the grown-up Cary Grant, he was fond of saying via his *Who's Who* entry that he had been educated at "Fairfield Academy, Somerset". While it was true that Bristol was at that time in Somerset, the county has rural and slightly misleading associations – since Fairfield School was and is in the midst of a densely urban area. As for 'academy', though the term is used in Scotland, it is all but unknown in England, except as used to dignify such titles as the Royal Academy of Dramatic Art. In short, whether they knew the school or not, Grant's *Who's Who* entry would mildly amuse English readers.

In external appearance, Fairfield School has changed scarcely at all in the sixty-odd years since Archie Leach last saw it. (*Archie* – let it be stressed; Cary Grant has seen it more recently.) Victorian and unwelcoming, it stands looking impressively ugly on an improbable triangular site defined by Fairfield, Fairlawn and Falkland Roads. To the north of it, tangential to one of the angles, runs a deep railway-cutting – a mysterious chasm that must have proved an irresistible lure to generations of schoolboys and some schoolgirls, too. At one end of Fairlawn Road, there is the Black Lion Theatrical Costumier – almost a reminder that Cary Grant once attended Fairfield School, certainly an attestation of the fact that Bristol is still a theatrical city.

In 1915, Archie Leach was eleven, and much of his life for the next two and a half years was to be centred on Fairfield. It is now a grammar school, but in those days the gap in secondary education between the so-called 'elementary' schools, to which admission was free, and the grammar schools, where most pupils were fee-paying, was filled by such establishments as Fairfield Secondary School. Of its kind, it was one of the best, and by any reckoning it was a good school. It had between three and four hundred pupils, and it was, surprisingly for the times, co-educational. It produced some fine scholars, most of the sixth-form boys entering the Civil Service.

Its first headmaster was Augustus Smith, BSc – known, behind his back, as 'Gussie' to all and sundry. He was an impressive but kindly figure, who would have cause to know Archie Leach well. Caning was much in vogue in those days, both for boys and girls, but though discipline was strict in the school and one girl was caned merely for eating an apple,[2] 'Gussie' Smith hated administering corporal punishment.[2] To Doris Guest, who was Headmaster's Clerk for two years and thought him a 'dear', he once said, mindful of how often they sent naughty pupils to him, "the staff are more trouble than all the children."[3]

The nation was at war, and at the end of Archie's first term at Fairfield, 'Gussie' Smith sent out a school Christmas card that contained a photograph of him in military uniform – possibly that of the school's cadet corps, which Archie desperately wanted to join. In that picture, the headmaster, despite his fierce moustache, looks much more scholarly and frail than he does stern or military. (Even so, one old Fairfieldian, Bob Bennett, remembered him as "a fatherly figure, but very strict".) Opposite the photograph is a message: "We are still in the throes of war, and my wish to all Fairfieldians at home and abroad is success to our cause, then Peace and Prosperity for the future. Yours sincerely, Aug. Smith." With or without a war, it seems unlikely today that a headmaster would send such a card, which evokes an age that has gone forever, less impersonal and with unquestioned values.

'Gussie' Smith became a familiar figure of authority to Archie, and he also learned to know well the rest of the staff: Henri Audcent, a teacher of French, as the name suggested; J.D. Arnold, who taught music; 'Maps' Madkins, who taught Geography and English; and the two Georges — Kendall and Senior. There were at least three women teachers — Miss Craigie, who was Scottish; Miss Truscott, who taught gymnastics; and Miss G.E. Quinton. The last named had gone all through the school as a pupil and then returned with an MA to teach there, leaving in 1921 to become senior Latin mistress at Kingswood Grammar School. "She had no time for Archie Leach," Doris Guest reported.[4] One of the most colourful characters on the staff was the gym instructor Henry Howard Hyatt — a name that he immortalized be invariably signing himself 'H₃'.

If Fairfield left its mark on Archie, as it did, he also left his mark on the school, and old Fairfieldians remember him well — and not just because he later became Cary Grant. Though he has been called by one of his classmates "a very happy boy" and "great fun at school",[5] there was another, less obvious side to his personality. He was "a good scholar" who "could soak things up", and his favourite subjects were art, geography, history and chemistry — the last an interest that led him, indirectly, to the theatre. Archie was, nevertheless, "always a naughty boy"[6] who was continually being sent up to the headmaster by one teacher because he upset the whole discipline of the class by making them laugh. "He used to stand on the mat outside," Doris Guest recalled, "and if Mr Smith wasn't there, I'd say, 'You here again?' More than once, I sent him back and said, 'I'll tell Mr Smith you came up. You go back to class and don't answer any questions' — Because you see, if this teacher said, 'Did you get a whacking?' ..."

Doris Guest was little older than most of the pupils at Fairfield School, which she herself had attended until the summer of 1916. For the next two years, she was Headmaster's Clerk — at first unpaid until

'Gussie' Smith insisted that, as she carried out the duties of a private secretary, she must be put on the payroll. Thereafter, she received the princely sum of fifteen shillings per week. In the early 'twenties, she was sports mistress at St Goar's Preparatory School in the Clifton district of Bristol, but Archie Leach gave her her baptism of fire at Fairfield School. She recalled: "We were very short-staffed at Fairfield once, and Mr Smith didn't know what to do, because Archie's class was without a teacher, without any supervision at all. Mr Smith said, 'Miss Guest, will you go down and just try to keep them in order?' Of course, I was seventeen or eighteen then. Somebody had set them some work to do, and it was the first time I had ever been in charge of a class. I said, 'Now get on with your work.' I was reading or writing or doing something. All of a sudden, a paper-pellet whizzed close to my ear. I didn't take any notice, but I kept watch, and up in the corner was Archie Leach with a catapult. He despatched another pellet. I said, 'Archibald Leach, bring that catapult to me.' He brought it out, and I said, 'I'm going to confiscate this.' I kept it, but much later the same day he saw me in the gym (because his class led out into the gymnasium hall), and he came up and said, 'Miss Guest, may I have my catapult?' 'You may have it back,' I said, 'if you promise never again to use it in class.' But I often wished I'd kept that catapult."[7]

When he entered the school, Archie was "a scruffy little boy", though there was "something very endearing and fascinating about him — a pathetic little figure" (and not so little; he was growing rapidly). "He had those big lovely eyes, and he always seemed to be plastered in ink. He was a lively boy, there was no doubt about that." Doris Guest "saved him from one whacking definitely and possibly from several."[8] Other contemporaries remembered his big voice and big laugh. Most agreed about the aura of pathos that his pranks and minor acts of delinquency could not entirely dispel. He might have been "a very happy boy" (though Cary Grant was not to remember him thus), but there were those who would recall "a poorly dressed lad running around the streets".

Of course, those were lean times for many people, and lots of boys, then and now, have been scruffy. But Archie lacked a mother's care, and it showed. Eddie Plunkett was one of the boys who played with him 'around the streets': "One day remains in my thoughts because Archie, sitting more or less chin-on-knees, in short trousers, with socks halfway down his legs — indeed, we were all like that — had a hole in his pants, and I remarked on it. Holes in pants and socks in

those days were commonplace, but we were happy kids. We most of
us had an idyllic life, as dads were at the war and loving mothers
didn't have the worries that they have today. We went in fear of the
policeman and park keepers in those halcyon days."⁹

The socks halfway down the legs strike an authentic note. English
schoolboys wore black or grey woollen stockings, turned down about
two inches below knees that were usually chapped, scarred or bruised.
Before he went to Fairfield, Archie had been accustomed to wearing
Eton collars – a celluloid one during the week and a linen one during
weekends. Although soft collars were permitted at school, the boys
were expected to wear the stiff Eton variety for formal occasions.

If Archie occasionally presented a bedraggled appearance ("He
wasn't one of the smartest boys – he was scruffy looking. But, then, a
little boy of twelve often is"), there nevertheless began in his early
teens a veritable obsession with cleanliness that was later to be
symbolized and epitomized by the white silk shirts, designed by Edith
Head and other famous names, that Cary Grant invariably wore in his
films.

Cleanliness and realism flourished at the same time. Through the
incidental expenses of school life, even with a 'free place', Archie
realized that one of his ambitions had to be relinquished. By gaining
other scholarships, he had hoped to go on to university, possibly even
Oxford or Cambridge. But books, fees and uniforms at Fairfield were
almost more than his father could afford. How could he or Archie
cope with the even greater incidental costs of varsity life? He shelved
his ambitions of higher academic accomplishments.

As well as figuratively, Fairfield School left its mark on him
physically. One winter day, he slipped on a slide in the ice-covered
playground and fell forward, snapping off a front tooth in the process.
Dentistry in England was not the skilled profession it has since
become, and in any case dental work cost money – the ever-short
commodity. Archie decided to have the remaining half extracted, and
his teeth obligingly grew to fill in the gap thus left. To this day, though
probably only an expert would detect the fact, Cary Grant has one
front tooth where most people have two.

Archie might frequently have been in trouble at school, but he was
useful to the larger society outside. Too young for the army, he served
as a junior air-raid warden. One vacation, he found work as a
messenger and guide at Southampton Docks, a restricted area at the
time, where he grew used to the sight of thousands of young men

embarking on transports for the battlefields of France — many of the youthful soldiers literally mere hours from death by drowning in the English Channel. German submarines were lying in wait. For all the sadness of these departures, this was an exciting time, the pitch of activity being all the more thrilling and mysterious for taking place at night.

Ships and sailing exerted their eternal fascination on a young mind. When he returned to Bristol, Archie would spend much of his spare time at the docks during a period when steamships, by sailing up the Avon, came right into the centre of the city. He even contemplated signing on as a cabin-boy on one of them, but, again, he was too young. Loneliness and restlessness, aggravated by his unsettled home life, were the itch in his soul. There was a bigger world than Bristol, and one day he would explore it. This was an ambition he confided in few.

Meanwhile, he at least felt valued for his war work, for which he was automatically considered qualified by virtue of the fact that he was a Boy Scout.

The Scout movement was in its infancy, having been founded in 1908 by Lt General Lord Baden-Powell. The baby was a lusty one, though, for Baden-Powell had toured the country on what amounted to a successful recruitment drive. One of those who heard of the movement and what it had to offer in the way of outdoor life, adventure and the acquisition of woodland skills was Archie Leach, who joined the First Bristol (YMCA) Troop, probably in 1913. He was not disappointed, for though the war came along almost immediately, he enjoyed the good-fellowship and the rough-and-tumble games. L.E. Grogan summarized the impact of the outbreak of hostilities on the fortunes of the troop: "This had been the finest and largest troop in the area, being made up of junior and senior troops, making in all about one hundred and fifty scouts. The 1914-18 War brought many changes, for all our scoutmasters — there were several — joined the armed forces, and having suffered the loss of premises, we were brought under the control of the Senior Patrol Leader, Vic Smith. Like many other activities, the troop declined. We lost our bugle-band, cycle-patrol, King's Scouts and Red Feather Scouts as the war years went on. On Saturdays, there used to be scouting games on the Downs or up over Purdown or similar places, and on more than one or two of these, Archie Leach would start out with the troop, but sometimes during the afternoon he and his particular pal would be missing, presumably after other game!"[10]

Archie was certainly "a lively youngster"* and "a very likable chap". One of the scouts who enjoyed his company then and later, after he had become Cary Grant, was Bob Bennett, who as an adult was a popular cartoonist on the *Bristol Evening Post* and is now in his eighties: "Scouts in those days went out every Saturday afternoon, complete with poles – the lot, you know. I was a patrol leader, but I don't think Archie had a stripe. I joined in 1913, and as far as I can remember, he was in the troop then. There weren't many troops in the suburbs then, and a lot of chaps interested in scouting went to the Central YMCA from all parts of Bristol. We originally met in the Central YMCA Hall in St James' Square. Whether they suggested the troop might move somewhere else, I'm not sure, but we went to several other headquarters. There was one halfway up the Croft in the Christian Science church, and we went to Portland Square for a time, which was the headquarters of the scout movement – 27 Portland Square. Archie must still have been living at Picton Street. I remember having a scrap with him several times in the 'wide games'. The idea was to put a woollen band on your arm, and if you broke the other chap's wool, he was dead. All scouts did this. We went to Leigh Woods usually. You'd see a chap hiding behind a bush and pounce and roll over with him – he with his arm in the air, and you with yours, trying not to get your wool snatched off. I remember a real 'wide game' was when the [whole] district was involved, and there was one I remember that I expect Archie was in.

"There was a king or a potentate of some kind with a certain route to take up through Coombe Dingle, and he had his scouts on ahead to clear the way, and then he followed. Actually, the 'potentate' was a parson who lived in St Andrew's Vicarage – the Rev. Havard Perkins. He was under a sort of canopy as the king, and before he could reach his destination, the other half of the scout troop had to bump this chap off somewhere along the route. So we hid ourselves in various positions with, I think, balls of cotton wool or something like that, possibly newspapers, and we had to hit the king. Of course, his spies moved up to make sure there were no opposing spies or ambushing parties *en route*. If you dodged them, you stood a good chance of getting in a shot at the king."[11]

---

* So lively that his after-school pranks provoked one adult to throw a bucket of water over him.

When Archie Leach was in the midst of his career as Cary Grant, he must have found the plot of one of his films at least, *Gunga Din*, strikingly reminiscent of those scouting fantasies he had acted out so strenuously a quarter of a century before. The young Archie's physique was sturdy then, but it was in his middle to late teens that he became outstandingly tall. During his schooldays, "He was about average height. He wasn't what you would call a big chap."

Ironically, Bob Bennett, though he vividly recalled Archie in the scouts, possessed no recollections of him at all at Fairfield School. The explanation was quite simple. No other social institution has a more rigidly organized stratification than a school, in which the pupils are not only separated through the school's selection procedures and the classes into which they are put but also self-segregated by their own exaggerated consciousness of age differences. Bob Bennett was older than Archie and of course in a higher class.

The freemasonry of the scouts was another matter, however, and outside school, the two boys were frequently together. One negative aspect of Archie's personality, made more remarkable by his later history, stuck in Bennett's mind: "He never talked of theatrical ambitions." When they eventually appeared, these were to surprise most of Archie's contemporaries. If he was interested in the cinema, so were a good many other youngsters. He took no part in amateur theatricals, but not surprisingly he and Bennett tried to transpose and imitate what they saw on the screen, which often seemed ideally suited to scouting games.

Bennett found a particularly agile hero to emulate: "There was a chap in films – I used to model my life on him. He had umpteen little tricks. When he was being chased, he'd suddenly fall down in front of his pursuer, and the other bloke would be knocked for six. I tried this out, and it was most successful. As Archie went to the same picture-house in Zetland Road (it later became the Scala cinema), in all probability he used the same stunt. This chap I imitated was Eddie Polar or Polo – this acrobatic chap in the film. When he was being chased, he'd run round a corner, and as his pursuer came along, he'd dive out full length in front of his feet. We used to do this. I remember nearly killing one chap."[12]

At this distance in history, with adolescents who are now more sophisticated (but not necessarily wiser or more alert to the promises of life), it is easy to deride the scouting movement, with its links to imperialism, its reinforcement of the male stereotype and its emphasis on a rather simple mind in a healthy body. For whole generations, though, it provided adventure, comradeship and the tolerant experience of communal existence that helped form men like Bob Bennett.

Something more, too: it encouraged the self-reliance that was already more than nascent in Archie Leach. "He was a bit of a loner," said Bennett.

Though Archie might not have regarded physical training as one of his favourite school subjects, he was athletic, if not greatly gifted in that direction, and 'H$_3$' (Henry Howard Hyatt) "was a very good gymnast". Self-reliance and physical proficiency in themselves added up to little, but there was taking place in those years the chance coalescence of random elements that would give thrust and drive to Archie's personality long before such powerful motivation was usually called for in one so young. It was not that Archie had shown special gifts; it was that his nature, restless and frustrated, needed to seize on whatever was available to shape a new life, an existence that had more to offer, perhaps, than either formal education or domestic circumstances that fell sadly short of the ideal.

One more ingredient remained to be added to the mix.

3

Nudged by Destiny?

Life at Picton Street had its ups and downs, and during one of the downs, the landlord called for the rent, which Elias Leach could not pay. As the arrears piled up, though, Elias offered the landlord a painting of lions in lieu of rent. It was thought that Elias himself had done the painting, but it seems more likely that it was executed by a relative, one of Archie's uncles, who painted for a circus and rented a room as a studio over a workshop in the Ashley Hill district.[1]

In itself of little account, the story is of more than passing interest to anyone attempting to explain Archie Leach's otherwise somewhat inexplicable enthusiasm for the theatre, which was to burgeon suddenly and to profound effect when he was thirteen. Of course, he had heard his father, in an untrained voice, sing music-hall songs, and his addiction to the cinema gobbled up much of his limited pocket-money. But an uncle who painted for the circus was different – the sort of coincidence that might have provided first-hand and intimate experience of the intoxication of sawdust and spangles.

If sheer lack of evidence leaves such ideas tantalizingly in the realm of speculation, there can be no doubt, however, about the most powerful stimulus of Archie's quite unheralded yet spectacularly potent absorption in the theatre.

One of his favourite subjects was chemistry, and at Fairfield School, he encountered an electrician who was helping out in the laboratory as a part-time assistant. He invited Archie to visit the Hippodrome Theatre, which had been built as recently as 1912 and seated nearly two thousand and in which he had installed the switchboard and lighting system. Archie jumped at the chance – not because he was particularly interested in the Hippodrome but because anything electrical had his instant curiosity as part of the miracle that was replacing gas.

All that casual expectation changed as soon as Archie got to the

Hippodrome's Saturday matinée, which he was allowed to watch from back-stage. Cary Grant has since used the word 'destiny' for that chance encounter with the electrician and the deep impression created by the colour, bustle, smells and excitement of a large modern theatre in full swing during the prime of live entertainment.

The adolescent Archie Leach had met his apocalyptic moment.

Thereafter, he began to haunt the Hippodrome and the Empire – though not so much the Theatre Royal. Years later, Cary Grant said, "The Theatre Royal was in a forbidden land then. The surrounding area was rife with drunkenness and prostitution. But I snuck in a couple of times to catch a particular show." Mrs Lillian Pearce, a classmate of Archie at Fairfield School, had an anecdote of those years. Largely because of clowning around, he continued to be sent out of the room. The young Lillian would be ordered to fetch him in, only to find that he had disappeared – "Probably to the Hippodrome".[2]

The electrician, a kindly family man who was much impressed by the enthusiasm he had triggered in Archie, found him a job of sorts at the Empire, where he became a general factotum for the men working the lights – a post that, given his age, was certainly unofficial and definitely unpaid. The boy became precociously wise in the ways of show-business folk, greedily absorbing the lore and superstitions of the theatre. The manager of the Empire probably thought that he could not lose by having so willing a helper around. Archie proved otherwise.

At one performance, he took control of the balcony spotlight while the Great David Devant, illusionist extraordinary, presented his magic act. Ill-briefed, Archie, unaware that the beam should have been centre-stage at all times, allowed it to wander, thus revealing mirrors that should have remained concealed and thereby ruining the trick. The welcome mat was withdrawn at the Empire as a result, but Archie, scarcely crushed, transferred himself back to the Hippodrome, where he became a familiar sight – the boy who was eager to run errands or deliver messages. Nevertheless, he was not beyond parental control, and if he was to keep out of hot water with his father he had to depart before the evening was very old.

All this time, it might have been guessed, he was racking his brains for a way to enter this enchanted world into which he had stumbled as a stranger and in which he was allowed to stay only as a visitor, tolerated for his services as what a later generation would call a 'gopher'. ("Hey, Archie, go for some cigarettes, will you?") Archie

Leach knew where he wanted to be in the theatre, too, and it was not
behind the scenes as a call-boy or a stagehand. He wanted to become
a performer. But how? There was no end, it seemed, to what he
couldn't do.

He could recite, of course, but hardly up to professional standards.
Though he knew some of the music-hall songs that Elias Leach would
sing as party pieces, renditions of such ditties by boy sopranos were
not in demand. He knew nothing of dancing or acting, juggling or
conjuring, and though he played the piano well enough for school
assembly, he could not, by any stretch of the imagination, have been
called an instrumentalist.

Then Archie was struck by an idea the shrewdness of which
presaged the later astuteness of Cary Grant. He had heard of Bob
Pender and his troupe of knockabout comedians – youthful acrobats
whose numbers were hard to maintain as the war continually skimmed
off the older ones for military service. Archie reasoned that Pender,
having difficulties in keeping the troupe at its full complement, would
not be too worried about lack of experience in a would-be recruit and
that he might also not question too seriously the statement that Archie
had reached the age of fourteen – the legal requirement for a working
lad. Accordingly, pretending to be Elias Leach for the purpose, Archie
wrote a letter to Bob Pender and enclosed a snapshot of himself. He
was, he told himself, tall for his years and looked older than he was.

Nervously, he waited for a reply, which, since it would be addressed
to Elias Leach, he would have to intercept before his father spotted it.
All went according to plan, and the purloined letter from Pender lived
up to Archie's most optimistic expectations. It expressed interest in
Mr Leach's son, suggested that he should go to Norwich – where the
troupe was currently engaged – for an interview, and enclosed the
train fare.

There were no other problems to solve. To a great extent, Archie
and his father lived parallel but separate lives, often leaving home at
the beginning of the day without seeing each other. The boy could
scarcely wait. In the end, he packed a bag, departed the house in the
middle of the night and caught an early-morning train to Norwich,
where he arrived at ten o'clock after a lengthy journey. He went
straight to the theatre to find Pender putting his performers through
the daily drill.

Bob Pender was about forty-four, a short, well built man who had
been famous as a Drury Lane clown and knew a great deal about the

theatre and the ways of young boys. To borrow a nautical expression, he ran a tight ship, helped to do so by his wife Margaret, a dancer who had once been ballet mistress at the Folies Bergère. Pender died in a Southend hospital in 1939 at the age of sixty-eight, having ended his career ingloriously, owning a toyshop in that town.

The complete professional, he looked Archie up and down and probably guessed immediately that the boy, if not actually under age, had written the letter signed "Elias Leach". Pender made a brisk decision. Archie could begin immediately as an apprentice to the troupe. With his father's approval, of course. Archie did not even have to submit to anything that might have been described as an audition.

If his spirits had been high earlier, he was now truly jubilant. His apprenticeship beginning without delay, he was taken to the lodgings in which the Penders and the youngest members of their troupe were staying. There commenced a new schooling, with tumbling and eccentric dancing coming first in the syllabus, followed by the arcane practices of make up. Beginners did not go straight on to the stage, as Archie learned with a resignation that was offset by his perception, even over a short time, of slow but recognizable improvement in the techniques he was being taught. The troupe moved on to Ipswich, where, having only just begun, his instruction was interrupted – but not before he had started to enjoy the flavour of his new existence and the pride of being a working-stiff (he earned his keep and ten shillings a week pocket-money).

Elias Leach was neither an indifferent parent nor a fool. It took him a mere ten days to catch up with his errant offspring, the necessary detective work causing him little trouble. Even so, he might have been expected to be angry. In fact, he rapidly established a rapport with Bob Pender that was no doubt aided by their discovery that they were both freemasons. Over a drink, they decided that Archie would have to return to Bristol to finish his education.

Without chastisement but sufficiently punished by sheer disappointment, Archie went back to Fairfield School as a celebrity – the boy who had run away to join the stage. Everyone, however, must have known that the title was only technically accurate; he had not even performed in front of an audience, because there had been no time for him to make his début.

Distinguished by this colourful episode, he continued also to be notorious for his bad behaviour – not vicious delinquency, but the hundred small infractions by which youngsters can run foul of teachers. His conduct came to a head, however, with one prank too many. Or did it?

The story told by Cary Grant was clear enough. Archie and another boy took it into their heads one afternoon to investigate the interior of the girls' lavatories. While Archie kept watch, his partner in crime made the first foray into the forbidden territory, but before Archie himself could follow suit, he was grabbed by one of the women teachers – powerful enough, whoever she was, to hold him, though the other boy escaped. (In her tightly compressed account of the events for *Photoplay* in the 'thirties, Julie Lang Hunt stated that Archie was expelled from school for the misdemeanour of another pupil, the identity of whom he refused to reveal as a matter of honour.)

In itself, this escapade was not inexcusable, but, according to Grant, coming as a culmination to a whole string of malefactions, it provoked 'Gussie' Smith, who was tired of seeing Archie Leach waiting outside his study, to the ultimate sanction. The next morning, Archie was called out in front of the whole school while the pupils were still assembled in the hall after prayers. Smith recited the entire catalogue of the boy's misdeeds before publicly expelling him. When Elias Leach got home from work that night, Archie broke the news to him.

Two aspects of this story are puzzling enough to provoke questions. After Archie had been sent packing in a near-ritual that would surely have struck terror into the hearts of the other pupils, why is it that it is so hard to find any of his contemporaries who remember the public expulsion? Among those who do, often with notable vagueness about detail, one at least, while recalling that Archie did stand on the platform with Augustus Smith in the presence of the whole school, refutes point-blank the notion that the headmaster itemized Archie's transgressions in terms such as "irresponsible and incorrigible". Would Smith, described as "a dear" by one who knew him well, have been capable of this act of calculated cruelty – especially for the prank described? (If rare, co-educational schools were by no means unknown in England, and that sort of 'crime' must have been familiar to them.)

Though to dismiss the recollections of the mature Cary Grant would be rash, our acceptance of the story of public expulsion might be modified by an understanding of its importance, relatively, to the different people involved. Naturally, the experience was disturbing, if not permanently wounding, to the youthful Archie. To many, perhaps most, of his fellow pupils, however, it was ordinary enough to be forgotten with ease. Remarks from Augustus Smith that weighed heavily on the sensitive Archie seemed unexceptionable to the rest of the school.

Another version of how Archie Leach left Fairfield Secondary is persuasive, if merely as a hypothesis. His record was not good, and his truancies had been repeated since his return from Ipswich. More than one member of staff had been exasperated by his conduct. It seems not impossible, as some of Archie's contemporaries assert, that Augustus Smith sent for Elias Leach and that the two of them talked matters over, reaching the conclusion that it might be best for all concerned if Archie, who had anyway attained the age of fourteen, should leave the school. Such an ending to his academic career might have been less dramatic than the reported expulsion, but it had the virtue of plausibility.

Archie Leach's severance from Fairfield School remains a matter of mystery, inviting speculation. "I have heard various accounts of the reason for his leaving the school," its present headmaster, G.H. Calvert, commented, "but have no reason to suppose that any one of them is truer than another. Probably only Mr Grant and the headmaster of the day knew the facts of the matter, and memories play tricks after sixty years."[3]

We are left with the fact that Archie left Fairfield Secondary on 13 March 1918, nearly two months after his fourteenth birthday.

Three days later, he had rejoined Bob Pender and his young knock-about comedians in a return that appeared unpredictable but could have been planned. His father certainly did not attempt to detain the boy, and there was no legal hindrance to his re-employment. Elias might have been saddened at the need for his son to be removed from school, but he recognized the validity of Archie's desires and that his heart was set on doing what he had previously been prevented from doing.

Just over two years later, his new life was to lead him to America.

In 1918, however, he left behind him acquaintances and fellow pupils shocked by his sudden departure and ill informed of the reasons for it. Garbled stories about him proved to be the stuff of legends. For the rest of their lives, some of his contemporaries reflected in their words and attitudes the legends rather than the truth. Thus: "He ran off because he wanted to do what he wanted to do. In these days, it would be called initiative."[4] (Fine – for the first excursion; the second time, he was not running away.) Or: "When he went to America, it all seemed to be a sudden decision. He left the troop and Fairfield School, and we scouts were led to believe the school headmaster had had talks with his parents [sic] and he had gone to farming-relations or friends in America."[5] (Interesting, but inaccurate as to detail.) "I know I had a cry when I heard he had run away to America so young." (Again the running away to America; and when Archie finally *did* reach America, he was sixteen — still young, but two years older than he was when he left Bristol in 1918.)

But perhaps the sadness, after all, struck the appropriate note. For even though Archie Leach had become infatuated with the theatre, it might have been said that the motherless boy was not going towards something eagerly but rather leaving behind things that he was not sorry to forget.

4

Rough and Tumble

He had one more visit to make, but otherwise he was bidding a long farewell to Bristol.

He resumed his training with the Penders, learning timing, the art of mime, how to control and 'work' an audience, as well as dancing, tumbling and stilt-walking. In the act, there was no dialogue, all emotions being conveyed by gesture and expression. Though he had no means of knowing it, Archie Leach was laying the groundwork of the formidable technique that would be used by Cary Grant.

Less than three months later, he was back at the Bristol Empire, but this time as part of the Bob Pender act. Backstage, his friends crowded round, and his father, who had watched from the audience, was reunited with Archie and filled with paternal pride at having seen him perform − not so well as he eventually would do, but as a practising member of the troupe. After the show, the two of them walked home together through the June night, and Cary Grant was to look back on that visit as one of the closest chapters in their relationship.

The Pender troupe toured the English provinces and played the Gulliver chain of music halls in London. If they were working 'in town', most of the boys stayed with Mr and Mrs Pender in the big house they owned in Brixton in South London. In those days, Brixton was a vast camp for performers who worked not so much in London as in the many theatres of the south coast. The area was crammed with 'digs' (short for 'diggings' or lodgings for actors), and anyone seeking a magician, a performing-dogs or fire-eating act, a juggler or a monocyclist, a singer of songs or a specialist in humorous monologues, had only to wander down Brixton High Street to find what he was looking for. It was a showbiz town, even though the term was not then current. In the large Pender home, the boys slept in a kind of dormitory and were kept to a fairly strict regimen, part of which was the drill or training exercises they were made to practise every morning.

Fourteen was an impressionable age, one at which a boy, besides being receptive to new methods and ideas, adopted with the unquestioning flexibility of youth, was apt to mimic and imitate, especially if by so doing he could gain ready acceptance with his peers. Most of the people with whom Archie associated doubtless had Cockney or at least London accents. The concentration of population in the South-east of England has always been fierce, and the results could be heard again and again in the accents of performers in the music halls and, to a lesser extent, in the legitimate theatre. (Even today, so great is the influence of London, home of the famous theatre schools, that it does not take a particularly keen ear to be amused by the numerous families in television commercials made up of parents speaking 'standard' English and children talking with pronounced Cockney accents.) Of course, Archie would hear all sorts of speech and dialects in his new life, but it is certain that he chiefly listened to the sounds of the south, more specifically London. He had only to step outside on to the streets of Brixton to be exposed instantly to that unmistakable style of talking – a matter of both vocal inflections and tricks. (He came to know well the Cockney's vast vocabulary of rhyming slang – 'apples and pears' for 'stairs', 'trouble and strife' for 'wife' and so on, shortened by real experts to 'apples' and 'trouble'.)

The effects of this exposure may be heard today in the speech of Cary Grant, which, besides being unique and therefore much imitated by entertainers, is tantalizingly strange to English ears. If there is comparatively little American in it, there is scarcely any of the English West Country, either. But it does reveal traces of those years working with Cockneys or near-Cockneys and associating with the people of southern England, who not only provided many of the music-hall artists but also popped up in large numbers in Hollywood during the early days of the colony.

The voice that Cary Grant the man was to inherit from Archie Leach the boy has mystified many, not least those who knew both him and the area in which he was born and raised. Ernest Kingdon put it this way: "He was trying to maintain English speech, and he had trouble with his diction ... I've given thought to this. People say, 'What makes him talk in that queer manner?' It's not cultured English talk ... A very precise talker, as if he'd been taught elocution."

The analysis was accurate, and the lack of "cultured English talk" helped to give vitality to his manner of speaking. Archie Leach absorbed much of the atmosphere in which he was maturing, later, as

Cary Grant, he taught performers such as Rosalind Russell, the Cockney and music-hall songs that became familiar to him. They were part of a process, one of the by-products of which was a special, unique voice that was to make Cary Grant instantly recognized, not to say loved, by generations of movie goers.

The war ended on 11th November 1918, a date that Archie remembered by the fact that the Penders were playing in Preston, Lancashire, where the news of the armistice was received without jubilation, many of the local families having lost menfolk during the hostilities. In like manner, he would recall that Christmas because he was at Colwyn Bay, Wales, walking on stilts in pantomime.

So the months went by, gradually stretching to over two years, during which he learned more and more and the Pender troupe was much in demand – so much so, in fact, that Bob Pender not only engaged more boys but also doubled Archie's pocket-money to an exhilarating one pound a week.

At last, Pender hit what might have been called the big time, and it meant an exciting trip to the United States. Charles Dillingham made an offer for Pender and eight out of the twelve boys to appear at the Globe Theatre, New York. Who should go and who should stay must have caused some flutterings of pulses, but Archie was one of those selected, and in July 1920, he joined the others sailing on the SS *Olympic* for America and adventure.

The adventure began before the ship even docked in New York, for on board were Douglas Fairbanks Sr and Mary Pickford, just married and, of course, the world's sweethearts. For the sixteen-year-old Archie, the encounter with the athletic, tanned Fairbanks was even more impressive than he realized at the time. Later, as a man, he was to emulate that healthy, bronzed appearance, without at first realizing upon whom he had modelled himself. He could scarcely have guessed, either, that the actor's son, also to become a famous moviestar, would one day be one of his valued friends. America might have been the land of opportunity, but whatever Archie's dreams were, they did not presume to such magnitude.

The Penders were fated never actually to play at the Globe Theatre, because the act was switched to the Hippodrome – a disappointment, at least at first, since they would have been in a show starring Fred Stone, the musical comedy star.

To Archie, everything in New York seemed bigger, louder, gaudier and more imposing than anything back home – at once, in a sensation experienced by most addicts of the cinema who visited the town, familiar and strange. Of all America's qualities, sheer size was perhaps the most difficult to cope with. Take the Hippodrome Theatre on Sixth Avenue. Archie wasn't to know at that time that it was the world's largest theatre; all he knew was that it was enormous – at least five times as large as its namesake back in Bristol. Among the statistics with which he had to grapple was the fact that the show in which they were appearing had one thousand performers plus eight hundred people who didn't actually work onstage. Small wonder that the boy at first felt lost.

He was given time to acclimatize. Their show, *Good Times*, ran for 456 performances, and during its run, Archie explored New York from end to end, often by means of the open-top buses that travelled for so many years along Fifth Avenue. Still closely supervised by Mr and Mrs Pender, the boys had a rota of duties to make communal and cramped living smoother, and Archie would occasionally find that it was his turn to cook, a skill he had acquired as a Boy Scout. His stew was a *specialité de la maison*. Archie was happy – a gregarious boy among people he liked, performing with confidence, making his way in the world with independence and a strong sense of expectation. For all their evils, the so-called Roaring Twenties were a bracing period.

After *Good Times* closed, the Penders embarked on a six-month tour of the Keith vaudeville circuit that took them to Chicago, Philadelphia, Boston and other cities of the east. In mid-1922, the tour closed on a climax, an appearance at the famed New York Palace. A big decision then faced Bob Pender and his troupe: without definite prospects, they could stay in the United States or they could return to England. In the end, that decision was not unanimous. Some of the members, including Archie and Pender's younger brother, decided to try their luck in America, while Bob Pender departed with a depleted company. To those who remained, he gave a sum equivalent to their return fare to England, and in later life, an honourable man, he indignantly refuted suggestions that he had abandoned any of his boys in the States.

Archie might have been full of vague hopes and dreams, but he found himself facing tough times that summer. In the midst of them, he met John Kelly, a young Australian who was later to achieve fame as Orry-Kelly, the Hollywood designer who won an Academy Award for *An American In Paris*. At that lean time, though, Kelly was hand painting neckties and selling them, an enterprise in which he enlisted Archie.

At eighteen, Archie discovered just how hard life could be in the land of opportunity. But at Coney Island, he found a job on stilts, carrying placards for $40 a week. At weekends, he claimed double rate because children would try to trip him up. For a short time, he also touted tickets in the amusement park for the tunnel of love.

Eventually, he joined other refugees from Pender's troupe for an act as part of *Better Times*, the sequel to *Good Times*, which opened on 2nd September 1922.

He had made two discoveries, the one sobering, the other encouraging. The search for work had made him acutely aware that he had never spoken on stage and that *there* was a bridge that had to be crossed sooner or later if his career was not to remain in vaudeville and at a strictly physical level. On the other hand, experience and self-knowledge informed him that he was what was usually described as an eligible young man. There had been valuable social lessons to be learned once he was on his own. Though America might have its snobberies, it was none the less more democratic than England, where a man would be labelled in less than five minutes by his accent, his clothes and a few questions about his education. Categories were rigid then and social distinctions emphatically made and carefully preserved. The same barriers were not to be found in America, where, in any case, he had the advantage of speaking English without the disadvantages of an American background that *could* have made him a victim of snobbery. Only an expert in English social gradations could have slotted him exactly into a niche. To everybody else, he was a tall, personable, well-spoken and well-educated young man with dark brown eyes and a fascinating chin – plus a not-too-definable something else, the 'presence' that his theatrical training and experience had given him. A Sherlock Holmes would have placed him in a moment, whereas the average American would have been easily impressed.

Already, the youthful Archie had found that he could be in demand as a 'spare man' for dinner. He realized that hostesses actively sought young fellows like him for their parties and that such occasions might be the stepping-stones, by offering the chance to meet influential people, to advancement or employment.

With the same act he had performed in "Better Times", he began

to tour extensively on the Pantages Circuit, playing t[...]
and even in Canada, but later, in 1924, the group dis[...]
of disagreements. Though Archie had saved quite [...]
during his steady employment, disillusionment at th[...]
strong that he could easily have returned to England with some or the
others.

Once the summer, the dreaded slack season, was over, his career
was coughing and spluttering and yet, in its own way, persisting. He
had already, after a fashion, learned to speak — 'planted' in the
audience as a member of a mind-reading act. He began to obtain work
as a 'feed' or straight man and later had regular bookings and toured
numerous small towns. At least he was not starving. As the mid-
'twenties loomed, he was living in a small room at the National
Vaudeville Artists' Club on West 46th Street, New York, and had a
fair standard of living. (About this time, it was later reported, Jean
Dalrymple, who was to be for a lengthy period director of New York's
City Centre, gave him a job at $75 per week in her vaudeville sketch,
The Woman Pays. Because of his walk, he was called 'Rubber Legs'.)

Then, with New York his base, Archie met Reginald Hammerstein,
a stage director and younger brother of Oscar Hammerstein II, who
suggested his true talent might lie in musical comedy. Receptive to the
hint, Archie took voice lessons and was engaged on a run-of-the-play
basis by Arthur Hammerstein, Reginald's uncle, for *Golden Dawn*, the
opening production of the new Hammerstein Theatre. The book and
lyrics of this were by Otto Harbach and Oscar Hammerstein II and
the music by Emmerich Kalman and Herbert Stothart. The show
starred Louise Hunter and Paul Gregory, and Archie had a small part
as an Australian prisoner of war and doubled as understudy of the
juvenile lead. A member of the chorus was George Brent. The
production opened on 30th November 1927, and ran for 184
performances and six months, during which Archie was paid $350 per
week.

Afterwards, Arthur Hammerstein re-engaged him for another
musical, *Polly*, and though one notice praised him for his "strong
masculine manner", he opened to bad reviews in Wilmington,
Delaware. The show reached Broadway, where it lasted for only
fifteen performances, but without Archie Leach, who was replaced.

These ups and downs might have been, and indeed were, tough, but
they were all part of the evolution of a professional who could take
hard knocks, avoid panic and hang on for the next — in theory, bigger

– break. One seemed to have arrived when Archie had the chance to take over the lead in Arthur Hammerstein and Florenz Ziegfeld's *Rosalie*, having been chosen by Marilyn Miller to replace the comedian Jack Donahue. However, because of strife between the producers, Archie's contract was sold to J.J. and Lee Shubert, the impresarios whose shows were famous for their pretty girls, and they kept him employed for most of the next three years, first by casting him with Jeanette MacDonald in *Boom Boom*, a musical by Werner Jansson and Fanny Mitchell, for appearing in which Archie received $450 per week, which was good money. After seventy-two performances at the Casino Theatre, the show closed, and both he and MacDonald were tested at Paramount's Astoria, Long Island, Studios, though no contracts were offered. Archie was told: "You're bow-legged, and your neck is too thick."

The Shuberts next put him into *A Wonderful Night*, Fanny Mitchell's reworking of *Die Fledermaus*, which ran for 125 performances during the first year of the depression, having opened immediately after the Wall Street crash. Archie played the male lead opposite Gladys Baxter. He afterwards starred in the road company of *The Street Singer*, the tour of which ended in the spring of 1931.

In July and August of that year, Archie sang and acted with J.J. Shubert's Municipal Opera of St Louis, Missouri — eighty-seven performances in the open air, with roles in such productions as *Rio Rita*, *Countess Maritza* and *The Three Musketeers*.

He had little to complain of. If his career seemed to have taken him over rather than he his career, he was receiving excellent pay of $300 to $400 per week. He had not planned to be a singer in musical comedy, but a singer he was. Then the Shuberts cast him as the lead, Cary Lockwood, in *Nikki*. The star of this was Fay Wray, who was married to John Monk Saunders, the play's author, and who, in 1933, was to find a permanent place in screen history clutched in the fist of King Kong. *Nikki* was an unsuccessful work, set to music, evolved from a magazine serial and a movie already made (*The Last Flight*, First National, 1931) about aviators in Paris after the war. Archie's role had been played on celluloid by Richard Barthelmess. The production opened at the Longacre Theatre, New York, but lasted only thirty-nine performances.

Archie was becoming as used to these disappointments as he would ever be, and so he was not unduly put off by the next development — at once auspicious and abortive. He was cast as an American sailor in a

Paramount one-reel filler, *Singapore Sue*, written and directed by Casey Robinson, later to be one of Hollywood's greatest screen-writing talents. Impressed by the young actor's potential, Robinson wrote to Hollywood drawing the attention of studio executives to the relatively unknown Archie Leach. Nothing happened. As for the movie, it was not released until 1932, after a new star called Cary Grant had already appeared in feature movies.

Following three years' work, Archie decided to take a break and to drive with a composer friend to California, that golden land he had already seen on vaudeville tours and in which he knew glittering opportunities existed. Once there, he enjoyed himself. According to Robert Lord he was a frequent visitor to William Randolph Hearst's San Simeon, where he found himself attracted to Marion Davies, who was watched by guards supposed to keep her away from both liquor and the more eligible males, among whom Archie was definitely to be counted. With Lord, a producer who was then planning Davies' *Page Miss Glory* (1935), he played many games of tennis on San Simeon's superb composition courts.[1]

Before he broke into motion pictures, Archie had only a short wait. Through a contact, he met Marion Gering in December 1931. Gering was a former Broadway stage-director, then thirty, of Polish-Russian extraction, who had been in America only five years. He needed an actor to play opposite his wife in a screen test, and Archie seemed to have the necessary qualifications. When the test was made at Paramount, however, though Mrs Gering failed to impress, Archie was offered a long-term contract.

He was both surprised and yet not surprised. With hindsight, he would tend to talk of the fate that had taken him first to America and then to California. The truth, it might have been argued, was somewhat more prosaic. Chance had taken him to America, where hunger put an edge on his ambition. That ambition was vague and ill-defined. For example, though he was not about to turn down a career in movies, he had no clear idea of what he wanted to do – what sort of performer, if the studio would permit him, he intended to be. Nobody as astute as Archie Leach was becoming could have been blind to the possibility of work in front of the cameras. On the other hand, he had not counted on it. After failing one screen test and seeing nothing come from his role in *Singapore Sue*, he had certainly not set his mind on a long-term contract and had indeed taken care to leave open a road back to the New York stage.

If destiny *was* to be evoked, destiny pushed Archie, not vice versa. Merely wanting was not enough; luck had something to do with it. And though success fed Archie's ambitions, they had not been so well nourished to begin with.

He was too intelligent, though, not to see the infinite possibilities that now opened up for him. Many young hopefuls failed, and long-term contracts could be terminated – the power of the studios appeared to be unlimited. But if ever there was a time to work and strive, this was it.

One change had to be made immediately. Paramount, perhaps understandably, were dissatisfied with the name Archie Leach, which might have served adequately a knockabout comedian in vaudeville but ill suited the romantic leading man they had in mind. The name would have to go.

In January 1932 he was given a new name in two stages. First, over dinner one night, Fay Wray and her husband suggested Cary Lockwood, the name of the character Archie had played opposite Fay in *Nikki*. The studio, however, while agreeable to Cary, objected to the surname because there was at that time a Harold Lockwood in films, and confusion was to be avoided. Running his finger down a list the studio kept for occasions like this one, an executive selected Grant. When the choice was made, nobody seemed to be mindful of the fact that Paramount employed a big star called Gary Cooper – and that 'Cary Grant' presented the very opportunity for confusion they were anxious to avoid.

Nevertheless, Cary Grant it was. Long live Cary Grant. Archie Leach was not dead, of course, but the new name, if not identity, was fitting for what its owner sensed to be a great new chapter – or perhaps a series of chapters – that would carry him far beyond the most romantically unrealistic dreams of little Archie Leach of Bristol.

A late picture of Cary Grant's mother with his cousin Ernest's wife, May

The house in which Archie Leach was born

Fairfield School yesterday

Fairfield School today

Archie on parade (left, with sleeves rolled up) with 1st Bristol (YMCA) Scouts

School group; Archie Leach front right; 'H$_3$' in foreground

The Hippodrome Theatre, Bristol, today

Kingdon family reunion in London in the 'thirties; Grant in foreground

Billie Burke, Alan Mowbray and Grant in *Topper* (1937)

Roland Young, Constance Bennett and Grant in *Topper*

Victor McLaglen, Cary Grant and Sam Jaffe in *Gunga Din* (1939)

Ann Evers, Grant, Joan Fontaine and Douglas Fairbanks Jnr in *Gunga Din*

Grant and Jean Arthur in *Only Angels Have Wings* (1939)

In Name Only (1939) with Carole Lombard and Kay Francis

In Name Only (1939) with Carole Lombard

Grant with Jean Adair and Josephine Hull in *Arsenic and Old Lace* (1944)

5

She Done Him Right

The Hollywood of the 'thirties in which Cary Grant was soon to be a prominent figure was as prolific as it was lavishly endowed with talent. If there had been a slump in the movie business earlier, the advent of sound or, more specifically, the release of *The Jazz Singer* in 1927 had immediately lured back audiences who were staying at home to listen to the radio, and by 1932 the motion picture industry was moving into high gear. The coming of speech to the medium had ruined some, most notably John Gilbert, but Hollywood was more than learning to live with its new dimension. The effects of the Wall Street crash were still being felt, and yet memories of the terrible event, which had hit movie-makers in the West as well as more conventional businessmen in the East, were already receding. Furthermore, audiences were exhibiting, in the midst of the Great Depression, a seemingly limitless hunger for the products of Hollywood. Newcomers flooded into the colony — indigenously, from Broadway, and, as European expatriates, from Germany and Hungary. There was a seemingly inexhaustible demand for actors, if not leading men, who had English accents (or accents that might sound English to American ears) and could therefore readily play Bostonians, debonair men about town and the cultured sophisticates who would unfailingly lose the girls to all-American heroes in the last reels. (Among the exceptions was Ronald Colman, whom Grant would join before long.) In this boom period of Hollywood, every obvious and some not-so-obvious sources of talent were plundered, and the expenditure of money and expertise was prodigal. Both were merged in the actual process of making films, in which collaboration was the keynote. While powerful talents such as director Michael Curtiz created their detectable impact, the pressures were such that it is usually more meaningful to talk of a studio style in that decade rather than a director's art; the *auteur* theory of movie-making was not then current, but it would scarcely fit, in retrospect, the pictures being made in the 'thirties. During those ten years, a key figure like Curtiz directed a phenomenal forty-four movies. His fellow work-horse at Warners, Raoul Walsh, directed twenty-one. Sam Wood and Henry King made twenty-four and twenty pictures respectively. Even a comparatively late starter like Henry Hathaway crammed eighteen productions into a mere eight years. With output so high, it was inevitable that quality would fluctuate under pressure, that 'personal vision' would come a poor second to production-line efficiency. Treatment was often superior to subject-matter, arguably the more so once Hollywood, by the mid-'thirties, had arrived at the concept of the genre movie and increasingly inflexible formulae for those products on to which such labels as 'action movie', 'musical' and 'woman's picture' were attached. Simultaneously with the evolution of identifiable categories came the conscious 'typing' of stars. If movie-makers knew the category of a picture, then they also automatically knew the type of star to fit it, and if, conversely, they knew the type of star for whom they had to cater, fashioning the appropriate vehicle became relatively easy. The phrase "a Joan Crawford picture" was far more than an advertising-man's tag, and if there was one great constant in movie-making then and for years to follow it was the stars themselves.

In the first half of the 'thirties, Paramount, ruled by Adolph Zukor, lacked the rock-like business stability of, say, Metro, and the profit or loss incurred by one picture tended unduly to affect the studio's financial climate. But if Paramount experienced its business vicissitudes, it was hard to fault in terms of style. Nor was this a matter of trademarks as tangible as MGM's sumptuous artwork, Warners' proletarian subject-matter and strong emphasis on social problems, or Universal's profitable preoccupation with horror. Paramount's style was more subtle, less definable – an amalgam of warm photography, European wit and suavity, and a predilection for romantic or covertly sexual comedy (handled most deftly by Ernst Lubitsch) and historical pageant (directed inevitably and heavily by De Mille). If De Mille was Paramount's great indigenous talent, Lubitsch was a prime exponent of the European touch whose influence could be detected *passim* in the Paramount product and could even soften De Mille's extravaganzas at their most stolid. Both stars and technicians frequently came from Germany, the stars especially from UFA, the most notable example being Marlene Dietrich. At Paramount, Cary Grant's contemporaries included

Claudette Colbert, Maurice Chevalier, Jeanette MacDonald, Sylvia Sidney, Jean Arthur, Fredric March and the Marx Brothers, with Gary Cooper as perhaps the undisputed king of the Paramount crowd. In Hollywood as a whole, such stars as Clark Gable and Spencer Tracy were among Grant's rivals. Errol Flynn was to vault to instant stardom with *Captain Blood* in 1935, and Grant's exact contemporary, James Cagney, was making some of his most famous pictures under the auspices of the same studio, Warner Brothers. The year before Grant's career began (1931), Cagney's fame became assured when he rammed half a grapefruit into Mae Clark's face and later expired with the words "I ain't so tough" in *Public Enemy*.

By the middle of the decade, there were over 18,000 cinemas in the US alone, and cinema attendance totalled 87 million per year.

Then, as now, a Hollywood contract was a Hollywood contract. Grant was not about to become fussy over which studio he worked for. Whether he was aware of the truth or not, however, the year he joined them Paramount made a $16 million loss, with ensuing bankruptcy. The auguries might have seemed unfavourable, yet it was arguable that Paramount was always either up or down, a rollercoaster of a studio. Three years later, weekly movie-going attendance hit 220 million, with 80 million in the US, and Paramount showed a profit of $3 million.

Leaving behind his musical-comedy career, Cary Grant began work for Paramount at $450 per week at the age of twenty-eight. The bare statistics of his first year with the studio reflect the production-line smoothness of the times: he made seven movies in 1932, working a full fifty-two weeks. The figures scarcely compete with Clark Gable's eleven pictures made the previous year – his astonishingly active début with MGM; but they do show how eager the Hollywood factory was to capitalize on a discovery and to create and encourage his familiarity to the public.

Billed fifth, Grant first appeared in Frank Tuttle's farce *This Is The Night*, in which he looked conventionally handsome and attracted approving critical comment. At eighth in the cast list, he was less noticed and less noticeable in Alexander Hall's *Sinners In The Sun*, his first picture with Carole Lombard and a dispirited production in which the drama came a poor second to fashion parades. Equally factitious and even more devoid of chances for Grant was Dorothy Arzner's *Merrily We Go to Hell*, in which his role, billed ninth, was small indeed. His career picked up somewhat when Marion Gering gave him a minor part, lasting only for the first half-hour of the completed film, in *The Devil And The Deep*, the stars of which were Tallulah Bankhead, Charles Laughton and Gary Cooper. The part was arguably better than the purely supporting roles he had played previously, but with Cooper in the lead, Cary Grant excited little attention, especially as he departed so soon from the screen.

Cooper, Paramount's errant star, had returned to the studio in 1932, no doubt eager and even slightly fearful at the prospect of inspecting Grant, this new talent his employers had hired in part at least to keep their recently wayward older star in check. For Cooper, the news that Grant could *act* was alarming, or so he pretended, but he was soon to decide that he had little to fear.

Having joined Paramount in 1927, Gary Cooper, much in demand, made nine pictures in 1929 and seven the following year. By 1931, he was complaining that he was working too hard. After Paramount, apparently responding, had said that they would "split up [his] schedule", he found himself involved in two pictures at the same time, one by day and one at night. While he was filming *City Streets* in 1931, he suffered a near-collapse from the combined effects of jaundice and exhaustion and later took off for Europe. In Venice, he was charmed by the Countess Dorothy di Frasso, but his romantic interlude was abruptly disturbed by Paramount's summoning him back to make *His Woman*. That autumn once the picture was finished, he travelled to Africa where he was joined by the Countess. In a fashion typical of the studios and their treatment of the stars during that era, Paramount made the most of the publicity and slyly engaged Cary Grant. Neither the similarity in the first names nor the fact that the two men shared the same initials (if reversed) was lost on Coop.

These resemblances might have been dismissed as superficial and contrived, as indeed they were. But there were other striking parallels between the stars. Both Cooper's parents had been English, a fact often overlooked, and he had been educated in England. Though he had yet to prove his versatility in such pictures as *Bluebeard's Eighth Wife*, Cooper was to fit surprisingly well into Paramount's *salon* romances, in which sophisticated heroines were to respond convincingly to his vulnerability. Carl Sandburgh's "beloved illiterate" wore lounge suits as well as chaps and stetson (the same was not to be said for Cary Grant), and his flair for comedy was genuine and appealing. On the other hand, Grant, it might be suggested, was never to deteriorate, but his rival, whose on-screen virtues had been stoicism and simplicity, was to decline sadly in the 'fifties into self-pity and near-lachrymose self-indulgence.

One marked dissimilarity between the two actors deserves mention at greater length. Though Cary Grant, like Cooper and almost all other male stars, was to run the gamut of *macho* roles including naval lieutenants, aviators, playboys and gamblers, he never became a star of Westerns or even played in one of them during his entire lengthy career. To say exactly why would be hard, and it would be too facile to state that he was disqualified by his 'British' accent. Similar handicaps did not deter movie-makers from using Errol Flynn, that Warner Brothers 'Irishman', and later Stewart Granger as the stars of such films.

Overall, however, no matter how much Grant and Cooper might have had in common, they were essentially different actors – even though Paramount might not always have been aware of the fact. It was soon to be a complaint of Cary Grant that he was not an interchangeable type and that roles originally conceived with Cooper in mind could not readily be passed on to him as though those parts were suits and the two stars were exactly of the same height and build.

For a while, though, Grant buckled down and took what came his way. His fifth picture in 1932, was Josef von Sternberg's *Blonde Venus*. Ludicrous and rambling, the story was none the less conveyed in superior photography by Bert Glennon, with the result that Dietrich and Grant both looked their romantic best. In any case, he was rather good in his small role, playing second fiddle to Herbert Marshall, as an affluent playboy. During shooting, von Sternberg changed Grant's parting from left to right – a style to which he adhered ever afterwards. *Blonde Venus* was premiered at the Paramount Theatre on 23rd September 1932, and though it was poorly received, critical approval of Grant had Paramount announcing a version of *Blood and Sand* for him and Tallulah Bankhead. The planned remake did not, however, materialize. Instead, Grant went into *Hot Saturday* to portray yet another playboy in a romantic-triangle drama turned down by Gary Cooper. The property was clearly designed as a vehicle for Nancy Carroll, a declining Paramount star, but the exposure did Grant no harm, the *New York Herald Tribune* remarking: "The new Gable-esque [sic] leading man ... a dashing young man who seems destined for that screen popularity which comes when a player can seem a handsome juvenile and still make sense." The film gave him top billing for the first time in his career.

Making it, Grant encountered Randolph Scott, with whom he became firm friends, for a while sharing a house with him – an arrangement that elicited a mordant comment from Carole Lombard, who knew them both, about who paid the bills. Her remark no doubt helped lay the foundations of Grant's reputation for stinginess.

Madame Butterfly, the last of his seven screen appearances that year, reunited him with Marion Gering as director. In total, Gering was to direct five of the Hollywood movies of Sylvia Sidney, who was the female star of *Butterfly* – a film that, though she strove valiantly in it, enhanced the reputation of nobody concerned. Puccini's music was used only as a background score, but in yet another property rejected by Gary Cooper, Grant at last used his singing-voice on screen, the song being called "My Flower of Japan". *Madame Butterfly* did him no *obvious* good, perhaps, but at least it kept his name and appearance before a public – especially the female section of it – increasingly appreciative of his handsome looks and stiff but improving acting.

The legend, like any other, has more than one version. A familiar telling of it has him on the studio lot doing push-ups as she walks by and is deeply impressed by his appearance and physique. (Push-ups? Did that sort of 'discovery' ever occur, except in a now-defunct genre of showbiz-Hollywood movie?) Another, which she herself related in print, has her leaving an office in which she has been discussing plans with Al Kaufman, a Paramount executive under Zukor, and Bill LeBaron, producer of his first film, *Night After Night*. On the studio-street, she spots "a sensational-looking young man". Learning his identity from her companions, she declares that she has found her leading man. Kaufman protests that he has so far not made a picture – merely tests. She is not to be deterred. 'If he can talk,' she says, 'I'll take him.'

She, of course, was Mae West and the "sensational-looking" actor was Cary Grant.

The second version of the legend was told in West's autobiography, *Goodness Had Nothing To Do With It*, and its inaccuracies are surprising. By any definition, Grant, with seven movies behind him (he was actually making the seventh, *Butterfly*, when West met him), was a star. For the unwary, however, the anecdote, with its implication of placing a young known on an up-escalator, is a good one and contains more than an element of truth, as Grant himself acknowledged. Of

Mae West, he said, "I owe everything to her. Well, not quite everything, but almost everything. She knows so much. Her instinct is so true, her timing so perfect, her grasp of the situation so right."

Mistress of sexual innuendo and libidinous humour, she had made the first big splash in her scandalous and glorious career with a 1926 Broadway play called *Sex*. As author and star, part of her reward was a charge of immorality and a ten-day jail sentence – the sort of publicity money could not buy. She followed *Sex* with *Diamond Lil* and *The Pleasure Man*, which earned her another court appearance. By that time, her style and technique, formed largely by vaudeville, were set. Her figure and personality were both generous, and the combined effect of her gait, bearing, expressions and unique voice was to provoke, to suggest, to titillate, to satirize herself and, perhaps above all, to make insidious infiltrations past the rigid defences of prudery and decency. Her most natural way of speech was the seemingly artless double-entendre. *Night After Night* brought her to Hollywood in 1932. Men had so far dominated movie-making, but Mae West, as her act and shows implied, dominated men, and they agreed that she could write her own lines – a typical arrangement, still in effect when she made *Myra Breckinridge* nearly forty years later. In *Night After Night*, she was a sensational success, and her co-star, chosen for his muscles and virility, was George Raft.

She had a good idea of the male foils she needed to appear at her most effective, and Raft had been the embodiment of only one of her preferences. Without sacrificing the virility, Cary Grant represented another: 'class', good manners, the aura and bearing of a gentleman.

The film for which she wanted him was *She Done Him Wrong*, an adaptation of her stage success of 1928, *Diamond Lil*. (The title seemed too hot for Hollywood to handle, and the character played by West was renamed Lou.) She demanded and got a week's rehearsal before shooting, which began on 21st November 1932. Director Lowell Sherman completed the picture in a mere eighteen days, and for an outlay of $200,000, it earned $2 million within three months in the US alone. In effect, this one picture saved Paramount from bankruptcy.

For Cary Grant, it was a big, an enormous break. Running the Salvation Army mission next door to the saloon where West performed, he lent to the proceedings a spurious air of legitimacy or respectability. Spurious, because his implied morality existed merely to be slyly circumvented by her uninhibited lewdness, and his courtesy and breeding were not so much a rebuff as props to the expression of her outrageously healthy sexuality. In short, he was her partner. Even the role of Salvation Army Captain Cummings was not what it seemed: he turned out to be a federal agent on the track of white-slavers. Appraising him, West called him " ... warm, dark and handsome ..." In one scene, just before she exited, she looked at Grant from top to toe and murmured, "You can be had." Trying to pacify the saloon's revellers, he appealed to her for assistance, adding, "I'm sorry to be taking your time." Her retort: "What do you think my time is for?" It was in *She Done Him Wrong* that West uttered to Grant the immortal line: "Why don't you come up sometime ... see me?" (One of those lines that, like "Play it again, Sam", are almost invariably misquoted.) At the end of the picture, as Grant was about to put handcuffs on her, she said, "Are those strictly necessary? You know, I wasn't born with them." He replied, "A lot of men would have been safer if you had." The moral he appeared to be pointing on one level was eclipsed by what was essentially the punch-line of a hilarious gag. As if that were not enough, she went off personally escorted by the handsome captain in his car and wearing a new diamond ring. "You bad girl," he admonished her in tones that no one would take seriously. "You'll find out," she promised him.

Predictably, *She Done Him Wrong* belonged to Mae West. Her magnificently jutting hips, incredible swagger and teasing nudges to her coiffure were much on view. As usual her first entrance was carefully prepared, immediately preceded by the ambiguous praise of an admirer: "She's one of the finest women that ever walked the streets."* She sang songs with such titles as "My Easy Rider's Gone" and "I Like a Guy What Takes His Time". But, for Cary Grant, the film was also a triumph in which he emerged as much more than Mae West's straight man or a chance participant in a smash-hit. His looks, underplaying, and comic timing merged to suggest far greater accomplishments to come.

She Done Him Wrong set up a sigh of relief that was to be heard all around the Paramount lot. The studio had been considering the idea of

---

* A line that, for sheer effrontery, rates comparison with one in Raoul Walsh's *What Price Glory?* (1926). In that film, Victor McLaglen asked one of his soldiers, who had a pretty girl on his arm, where he was going. The soldier replied: "Captain, I'm bringing you the lay of the land." To complete a good circumstantial job, he took out a map from his pocket. There were no problems with censorship.

selling out to MGM, of converting 1,700 theatres to office buildings. Mae West changed all that, and in 1933 she was listed eighth biggest at the box-office.

For her, however, it was in a sense the beginning of the end, for though her success continued, her on-screen conduct affronted puritans and drove a horse and buggy through the Motion Picture Production Code. The Legion of Decency, formed in 1934, exerted pressure to curb her nose-thumbing at square sexual-morality, and though, as a big dollar earner, she had for a time been almost immune, censorship began to bleed her films of their vitality. Even Mae West, by the mid-'thirties uttering such lines as: "Any time you take religion for a joke, the laugh's on you", could sound cowed and unconvincing. In the 'forties, she returned to the stage, having already staked her claim in history as a legend. The servicemen of the Second World War confirmed her immortality through the iconography of the pin-up and the name that was spontaneously bestowed on the airman's inflatable life-jacket.

To paraphrase Oscar Wilde, appearing once opposite Mae West might have been counted accident or good fortune. But to appear twice looked suspiciously like good management; and Cary Grant, before 1933 was out, was to make a second picture as leading man to the star who had taught and given him so much.

The Woman Accused, Grant's second film of 1933, was an unworthy successor to *She Done Him Wrong*. Based on a magazine serial by ten (sic) popular novelists, the new movie perhaps understandably lacked coherence and credibility. But if the same flaws were to some extent present in *The Eagle and the Hawk*, this first World War flying-yarn based on a story by John Monk Saunders had strong characters and was well directed by Stuart Walker. Furthermore, although the sadistic aerial gunner played by Grant was to turn improbably noble at the picture's climax, the role was notable for revealing a darker side to the star's screen *persona*. By this time, the debonair Cary Grant was well on the way to becoming familiar, and to discover that the dazzling teeth might bite or the velvet touch give way to the flashing of unsheathed claws came as something of a shock. A small one, though. It was swiftly smothered by a string of more anodyne productions, and it was to take George Stevens and Alfred Hitchcock to explore the depths of the actor's range – and even then tentatively, in resolutely commerical contexts in which he turned out to be the good guy, after all.

Released in June 1933, *Gambling Ship* was Grant's fourth film of that year, an unexceptional romantic story that had him looking suave and vacuously handsome – in case anyone had been worried by the hard man he had played in *The Eagle and the Hawk*. After *Gambling Ship*, however, he was again teamed with Mae West – he is the only star of his stature to have appeared opposite her twice – in *I'm No Angel*. Predictably, it was uninhibited, not to say licentious, comedy, its mood epitomized by the exchange between a circus fortune-teller and West: "You were born in August." – "Yeah – one of the hot months." To add to the extravagance, West, playing a lion-tamer ("a girl who lost her reputation but never missed it"), uttered such immortal lines as "Beulah, peel me a grape" and "When I'm good, I'm very good, but when I'm bad, I'm better" (a sentiment later adapted as an advertising slogan for her films). In the face of such lusty good spirits, Grant, as leading man, might have had little to do, but he did it well. Though not without its flaccid sections, *I'm No Angel* fared even better than *She Done Him Wrong* and grossed $3 million. Its success and that of the earlier picture were not unconnected with a significant event that took place on 19th December 1934, when the bankruptcy of Paramount Public Corporation was settled and a new company, Paramount Pictures, Incorporated, was formed.

Still kept busy, Grant and other stars were glimpsed in one-reel Paramount shorts under the generic title of *Hollywood on Parade*, and to cash in on the 1933 Christmas-trade, he appeared, singing about "beautiful, beautiful soup", as the Mock Turtle in *Alice in Wonderland*. Contemporary publicity photographs have him contemplating his Mock Turtle mask quizzically – as well he might have done. Disguises, bizarre make up, 'stunt' performances have ever muffled star allure, and the tepid amusement of trying to identify such Big Names as Richard Arlen and Gary Cooper through their skins and masks did not prevent *Alice in Wonderland* from being an artistic flop. (Though perhaps the classic disaster in this line remains John Huston's *The List of Adrian Messenger*.)

6

A Brief Stab at Matrimony

If the release of two movies with Mae West had been landmarks in his professional life, Cary Grant found 1933 memorable for more personal and intimate reasons. It saw the quick ripening of a nascent interest in the woman who, almost before the year was out, was to become the first Mrs Grant.

In those days, the commissaries of the major studios were far more than places to eat. Their other functions included the provision of a stage on which to see and be seen, a staircase on which shifts of ascendancy could be detected or political drifts sounded, an exchange for rumour and gossip – who was in, who out, who sleeping with whom, who about to close which deal. Intangible lines could be drawn with daunting accuracy, so that one's mere presence, at, say, the executive dining table might be read as a sign of favour bestowed or power enjoyed. (Years later, when he worked for Columbia and was highly regarded, even by Harry Cohn, the studio's boorish czar, a man about as far removed from the socially deft Cary Grant as it was possible to be, Grant was invited to lunch regularly with Cohn. Mark of favour though it was, Grant eventually begged off, utterly bored by the inescapable talk of football.)

One day in 1933, the Paramount commissary was the setting (perhaps almost inevitably, certainly fittingly, in so busy a year of acting) for his first encounter with Virginia Cherrill, the blonde actress who had been a figure in society until Chaplin persuaded her to play the blind flower-girl in his 1931 silent, *City Lights*. Then in her mid-twenties, she had previously been married to Irving Adler and William Rhinelander Stewart, and, though a Fox contractee, she had just finished making *The Nuisance* (a.k.a. *Accidents Wanted*) for MGM, essentially a vehicle for Lee Tracy. Previously, she had made *Girls Demand Excitement* (an early John Wayne film) in 1931[*] and

_____
[*] Once described by Wayne as: "The worst motion picture in the history of the industry."

Delicious in 1932, but her career never flourished, she began to accept leads in minor productions, and she made her last appearance in *Troubled Waters* in 1936.

As soon as he was introduced, Grant was charmed by her. She was a thoroughbred who moved easily in a world that he was beginning to find extremely congenial, and though she was not a 'civilian', the disparity between their careers was such that, if matrimony ever entered their thoughts, there could be no argument about whose interests should come first. Furthermore, whether he was aware of the influence or not, the fact that Virginia was an Anglophile was certainly no deterrent for one who had adapted to working in American movies without shedding gestures and intonations that were unmistakably British. She had 'class'. Cary Grant would never have used the word, but Archie Leach might.

The two of them were to be seen dining out, at parties and at premières, but the courtship was a stormy one.

In November 1933, with Randolph Scott as company, Grant followed Virginia to England, and once there, he and she lost little time in going to Bristol, where the actor visited Fairfield Secondary, his old school. With M.J. Truscott, the then headmaster, he toured the buildings for an hour and renewed acquaintance with Henri Audcent and Miss Craigie, his old form mistress.

Grant had returned to his hometown as a combination of tourist and sentimental but essentially *dégagé* pilgrim. He found, though, that he had a large number of old friends, many of whom he remembered vividly, and perhaps an even larger number of relatives, many of whom were unknown to him.

Curiously, the last comment might have been made about Elsie and Elias Leach, the closest kin of all. He had known his father for longer than he had known his mother, but he severed the connection with both at an uncommonly early age. "I haven't seen Dad for three and a half years," he stated before he arrived in Bristol, "and I am just longing to get back to have a quiet time with the folks and get around to some of my old haunts." At least one of his reunions was not planned. He called on a performer he knew, Vera Pearce, who just happened to be appearing at the Prince's Theatre, Bristol.

Mainly because of his mother's stay in the institution at Fishponds, Grant had had no contact since his childhood with the Kingdons, Elsie Leach's side of the family. Of Archie Leach's departure from Bristol, Ernest Kingdon said, "It was as though he had fallen off the face of the earth."[1] To his mother's relatives, who had not kept in touch with the Leaches after her hospitalization, Archie's reappearance as a Hollywood star was a sensation, but having seen his name in the local papers, they contacted him again during his visit.

"A quiet time with the folks" was not so quiet, after all. There was a large-scale reunion at Picton Street, where Ernest Kingdon discovered that the house "had many, many pictures all over the walls of Archie at all ages ... It was pretty hot, stifling. Cary had sent his chauffeur to pick up my father, his Uncle David. Dad at the time was unavailable because my mother was pretty ill, but I was there and my brother was in my father's place. My brother said, 'Let's get out, take a walk and get some air in our lungs.' We went for a walk [with Cary Grant], and as we were walking around the different back-streets, Cary was digging up his memories. We passed a fish and chip shop, and my brother, who was then just back from the States, said, 'Good gracious, it's a long time since I walked along eating fish and chips.' Cary said, 'Same as me, Charles. Let's have some.' We went in, we bought them, and we walked along eating fish and chips ... His first visit to Bristol as Cary Grant."[2]

The actor's marriage to Virginia Cherrill was in the offing. "It would please me very much," Grant said, "if we could be married in Bristol among my own folks." (Some of these, together with friends, Virginia had met at an informal party at the Grand Hotel.) But Grant's plans changed from day to day, almost from hour to hour, and the marriage was not to take place in his home-town. However, as a second choice, it seemed appropriate that they should wed in London, where notice of the marriage was given in early December. There was to be a delay, even so.

On 1st December, Grant gave an interview in the capital after his return from Bristol and said, "I saw my father, my uncles, my cousins and my aunts and had a wonderful time." (One cousin by marriage had tangible cause to remember that visit, for Grant, who was never too fond of hats, gave him a brown trilby that he had worn in *Madame Butterfly*. Worn regularly, it was greatly admired but eventually, well past its prime, had to be thrown out.[3])

By mid-December, unpredictably, Grant was undergoing surgery at a Fulham nursing home. Whether the need for the operation had manifested itself suddenly or whether the operation had been planned, the marriage would have to wait. It seemed certain, however, that the surgery for "an internal complaint" was the result of a bomb explosion during the making of *The Eagle and the Hawk* in March of that year.

According to Mitchell Leisen, associate director on the picture, what had happened was that the star had been inattentive and as a result was injured in an explosion that was triggered prematurely. The rest of the cast were unhurt because they had followed instructions and were standing in the correct places. At the time, newspapers made much of the mishap, but the details were never clear.

With medical matters out of the way, Grant and Virginia Cherrill married on 9th February 1934, at London's fashionable Caxton Hall, leaving England immediately afterwards on the *Berengaria* sailing for New York. Grant commented, "We wanted a quiet wedding and no ballyhoo, but we didn't get a chance. So we timed the marriage to take place just before the boat-train left." It was true that once word leaked out, there was a crowd at Caxton Hall to see the famous couple. The "ballyhoo", even so, was nothing by American standards. (A parallel incident once occurred in Bristol when Grant was present for a family gathering in a small public house in Dean Street, St Paul's. News soon got around that a famous star was there, and rapidly the place became crowded, with people peering over the partition.)

Grant had been upset by the mob at Caxton Hall, and Virginia had not accepted his stay in hospital too graciously. If there could be seen in the circumstances omens that were not exactly propitious, the auguries proved depressingly accurate. In all but name, the marriage was to be over in little more than six months.

Probably neither party was to blame. But just as part of the cause may have been in Virginia Cherrill, part, by his own admission, was in Cary Grant.

In 1934, he was thirty – four years beyond what Scott Fitzgerald called "the very acme of bachelorhood". Arguably, though, the bachelorhood should have been extended longer – perhaps indefinitely. Later, Grant could say, "When I'm married, I want to be single, and when I'm single, I want to be married." There, however, spoke the wisdom of hindsight, as when he said to journalist Michael Roberts in 1974, "I like doing the things one does alone."

Cary Grant in 1934 was both more and less than the roles he played. There had already begun to emerge the man of unbounded sophistication who could suddenly be eclipsed by a confused, suspicious *alter ego*. Elusive, too. The superb health, assiduously cultivated by temperate habits, would become a trademark and encouraged thoughts of solidity and assurance. But he had a well-developed knack of eluding one's grasp.

In print, David Niven has described him as a "will-of-the-wisp". Much earlier, Julie Lang Hunt, in charge of magazine publicity at Paramount when Grant signed his contract in 1931, observed how adroitly he could escape the question that probed. She set up interviews at which he was charming and a good host, offering lunch, tea or cocktails. But he deftly deflected attempts at personal exploration and delivered a mere handful of facts about his antecedents and stage experience. Nor was the on-screen assurance entirely accurate. Both Julie Lang Hunt and his friend Randolph Scott confirmed in *Photoplay* in the mid-'thirties his sensitivity (abiding, as it turned out) to criticism. Inaccuracies and misquotations in the Press might have been the inevitable lot of public figures, but they could upset him deeply.

Though others have successfully married in parallel circumstances, he was intensely involved in his career, which was thus far, however successful, neither the source of satisfaction he hoped it would be nor the glittering triumph it would later become. In professional terms, he had hardly even begun to evolve the unique Grant *persona* – the bow-legged walk that needed no simulation, the incredulous stare, the spontaneous grunts and apparent ad libs, the sceptical or disturbing scrutiny (anatomy improbably awry). These were more than tricks, and it would take directors as gifted as George Cukor and Howard Hawks to liberate the richly comic spirit of which they were a part. If, as he was later to assert, Grant played himself, his personality by 1934 was in one sense already coming close to the unfailingly courteous, suave and experienced star so popular in the 'forties and 'fifties. What he yet lacked as a leading man, maturity and more pictures would provide. But Cary Grant the world's greatest light comedian was another side to that star – and scarcely nascent in the mid-'thirties; and it was this aspect to his talent that would stake his claim to originality.

To an outsider, it might have seemed that he already had it all – money, fame, a screen image both flattering and unique. Without a fierce or aggressive masculinity, he was nevertheless proving as popular with men as with women. He had, it could have been argued, merely to polish and refine.

Grant, though, did not see matters so simply. To start with, he resented being a recognizable type – not unique at all. He would put a stop to the plucking of his eyebrows and the excessively cosmetic use on him of make up. But he was almost as unhappy about his roles, later remarking, "They had a lot of leading-men at Paramount with dark hair and a set of teeth like mine, and they couldn't be buying stories for all of us." What rankled most was living in the shadow of another, then greater, star. "I seemed to be getting all the roles that Gary Cooper didn't want," he was to observe. "I saw no reason why Gary and Cary should be confused."

The rewards might have been great, but the struggle had been fierce, and the privations of early days had left him with an enduring fear of poverty. To be Cary Grant took time and application – to say nothing of concentration. No wonder he was sometimes described as aloof. By the mid-'thirties, he was, as he himself has confessed, self-engrossed and difficult – a not-uncommon condition in artists who are striving to perfect a technique or at least solve the problems of their craft.

All these factors in his make up were pertinent to his marriage with Virginia Cherrill and any prognosis concerning wedded bliss. One more feature of a complicated psychology deserves mention. There had to be a coincidence between the on-screen and off-screen characters of Cary Grant, since his career up to this point had revealed a personality actor rather than a virtuoso who relied on sheer technique to transform his presence from role to role. And there was. Time and subsequent marriages were to show that he could be just as romantic as the heroes he played – and just as ready nobly to assume blame when romantic insubstantiality foundered on hard facts.

Incipient or developed, these were the traits Grant brought to his first marriage.

That year, 1934, he made four somewhat rapid comedies that might have been designed as much to illustrate his limitations as to exhibit his growing skill in underplaying. The first was *Thirty-Day Princess*, which again brought him together with Sylvia Sidney as co-star and Marion Gering as director. Its plot, about a newspaperman involved with an American girl standing in for a foreign princess prevented by illness from making a goodwill tour (a dual role for Sidney), strikingly prefigured William Wyler's *Roman Holiday*, the better known and more successful film of 1953. Oddly enough, the latter picture was at one stage planned for Grant, with Elizabeth Taylor opposite him and Frank Capra directing. In *Born to be Bad*, Grant was a rich trucking executive, married but pursued by a calculating Loretta Young, while in *Kiss and Make Up*, he was the owner of a Paris beauty salon who fell in love with his greatest cosmetic triumph, only to find, after marrying her, that she was hopelessly narcissistic. The film was decked out with songs, one of which, "Love Divided By Two", by Leo Robin and Ralph Grainger, Grant sang and which achieved some popularity. Farcical and resolutely superficial, *Ladies Should Listen* was perhaps the least of Grant's 1934 quartet of movies, notable largely for the fact that in it, as in the preceding *Kiss and Make Up*, a 'bit' was played by Clara Lou Sheridan. Fifteen years later, as Ann Sheridan and a star in her own right, she would join Grant to set up a remarkable on-screen chemistry in *I Was a Male War-bride*.

This was the period when Grant, though no longer exactly a tyro, was still imitating British actors such as Jack Buchanan and A.E. Matthews, most obviously by keeping his hand in his pocket – "but only because I was so nervous I couldn't pull it out again." Or, as he said once, looking back, "I used to be Noel Coward ... It took me three long years to get my hand out of there, and they were three years wasted."

More prosaically, the observation might have been made that his early films had sometimes shown the star making gestures whose expansive dimensions were ill suited to the cinema and that directors, seeing the problem, had advised him (as a remedy often resorted to in the theatre) to anchor his arms by keeping his hands in the pockets of his impeccably cut suits. In that pose, some men looked merely sloppy and poorly tailored. But never Cary Grant.*

Besides refining technique, he had other matters to worry him that year. By the fall, his marriage, the paint scarcely dry on it, was in trouble, and Virginia Cherrill left him, stating to the Press on 30th September: "It's true we have had a quarrel. Whether it is permanent or not is up to Cary. I left Cary two weeks ago and consulted a lawyer, but we later patched things up. I hoped that we might make a go of our marriage, because I am in love with my husband and have been very unhappy over our inability to adjust to our differences."

For all its positive aspects, the statement seemed ominously

---

* There are other cures for this ailment. Richard Burton tells the tale of how he passed through a 'Gielgud-phase', throwing his arms about in imitation of the famous Shakespearean actor. One day during rehearsal at Stratford-upon-Avon, Burton's palm was extended on stage when fellow-player Alan Badel thrust a sausage-roll into it.

hemmed in by qualifications and conditions. Grant was cultivating optimism or putting on a brave face when he announced almost at the same time: "It is silly to say Virginia and I have separated. We have just had a quarrel, such as any married pair might have. I hope when I get home tonight Virginia will be waiting for me."

His long-term hopes were to be dashed, however, and a week later Grant was front-page news in the Los Angeles papers. On 5th October, it was reported that a servant called an ambulance at 2.30 am after having found the star unconscious in bed. On a nearby table was a bottle containing tablets ("Poison tablets" – in some accounts.). Doctors asserted that Grant, by his own admission, had taken one. Detectives, on the other hand, insisted that the bottle was sealed and unopened.

Grant said afterwards, "All I know is that police crowded into my room and rushed me off to hospital. I was in a somewhat dazed condition after a late party. I believe that friends, knowing this, played a joke on me." If so, it was a cruel hoax, for a stomach-pump was used on the actor. The situation became no clearer when Virginia Cherrill added, "Something did happen, but it was a question of nervous prostration. He was taken to hospital, but it was a mistake."

Behind all the stories, it could be surmised, was the prime concern that the whole event should be minimized in the eyes of Elias Leach and others, who might well have presumed the worst.

Later, Grant was to dismiss the melodrama with the simple explanation that he had been drunk – a not unnatural reaction to his marital difficulties. "You know," he said, "what whiskey does when you drink it all by yourself. It makes you very, very sad. I began calling people up. I know I called Virginia. I don't know what I said to her, but things got hazier and hazier. The next thing I knew, they were carting me off to the hospital."

In the late 'fifties, he repudiated notions of a suicide attempt even more categorically with the remark: "The only time in my life I ever considered death was when I had jaundice – in '49 while I was making *I Was a Male Warbride*."

Who said life imitated art? (Wilde did – doubtless skipping off down the street to see whether he had beaten Whistler to the simple inversion.) There was irony in the fact that the split with Virginia should come towards the end of a year that had seen Grant sorting out his amorous problems with increasingly familiar style and aplomb *on screen*. To a romantic like him, the failure of his marriage must

have been a bitter blow, perhaps the more so because he was no
quitter and his bride had left him. (In Hollywood, a wife, whether of
six months or six years, remains a bride.) Who left whom was far from
being a trivial matter to Grant, if only because journalists seemed so
ready to misquote him on the subject. "I never loved any of my wives"
– was the remark once attributed to him by one news agency, which
he considered suing. To Roderick Mann, he complained, "I never said
it. What I said was I never *left* any of my wives. They all left me."[4]

The distinction might seem a sad one, but it was – and is –
important to him.

And maybe not just to him.

When he explained to Virginia, still a friend, what he had actually
said and what he had been *reported* as saying, she commented, "I
knew you'd never make a remark like that."

7

The Break with Paramount

In 1935, Grant's exact contemporary, James Cagney, just made it to number ten in the list of top box-office draws. His pictures had been big money-makers, giving him legitimate grounds to complain about his comparatively low salary. That year, six Cagney movies were released, including *G-Men*, perhaps his best since Darryl Zanuck, and William Wellman, having viewed three days' rushes, engineered an exchange of roles between Cagney and Eddie Woods (the nominal star) in 1931's *Public Enemy*. In 1935, Cagney also scored a personal success as Bottom in the otherwise critically mauled Warner Brothers version of *A Midsummer Night's Dream*.

At the same time, *Captain Blood*, another Warner picture, was turning Errol Flynn and Olivia de Havilland into stars of the first magnitude. Cary Grant's fellow countryman Ronald Colman shed his moustache and triumphed in 20th Century's *Clive of India*. Clark Gable was a hit, together with Wallace Beery and Jean Harlow, in *China Seas* and also in *Mutiny on the Bounty*, not only one of MGM's biggest money-spinners but also winner of the Academy Award for best picture. With the same studio, Spencer Tracy somewhat inauspiciously began a twenty-year contract with *The Murder Man*, having been fired by Fox after being arrested, drunk, near the end of location-shooting on *It's a Small World*.

Maurice Chevalier, formerly of Paramount, then with MGM, was loaned to 20th for *Folies Bergère*, which fared indifferently at the box-office. As for Gary Cooper, Grant's *bête noire*, he had two flops in *The Wedding Night* and *Peter Ibbetson*, but also his greatest hit up to that time, *Lives of a Bengal Lancer*.

One of his co-stars in that picture was Franchot Tone, who picked up an Academy Award nomination for *Mutiny on the Bounty* and was to figure, indirectly, in Grant's eventual split with Paramount.

Compared with his contemporaries of similar stature, Grant did particularly badly that year. At best, it might have been argued, he was standing still. He had a solid reputation as a leading man together with that reputation's concomitant limitations, plus a slight ponderousness that was all his own. Paramount was to do nothing in 1935 that would enchance the conventional lustre of its star. But it would deprive him of what he saw as a great chance.

In the old Hollywood studio set-up, there was to be found the nearest modern approximation to the system of patronage enjoyed by Mozart and Haydn in the eighteenth century. It would be a truism to say that Hollywood's way of dealing out rewards and punishments had all the virtues and defects of the older system, as well as devices that were the film colony's own invention. By loaning their stars to other studios, the Hollywood majors could both reward and punish. However real the rewards (and in Hollywood they were much more lavish than any offered by the court of Salzburg or the Esterhazy family), an artist caught up in the system had little genuine power and existed at the whim of the front office. If, then, a star refused a picture to which he was assigned, or turned down a loan-out to another studio, he could and probably would be suspended, any time so lost being added to the term of his contract — with the studio garnering valuable publicity over his 'rebellion' until, having had enough, it cracked the whip for the offender to come to heel.

Before Olivia de Havilland effectively brought to an end their abuse of power, the studios had it all their own way (and mainly their own way afterwards). The issue was suspension. When, in 1943, her contract expired, Warner Brothers informed de Havilland that she had an additional six months to 'serve' because they had added her periods of suspension to the end of her contract. De Havilland took Warners to court, and though Bette Davis had earlier lost her battle to free herself from similar ties with the studio, de Havilland won, the ruling becoming known in legal texts as the de Havilland Decision. (The cost to the star was $13,000 and an enforced absence from the screen for two years while the dispute was *sub judice*.)

Such litigation, however, was well in the future, and it did not materially change a studio's right either to loan a star to another studio (often for vast sums, while the star himself was paid at his usual rate) or to refuse to do so when the deal might be highly advantageous to the star's career. Thus the laws that bound actors to studios were practically unchallenged when Paramount vetoed the idea of loaning Cary Grant to MGM for *Mutiny on the Bounty*.

As a sin of omission, it was especially provocative in a year that saw the release of three indifferent Paramount productions that made predictable use of his services. In the event, Franchot Tone played in *Mutiny* the role that Grant had coveted and in which he had believed that he would be at least as good. He was surely right, for as David Thomson observed, looking back, Tone "could not exceed handsomeness as the midshipman". Additionally galling were the facts that Grant's British antecedents had made him particularly suited for the part and that he would, for the first time in his career, have been associated with a prestige production, handsomely budgeted, even if it was not in colour. He had acted with Charles Laughton before, in *The Devil and the Deep*, and he would willingly have taken his chances at being overshadowed by Clark Gable in the plum role.

Paramount's refusal to loan their star was to have a perverse sequel. Against this background of patronage or well-paid serfdom (according to who did the talking), the studio was soon to send Grant to MGM for a vastly inferior picture – thus adding a cellar of salt to an open wound. With the affair of *Mutiny on the Bounty*, the first big step had been taken towards the inevitable divorce between Paramount and its star, and the second and final one would follow before long.

Meanwhile, they gave Grant for his first picture that year *Enter Madame*, which had an operatic background and again showed him resolving on celluloid the sort of romantic entanglements that proved less susceptible of management in real life. The film did no harm at all to co-star Elissa Landi, but it provided old ground for Grant to tread as he played Landi's husband, resentful at taking a back seat to her singing-career, having an affair with another woman and finally being reunited with his wife. This concoction was farce rather than comedy – and stodgy fare, at that. If Grant had played second fiddle to Elissa Landi in *Enter Madame*, he at least dominated *Wings in the Dark*, in which he co-starred with Myrna Loy (though she took top billing), but the picture was fatuous melodrama, redeemed only by the consoling proof that his performance could be superior to its context.

Wearing a moustache, he starred in *The Last Outpost*, which began well and then petered out, Claude Rains stealing the acting honours. In a contemporary review, however, Graham Greene remarked that Grant performed "extremely well" in what was yet another love-triangle played out against a backdrop of the Sahara.

Grant was then looking superb in his pictures, but his handsomeness was relatively conventional and seemed destined to leave him as just another leading man, doomed to pick up for Paramount what Gary Cooper disdained. The least of Coop's films in 1935, however they fared at the box-office, was more interesting than any of Grant's. Furthermore, *The Last Outpost* bore all the signs of an attempt to cash in on the success of Cooper's *Lives of a Bengal Lancer*. (The first half of *The Last Outpost* had been set, like the earlier picture, on the Indian frontier.)

Something ended, something began. Grant's marriage, after little more than a year of uncertain life, wound up inexorably in court, where the predictable allegations were made – the familiar scatter-gun blast of marital recrimination. For Virginia Cherrill, it was stated that Grant "used liquor excessively, choked her, beat her, threatened her life, was sullen, disagreeable, refused to pay her bills, told her to go out and work – and then discouraged her every time she had a real opportunity". On 26th March 1935, Grant and Virginia were divorced in the Los Angeles Superior Court.

Par for the course? It might seem so to us today, after several decades in which we have had time to become inured to divorce action denouncements – often more a matter of legalistic expedience than complete sincerity. Grant, however, took the whole experience hard and told Randolph Scott that he would never marry again. (A parallel depression was to seize him after the break-up of his marriage with Barbara Hutton, when he took a six-room house in Beverly Hills and, except to work, rarely left it.

Returning to England, the former Mrs Grant later married the Earl of Jersey, though she subsequently divorced him and came back to California, where she took a fifth husband. Grant resumed living with Randolph Scott, this time in a house on West Live Oak Drive, near Griffith Park. At this time, he became a sun-lover, becoming so tanned that he began to film with almost no make up.

There commenced a new strand to his career. On 5th May, in the play *Adam and Eve*, he first broadcast on Lux Radio Theatre, on which he would be an occasional guest over the next twenty years. This aspect of his activities continued well into the 'forties, taking in such programmes as Groucho Marx's Kellogg Show and the Eddie Cantor Show. Grant was also a pioneer on George Faulkner's "The Circle", an early chat-show that flopped. Fellow guests included Carole Lombard and Groucho Marx, and the chairman was Ronald Colman. (At the time of writing, there is a legacy of this side of his art in "Silver Theatre – Cary Grant", Mark 56 738 – a record album of more than average interest. It presents a condensed version of *Wings in the Dark* sponsored by the International Silver Company and transmitted as an afternoon programme some time before Grant appeared in *Gunga Din*. He recreates his original role, playing opposite Phyllis Brooks in a production directed by Conrad Nagel. While the show is not without its laughable aspects, many of them inherited from the film itself, the star's performance is vigorous, intelligent, even nuanced – vastly superior to the performances of the other players and also, let it be said, to the radio efforts during the same period of many other film actors, who tended to give wooden, inhibited readings in front of the microphone.)

Loan-outs could work for a star as well as against him, and when Grant moved over to RKO Radio for *Sylvia Scarlett*, released in 1936, it was to play a role for which he might have been born.

The picture was made by George Cukor, a highly accomplished, perhaps even a great, director but in any case the first movie-maker of true calibre with whom Grant had worked. The screenplay was an adaptation of a novel by Compton MacKenzie published in 1918, the very year Archie Leach left school in England, entitled *The Early Life and Adventures of Sylvia Scarlett*. Despite inherent weaknesses of plot and construction, to say nothing of studio intervention that led to re-editing, the resulting film exerted a certain fascination, its characters and their dialogue sufficiently interesting to generate regrets that the concept was not more fully rounded. Grant played a cockney con-man (the first time his English background had been utilized in a way that was not pure cliché) who was involved with Katharine Hepburn, the daughter of an embezzler (Edmund Gwenn, well on the way to being another British stalwart in Hollywood). These wayward characters transformed themselves improbably for the needs of plot into itinerant theatricals, and reviews complained that Hepburn spent most of the picture disguised as a boy. (Times change: the movie was overdue for revival in the androgynous 'seventies.) The petty crook played by Grant was devious, somewhat seedy, decidedly not admirable, and yet, though he did not get the girl, of undeniable appeal. A suitably loud wardrobe was the most obvious outward sign that Grant had strayed from territory that was becoming predictably familiar. Uncouth speech and less than polished manners confirmed his departure from stereotype.

The biggest transformation, however, was internal.

George Cukor has since said that at the outset of filming Grant was "rather wooden ... inexperienced, too". But then the chemistry of playing against superior talents and taking direction from a man of great gifts began to have its effect. "He suddenly burst into bloom," Cukor stated, and his performance assumed assurance and authority.

Though *Sylvia Scarlett* had a tepid reception from the Press and indifferent receipts, Cary Grant enjoyed a personal triumph. "Grant ... practically steals the picture," *Variety* conceded, while the *Motion Picture Herald* was less tentative: "Grant's is the most convincing performance."

Malcolm Cowley once wrote of that key moment in a novelist's career when, all at once, he "becomes capable of doing his best work"; he at last discovers that "fable that expresses his central truth and everything falls into place around it, so that his whole experience of life is available for use in his fiction." Parallel experiences are to be found in the other arts ("One harbours emotion to project it at the right moment," said Maggie Teyte.) and for an actor, the nourishing stimulus and revelation lie in his divining the natural strength of his craft, his precise range and the innate flair that will lead him in future to select, if he can, one role rather than another. *Sylvia Scarlett* provided Grant's almost apocalyptic moment: he was a light romantic comedian. Once he had found that central truth about himself, he never seriously questioned it during the next thirty years of his career.

"Hollywood is the capital of missed chances and strange victories," declared Abraham Polonsky; and Grant's victory in *Sylvia Scarlett* had been of the strangest. Paramount had loaned him to RKO not with the idea of providing him with an actor's *tour de force* but – much more practically – in order to take advantage of a shrewd business deal. Involuntarily and coincidentally, they had loosened the strait jacket that had been stifling his creativity; they had placed him among exciting talents, two of whom would be eager to repeat the chemistry; and they had given him a taste of artistic success, even if in a flawed, inchoate venture. He could hardly fail to note the moral: he had found himself *outside* Paramount.

The corollary was that he was returning to all-too-familiar, unstimulating vehicles. Paramount wound up his contract by putting him into, first, *Big Brown Eyes*, released 3rd April 1936, and then *Wedding Present*, released on 9th October of that year. Neither movie had the qualities that would make it memorable. Though *Big Brown Eyes* was directed by Raoul Walsh, whose stature was comparable with Cukor's, it was derivative of *The Thin Man* and turned out to be

an inhibited production, a comedy-thriller in which Grant seemed
uneasy as the sleuth. He co-starred with Joan Bennett, who also joined
him for *Wedding Present*, a sub-standard farce that prefigured, in
certain features of its plot, Grant's great hit of 1940, *His Girl Friday*.
(Perhaps because screen-writer Paul Gallico based the antics of the
characters on the real-life exploits of Ben Hecht and Charles
MacArthur, and upon their play *The Front Page*, which was directly
derived from the co-authors' experience as newspapermen. Nothing
succeeds like cannibalism.) *Wedding Present* was coldly received by
the Press, among whom the *New York Herald Tribune* accused Grant
– possibly with perception – of "walking through" his role.

   1936 was the year in which Paramount, having refused to loan
Grant for *Mutiny on the Bounty*, allowed their star to be exploited by
the same studio, MGM, for *Suzy*, in which he appeared as a French
aviator opposite Jean Harlow. Implausible melodrama, *Suzy* must
have been singularly galling for Grant: it was not that the picture was
so bad but rather that *Mutiny on the Bounty* had been so much better
– or at least more successful in a highly commercial world.

   Suzy sported no fewer than four names on its screenplay – a sure
indication to the initiated that the genesis of the movie had not been
without its problems. (In this respect, the production was like those
Italian epics of a few years ago that had so many cooks labouring
over their scripts that the spoon would stand up in the thick broth
resulting from their combined and cumulative efforts.) In her book
Story-line: Reflections of a Hollywood Screenwriter, Lenore Coffee
has provided her own vivid impressions of the evolution of the final
script. Called in by Eddie Mannix to perform a salvage operation on
Suzy, she learned that Grant had not actually signed his contract and
was refusing point-blank to accept the role as written. Slightly
mystified, Miss Coffee formed an initial opinion that both Harlow's
part and the storyline itself were acceptable. A conference that
included a gloomy Grant, his agent Jack Bachman and the producer
Maurice Revnes at least made unmistakable the star's total aversion
to his putative role. When Miss Coffee suggested that the part might
be tailored to fit him almost to perfection, Grant expressed incredulity.
He was prepared, however, to listen to reason, and she persuaded him
to adjourn to an upper office with her in order to go over the script
that very afternoon. Her own position in the conflict was ambivalent.
As she explained to him, her job was to rescue the studio from what

appeared to be an impasse; but she wanted, on the other hand, to aid Grant to become a star of the first rank.

At these words, not surprisingly, his confidence in her grew, the more so when she told him to take notes of the revisions upon which they agreed, so that he would have his own record of the planned changes – or, in effect, the promises of improvement that she was making to him. Deliberately deflecting her attention from the "incredibly handsome" star to the job in hand, she observed the strong interest that her tactics had generated in him. Together, they improvised scene after scene, with Grant making suggestions not in terms of his own ego but in order to enhance the characterization and the story. If he said a simple "no" to a scene, she knew that it would require complete reworking. This shared process of revision had the desired effect. Before the afternoon was over, though the work had only just begun, Grant changed his mind and went downstairs to sign the contract.

What is revealing in the anecdote is Grant's concern not merely for a fat part or the leading role but also a part that would *suit* him, one into which he could breathe his own humanity as he had in *Sylvia Scarlett*. Big parts in big pictures was an oversimplification of what made stars. The parts had to be right, and they had to be interesting. The pictures had to be good, too.

Lenore Coffee's literary gifts and her flair for applied psychology might have worked well, but his loan-out to MGM was not a happy experience for Grant. On the contrary, *Suzy* represented one dissatisfaction too many.

With *Wedding Present*, his contract with Paramount was worked out. All set to renew, the studio was prepared to increase his salary to $3,500 per week, but Grant refused to sign without script approval – a privilege granted at that time only to such stars as Mae West and Marlene Dietrich. There was plainly an impasse, and in the face of it, Grant declared his intention to work free-lance – a daring decision at that stage in the history of the stars, who had seemed inexorably wedded by contract to individual studios.

With hindsight, one can detect inevitability in his choice. All the signs were that the purely personal failure of his marriage had whetted an already steadily growing professional ambition. Furthermore, he was so dissatisfied with his existence at Paramount that he was prepared to take a real, a great, risk. As late as 1963, Grant could talk in terms indicative of both accurate awareness of the Hollywood of the 'thirties and his own frustration at being if not eclipsed by Gary Cooper then at least seriously impeded by his pre-eminence at Paramount: "I see Hollywood as a streetcar, a streetcar called Aspire. It fills up at the back and empties out at the front, and there's only room for a few. Gary Cooper got on just ahead of me, and Ty Power was just behind me. Cooper stretched out his long legs and let people trip over him."[1]

Whether it was deliberate or involuntary, the perpetual dislocation of his career by Coop had become too much for Cary Grant. There had to be a better way.

It was not, however, immediately apparent.

The climate was healthy. The movie industry was working flat out to feed over 18,000 cinemas in the US alone. But Grant's free-lancing was virtually without precedent, and his first move was puzzling. Returning to England, he made for Grand National *The Amazing Quest of Ernest Bliss* (a.k.a. *A Rich Young Man, Romance and Riches* and *Amazing Adventure* – a variety of labels that speaks eloquently for the picture's problems in finding acceptance).

Grant was to remember *The Amazing Quest of Ernest Bliss* for more than one reason. During its making, his father, after two operations on 2nd December 1935, died in Bristol of "extreme toxicity". Unable to divorce his wife, he had lived for some time with a woman who bore him a son. Although Grant was remarkably reticent on the subject of his bereavement, he has left the sort of epitaph that any father might wish for from his son: "I worshipped him, and I learned a lot from him." Had Elias lived a little longer, he would have seen Cary Grant become a superstar long before the term was coined, but as matters stood, he had witnessed the first lustrous years of that superstar's career and the sort of success that he had no doubt never even dreamed about for the teenage Archie Leach. If most sons, for a variety of reasons, wish that their fathers might tarry awhile longer, Grant must surely have been philosophical, if not sanguine: he had begun to win the biggest prizes; he had repaid, if he ever could, the debt he believed he owed to Elias Leach.

On paper, nothing about the venture that had taken Grant to England looked reassuring, not least the fact that in *The Amazing Quest of Ernest Bliss* he was starring opposite Mary Brian, an American actress whose career was scarcely blooming and who retired later in the decade. At this distance, Grant's motives, about which he never expatiated in public, seem inscrutable. England was of course his homeland, and at that time its motion picture industry was flourishing. It was not, therefore, impossible that he dreamed of dominating the British scene – a somewhat smaller pond than he had been used to but having definite attractions if he could prevail in it as a star of the first magnitude.

The Amazing Quest of Ernest Bliss was not, however, the sort of production that could do anything but harm to its leading players, and this light comedy, despite its success on the stage, flopped on the English-speaking market. To his credit, Grant, having had the nerve to sever his ties with Paramount and not to sign up immediately with another Hollywood major, did not at this critical stage lose that nerve. The way ahead was signposted in two ways. First, after his experience with George Cukor he knew precisely what he wanted to do, how best to showcase his talents. Second, he discovered that *Sylvia Scarlett* and, less predictably, *Suzy* had done him no harm at all.

Cary Grant was 'hot' in Hollywood, and he lost no time in returning to the colony after his disastrous English experiment. Once back in California, he signed simultaneous, non-exclusive contracts with RKO and Columbia, securing the script approval upon which negotiations with Paramount had foundered. The logic of his actions was much more persuasive. He had made his impact in America and in American films. For all his English antecedents and the then encouraging prospects of the British movie industry, the opportunities in England were nothing compared with what Hollywood might offer – especially now that he had script approval. The time was ripe, and Cary Grant was in no doubt about the roles, if they existed, that he was seeking.

Almost immediately, he started to find them.

8

On His Nimble Feet

The death of Elias Leach had left an enormous loose end – the future
of Elsie Leach, his widow and Cary Grant's mother. There were those
intimate with the facts who were sure that Elsie should be released
from hospital, that she was quite capable of leading a normal life.
There were practical problems, but they could be overcome. The most
pressing, of course, was: who would support her? The answer was
obvious. Her only child was an internationally known film star, with
earnings commensurate with his reputation. The facts had to be made
known to Grant, who, once he had heard them, would know what to
do. With Elias gone, any decision had to be his.

Understandably, the Kingdons, Elsie's relatives, moved first.
Having never forgotten her, her brothers concerned themselves
actively for her well-being, and they – in particular, David and
Charles – contacted Grant and were instrumental in obtaining Elsie's
release. After it, she was properly reunited with her son in London,
where she stayed for a while with Charles before she came back to
live in Bristol. "She was," said Ernest Kingdon, "as normal as you
and I."[1]

Bearing in mind how long Elsie had been in the mental institution at
Fishponds, her son had no doubt assumed the worst. Her liveliness
and appearance must have surprised him. But there had been a
twenty-year lapse, with all that implied in terms of lack of familiarity.
The hiatus had worked its effect on both of them. Elsie remembered
Archie Leach and found herself looking at a world-famous movie star.

As Ernest Kingdon put it, "Cary Grant knew very little of his
mother. She was a stranger. Late in life, they had to come together
and learn to know each other. It was a tragedy, really – a great
tragedy."[2]

A tragedy, yes; but also – to turn the term on its head – a tragedy
with a happy ending.

With Elsie Leach's re-entry into his life, Grant made at least a beginning to a process that was to ripen into deep affection – the deeper as he came to understand more of that strange marriage between Elsie and Elias.

To re-acquire a mother at so mature an age must have been a strange experience. Grant had his own, strongly independent life, and his career kept him thousands of miles away from Bristol. But Bristol was almost all Elsie had ever known. Her roots were there, her memories – good and bad. There could have been little question of spiriting her off to southern California and a culture quite alien to her. Never robust psychologically, she was too old to make that sort of re-adjustment. She would, then, stay in Bristol, where friends and relatives would keep an eye on her while she led her own life.

And so she did – at first somewhat nervously, as might be imagined after others had so long been making her decisions for her. Mrs Doris Davis was married to the manager of the Commercial Cable Company in Bristol, and she recalled that "Cary used to cable regularly to his mother. More than once if a cable came, my husband would bring it, since Mrs Leach's house was *en route* between the office and our home. Elsie got very lonely and nervous. He often had a job to get her to come to the door, and he would call to her through the letter-box."[3]

Her nervousness was in one sense specific: a morbid fear of men. "I'm a virgin," she would protest again and again, and some of her friends agreed that, psychologically, she was. One of them, though, (a man) would occasionally tease her gently with the question, "In that case, Elsie, how did you come to have Cary?"

The more serious side of her fears and nervousness revealed itself in her behaviour when she was alone. After she had paid evening visits to him and his wife, the same man who had posed the unanswerable query about Elsie's 'virginity' would see her safely back to her own home. When he had bid her goodnight and before he was five paces away from the front door, he could hear the sound of bolts being shot. Elsie would not only lock every door in the house – a precaution that would scarcely have made her unique – but she would also bolt it and prop a chair against it on the inside. Overnight, she would barricade herself in her bedroom with heavy pieces of furniture. Friends who kept an eye on her and worried about her warned, "Elsie, if there's ever a fire in there, we're not going to be able to get to you to rescue you."

One occasion caused them genuine alarm. Though every light in the house appeared to be on, Elsie was not to be roused that evening or coaxed to the door. Had she been out, her friends reasoned, she would have turned out the lights as she habitually did as a measure of economy. In the end, they called the police, who reassured them somewhat by saying they were sure Elsie was not inside, though they had not at that stage gained entry. In the midst of all the consternation, a Rolls-Royce swept up to the property, and its occupants were Cary Grant and his mother − sitting together on the back seat and eating fish and chips out of newspapers. ("I miss fish and chips in the States," Grant would declare. "There's no better meal.") To the woman who had been principally concerned for Elsie's safety, he later sent a large bouquet of flowers.

His generosity towards Elsie frequently took the form of having delivered to the house large chests of food, two of which the same friend and near-neighbour saw unopened and with every likelihood of remaining so in the foreseeable future. "Why don't you open them up, Elsie?" the friend urged. "Come on. Let's have a ball." But Elsie was not to be persuaded. "I want to save them until they're really needed," she explained. "You never know ... Cary might be hard up one day."[4] It was almost as though there was too much for her to believe − her own good fortune and changed circumstances and the fame and wealth of her rediscovered son.

Nevertheless, Elsie's confidence increased, and in her maturity, she began to enjoy what lay ahead − decades, as it turned out. Apart from during the war years, her son would be a frequent visitor, and even in the midst of his longest absences, he would never forget her. As adults, they were to attain an almost unique closeness − something much wiser and perhaps sadder than a small boy's dependence on his mother. This was to be love of the give-and-take kind, a willed reciprocity that could be enjoyed only by mature people.

Meanwhile, Grant turned his immediate attention to a career that was clamouring for it.

Any year in which an actor starred in both *Topper* and *The Awful Truth* was a remarkable one, but 1937 did not at first augur so well for him. For one thing, he had and then lost, through no fault of his own, the chance of working with Henry Hathaway, renowned among directors. Grant should have starred with Carole Lombard and his friend Randolph Scott in *Spawn of the North*, which went into production during the closing months of 1936 and the first of 1937, beginning with location work in Alaska. Lombard, however, fell ill with influenza, and the picture was recast, with Dorothy Lamour substituting for her, and Henry Fonda and George Raft taking over the male roles.

At this juncture, it might be pointed out that a minor thesis could be written (and quite probably, in the prevailing American academic climate, already exists) on the roles lost or refused by Cary Grant. They serve as testimony to the fastidiousness with which he has selected his parts, and the following selection – presented now as a whole, rather than scattered piecemeal throughout the text – does not purport to be exhaustive.

In the late 'thirties, a production called *The Pioneers*, in which he would have starred with Jean Arthur, was shelved. Though eventually played by Melvyn Douglas, Leon in Lubitsch's *Ninotchka* (1939) was originally written for Grant, who also turned down the lead in Hitchcock's *Foreign Correspondent* (1940).

In March 1940, Scott Fitzgerald sold the rights of his story "Babylon Revisited" to the independent producer Lester Cowan as a vehicle for Shirley Temple as Honoria and Cary Grant as her father. (Fitzgerald would parade up and down before Sheilah Graham, the companion of his last years, abortively mimicking the male star's accent and saying, "Baby, can't you see me as the gorgeous Cary Grant?"[5]) The novelist debased his own tale in evolving a screen treatment, and the project was eventually shelved. Later, Cowan sold the screenplay to MGM, who had it completely rewritten before it emerged in 1954 as *The Last Time I Saw Paris*, with Elizabeth Taylor and Van Johnson.

In 1948, when de Sica was looking for financial backing for *The Bicycle Thief*, David Selznick was prepared to provide it on condition that Grant should play Antonio Ricci, the poor, unemployed hero of the neo-realist story. Star allure might have provided box-office insurance, but de Sica could not accept the notion. Grant missed *The Third Man* (1949) when a one-picture deal fell through, and in 1951, negotiations with Selznick for Grant to play Dick Diver in Fitzgerald's *Tender is the Night* foundered when the producer refused to meet the star's $300,000 per film. When the film at last appeared in 1962, Jason Robards Jr was as miscast in the role as Grant would have been ideal. As mentioned earlier, William Wyler's *Roman Holiday* (1953) was originally planned for Grant and Elizabeth

Taylor, with Frank Capra directing. In the mid-'fifties, Grant planned
to buy the rights to his earlier success *His Girl Friday* and remake it
with Grace Kelly, but the idea came to nothing. He turned down the
leads in both *A Star is Born* and *Sabrina Fair* in 1954, and he should
have played the William Holden role in *The Bridge on the River Kwai*
(1957). He had read the book and been approached by the producer
Sam Spiegel, but he debated too much about script changes and, since
he and his then wife Betsy Drake were tired of travelling, was
reluctant to do location work in Ceylon. "Meanwhile Columbia,"
Grant later observed, "knowing me, had also sent a script to Bill
Holden. Holden read the story, decided it was magnificent, which it
was, and said he'd do it. By then, of course, I realized what a great
part I had lost." And he had missed the opportunity to become, as
Holden did, an immensely wealthy man for the rest of his life on the
profits of a single picture.

Fox considered Grant and Burt Lancaster for Caesar and Antony
in their production of *Cleopatra*, but, as history remembers, that
notorious opus underwent many changes before it at last saw the light
of day in 1963. Even close to the end of his career, Grant turned down
at least two prize roles – for laudable motives. He passed on *Music
Man* (1962), insisting Robert Preston be used, and he similarly argued
that Rex Harrison, not he, was the obvious choice for *My Fair Lady*
(1964).

Besides these genuine chances rejected or otherwise missed, there
have been the roles postulated in a kind of affectionate game as ones
that Grant might have filled to advantage. For instance, Hitchcock
once said he envisaged the actor as Hamlet, and if Hitch was teasing,
it might have been assumed that he jested more about his directing the
play as a motion picture than about Grant as Prince of Denmark.
There can be no doubt, however, that Raymond Chandler, much as he
admired Bogart's toughness in *The Big Sleep*, was quite sincere when
he revealed that he had always envisaged Grant as his literary hero,
Philip Marlowe. The *Los Angeles Times* once perceptively nominated
Grant and Ingrid Bergman as admirably suited to play George and
Martha in Albee's *Who's Afraid of Virginia Woolf?* Only the
unthinking, heedless of the actor's past achievements and blind to his
unrealized potential, would automatically have dismissed even the
least of such notions as jokes.

Nevertheless, of all the films Cary Grant never made, the one
projected by Billy Wilder was the most gloriously frivolous – a true

joke as only Wilder can dream them up. Along with other directors, he was asked by a national magazine about unfulfilled ambitions. He replied that he would like to film the story of the Crusades. It would open on knights in gleaming armour preparing to ride off to war. The crusaders would kiss their wives farewell and then lock them into their chastity belts. The knights would thereupon ride off for the Holy Land. Cut – leading to a shot of the workshop of the character who would dominate the rest of the picture: the village locksmith played by Cary Grant.

Behind the impish tale is the admiration, returned by the actor, of a master director with whom Grant, sadly, never worked.

In the life of any major star, there are fascinating 'might-have-beens', but Grant's career probably had more than its share, largely because he chose with extreme care and therefore rejected more than a few interesting possibilities. In the end, even after the break-up of the old studio system with its inescapable imperatives, the pressure on a superstar is to accept *something* – anything – in order to satisfy the itch to work, the urge or need to remain in the public eye. (Against that must be set the somewhat inhibiting realization that each success means that there is more at stake with every selection.) His record, however, suggests that Grant's choices became more and more astute – at least in commercial terms.

Despite *Topper* and *The Awful Truth*, 1937 had its faltering aspects, more than a hint that the pioneering course on which Grant had embarked might prove rocky indeed. His first film for Columbia, released on 27th February found him opposite Grace Moore in *When You're in Love* (a.k.a. *For You Alone*), an intelligent farrago written and directed by Robert Riskin, the screen-writer who had helped Frank Capra turn Gary Cooper (that name again) into a comedian. Not that Grant needed *turning* into a comedian. Three years earlier, Grace Moore's immense success with *One Night of Love* had made the Metropolitan Opera soprano popular with the mass audience, and *When You're in Love*, replete with operatic arias and more easily digestible musical fare, was plainly a vehicle for Miss Moore. In it, she played an opera star (of course!) who, in order to enter the United States, contracted a marriage with a feckless painter (Grant), only to find her feelings for him deepening into genuine love. *When You're in Love* had charm and wit, but it was simply not a showcase for its male star and the talents he had displayed so arrestingly in *Sylvia Scarlett*.

Upstaged by his co-star, he might have been back in a Paramount programmer in which he had merely to look handsome and enhance the femininity of the female lead. Few could excel him in that somewhat passive art, but the exercise was not enough — far from the sort of opportunity Grant had in mind.

Nor did his first film for RKO exactly correct the impression that he was marking time. *The Toast of New York*, though spurious history about the nineteenth-century financier Jim Fisk and his mistress Josie Mansfield, was colourful and diverting, but Grant was inevitably overshadowed by a splendidly blustering performance from Edward Arnold, who took top billing as Fisk. Grant was still looking like the most handsome piece of screen furniture around, but for an actor of his aspirations, that familiar sensation was all the more galling for the impression created by his first two considerable films as a freelance that he might be limited to a career of lending suave support to other stars of greater magnitude.

The sense of waste and frustration, of bridges burned and hopes unrealized, must have been close to overwhelming. Into the third decade of his life, Grant had more than glimpsed the pinnacle of his profession. Yet, though he had come close, he still had not set foot on it — unless one counted *Sylvia Scarlett*, indifferently though it had fared commercially. But in that event, his subsequent career could be interpreted as — already — a descent from the heights.

In her posthumously published autobiography, *Will There Really Be A Morning?*, Frances Farmer, who played Josie Mansfield in *The Toast of New York*, sketched an impression of Grant during the film's making: "He was an aloof, remote person, intent on being Cary Grant playing Cary Grant playing Cary Grant. I considered him a personality, not an actor ..." Even without the desire to poison the well, it might be pointed out that Frances Farmer, tragically used and abused, almost throughout her life was suspicious and resentful in her feelings towards others. Furthermore, it would have been characteristic of her to look to Grant, however inarticulately, for help that he could not have given even had he been aware of her mute appeal. There remains, however, an authentic note in her depiction of the "aloof, remote" star. Grant has not hidden the fact that he was 'difficult' during this period, but anyone whose career was in the balance, as his was, had problems of his own, just as real as any of Farmer's. As she admitted in her autobiography, her behaviour on the picture was punctuated by neurotic outbursts to which Grant, to his credit, reacted with stoical detachment. "Polite but impersonal", he weathered the storms with self-discipline and at an appropriate distance. For, whether he was aware of the fact or not, neither he nor anyone else on that set could have helped poor Frances Farmer.

Grant's remaining films that year gave him precisely the opportunities he craved. Though both were perhaps more involuntary than they seemed, he made two wise selections in 1937. After Hal Roach had persuaded him to star in *Topper* for a fee of $50,000, he must have laughed at any reluctance he had felt initially. Norman Z. McCleod, the director, was a former gag-writer and animator who never managed to impose his personal stamp on the pictures he made, but *Topper*, inheriting the best qualities of Thorne Smith's *jeu d'esprit*, turned out to be one of Grant's early hits – a popular movie that was none the worse for being insubstantial and frivolous. He was cast opposite Constance Bennett, the two of them playing the ghosts of the Kerbys, a light-hearted couple killed in an accident. In their attempts to gain approval for entry into the spirit world, they had first to accomplish a good deed. The body of the film dealt with their endeavour to convert a stuffy banker to their own style of living during their earthly existence. Much of the fun derived from the Kerbys' ability to become visible or invisible at will – a gift that gave rise to superior trick photography. At least with hindsight, the male lead was a typical 'Cary Grant role', and it was observable that the actor had begun to relax, to insinuate his own charm and personality into his playing.

According to David Thomson, *The Awful Truth* was "made at Columbia as proof that the studio could manage without Frank Capra", but so bizarre was its gestation that Grant, having again signed at $50,000, began to mistrust his selection of property and first tried to switch to the Ralph Bellamy role, originally conceived with *Topper*'s Roland Young in mind. He then became so desperate to get out of the picture altogether that he offered to make another for free if Columbia would release him.

Among the principal players, Grant was not alone in his deep uneasiness. Probably he had been attracted by an idea rather than a worked-out screenplay, because almost everyone involved was upset by director Leo McCarey's feeding the script to them in small segments. Nobody at first believed in the picture. The cast might have been horrified had they known what was going on behind their backs. Having junked the original script, McCarey and his collaborator Vina

Delmar would improvise scenes as they sat in a car parked on Hollywood Boulevard.

Yet eventually everything clicked. McCarey, whose later decline was as sad as it was spectacular, was then at the height of his inventiveness. *The Awful Truth* endures as testimony to his talent – a timeless, universal comedy that hit below the intellect; a witty triumph of style over content, the latter being the sort of resolutely trivial story that would reduce any social revolutionary to foaming at his dogma. The plot largely concerned a canine Mr Smith, played by Asta of *Thin Man* fame, to whom Grant had visiting rights after he had divorced his wife, Irene Dunne. Presenting his master with the hat of a concealed male visitor, the dog precipitated an unforgettable slap-stick sequence that in no way undermined the comedy's sophistication and worldliness. On its highly coruscating surface, little emotion was visible, and yet genuine feeling was there, beneath the glittering veneer. *The Awful Truth* was a magnanimous, philanthropic movie that loved all its characters, among whom one of the most endearing was played by Irene Dunne, a superb screen comedienne, curiously neglected by historians of the cinema. (Yet one of them, David Shipman, asserted, "Few actresses could play comedy as she did.")

Opposite her, Grant personified a polished bon vivant with a surprising suggestion of vulnerability – the right role in the right film. This was his first unqualified success as an actor, and more than forty years afterwards, his performance is hard to flaw. Like so many of its successors, his display of burgeoning talents could be summed up by the Latin tag *multum in parvo*. In one scene, Grant, learning that Dunne is to marry Bellamy, an Oklahoman, speaks with urbane appreciation of the prospect of her exhilarating life in Oklahoma City. "And if it should ever get dull," he says, "you can always go over to Tulsa for the weekend." No one hearing that quip delivered for the first time could fail to realize that it comes from a master of comic timing and inflection.

Provocative, then, that Grant was overlooked at award-time. McCarey took 1937's Academy Award for best direction, and though there were four other nominations, the male star was mentioned in none of them.

(On 11th September 1939, a radio adaptation of *The Awful Truth* was broadcast by the Lux Radio Theatre, with Grant, Claudette Colbert and Phyllis Brooks. On 17th March 1940, the story was repeated on the Gulf Screen Guild Playhouse, with Ralph Bellamy,

Robert Young and Carole Lombard. On radio, *The Awful Truth* proved so popular that it was broadcast three times by Lux alone, though only twice with Grant's participation.)

By the end of the year, then, Grant had more than established himself as a free-lance star. From this time forward, a truly reciprocal process increasingly exerted itself: just as much as he sought plum roles, the finest movie-makers jostled one another to engage his services.

The first was one of the greatest.

In the late 'thirties, Howard Winchester Hawks had yet to achieve the stature he attained through such later masterly works as *The Big Sleep* and *Red River*, and there were still several years to go before French critics, in the mid-fifties, began lavishing polysyllabic superlatives upon him. He had already established himself, however, with a number of solid successes such as *The Dawn Patrol* (1930), *Scarface* (1932) and *Barbary Coast* (1935), and in the business, he enjoyed the reputation of being an unfussy, assured, inventive and deceptively relaxed director – a professional's professional. He was about to make what Pauline Kael subsequently called "the American movies' closest equivalent to Restoration Comedy" – a property whose lead-role had already been turned down by Ray Milland, Robert Montgomery and Ronald Colman when Cary Grant, after Columbia had cancelled *The Pioneers*, accepted it.

After he had had to be coaxed to accept the lead in *Topper* and had at first been deeply mistrustful of *The Awful Truth*, Grant, in selecting Hawks and *Bringing up Baby* for his next venture, showed the almost unerring commercial instinct that was to reveal itself again and again in his later career. Hawks had made only one previous comedy, *Twentieth Century* in 1934, but its flair had been undeniable, and *Bringing Up Baby*, if broader in conception and execution, was a worthy successor. The plot was inconsequential, improbable and eccentric, but the gags, though not particularly original, came thick and fast, and, against prediction, they worked – even the corniest of them, such as the set-up in which Grant, the back of co-star Katharine Hepburn's dress having been ripped completely away, shuffled along behind and in step with her to conceal her otherwise exposed flank. If anything, more happily paired with her leading man than she had been in *Sylvia Scarlett*, Hepburn played a strikingly different character from the earlier picture's transvestite heroine – an irresponsible heiress. Grant was a stuffy palaeontologist waiting to be liberated by her charm and zest for living, while the eponymous Baby was a pet leopard to whom both stars sang, "I Can't Give You Anything But Love".

Exasperation was the keynote of several scenes. Hawks thought that Grant sounded *genuinely* stuffy when he affected anger and, wanting the displeasure to come across as risible, asked his male star to think of someone he knew whose rage was habitually mirth-provoking, unintentionally funny. Grant couldn't, but Hawks himself recalled a man who would whinny like a horse at moments of high frustration, and the director induced Grant to employ a device that he was to use again and again, with incomparable control and timing, in subsequent pictures.

The anecdote, related by Hawks himself, provided a strong clue to the understanding of *Bringing Up Baby*'s artistic success. On paper, the screenplay by Dudley Nichols and Hagar Wilde must have looked less than promising. Rare rapport between cast and director and more than a little improvisation led to a transmogrification of the possibilities indicated by the script. Even the story's questionable recipe of regeneration through humiliation was made to seem plausible – at least in Grant's appealing personification of the transition. There was perhaps more – a sense in the movie of anarchy, of ultimate disaster, that was to be summed up in David Thomson's label: "a screwball comedy surrounded by darkness, for ever on the brink of madness". As much as in anything else, Howard Hawks' greatness lay in the extra dimension he could bring to a genre picture.

"Under the deft directorial hand of Howard Hawks," said *Time*, "*Bringing Up Baby* comes off second only to last year's whimsical high spot, *The Awful Truth*." Success makes everyone friends, and Grant and Hepburn both realized that their teaming could achieve happy results. Nevertheless, RKO despaired of making Hepburn popular, and *Bringing Up Baby* was her last movie for them. (She actually bought herself out of her contract with the studio.) Astutely protective of her career, she purchased the rights of Philip Barry's *Holiday*, later selling the play, director George Cukor, and herself in a package deal with Columbia. Since she had understudied the leading role on Broadway in 1928, she had a shrewd idea of the comedy's potential as a film. (There had, in any case, been an earlier version in 1930.) With Cary Grant opposite her, Hepburn believed – correctly, as it turned out – that the success of *Holiday* (a.k.a. *Free to Live*) was assured.

Grant played a dashing, somewhat iconoclastic hero who fell in love with one girl (Doris Nolan) only to transfer his affections to her sister (Hepburn), who was scarcely inactive in diverting his attention to her. Once again, as in *Bringing Up Baby*, the safe, respectable life was by implication rejected in favour of unknown, incalculable adventures. Grant's infectious sense of fun was well exploited by screen-writers Donald Ogden Stewart and Sidney Buchman, but they had little tailoring to do.

As a playwright, Barry was light, witty, deft, perceptive, unexpectedly moving – the sort of dramatist Grant seemed born to serve well. Furthermore, Barry's plays, in much the same way as *The Awful Truth*, represented the triumph of style over content, and this was also the feat that Grant had proved he could make singularly his own. In short, the alliance of Barry and Grant, as was to be demonstrated again in *The Philadelphia Story*, was hand and glove. The backward somersaults Grant executed in *Holiday* might have been grafted on – an interpolation from his earlier life with the Bob Pender Troupe – but the affinity that he exhibited with his role was spiritual and innate.

In November 1938, after a vacation in Europe, Grant returned to America. An event took place there that year that might have seemed of limited significance at first, even to some in the industry, but was to prove of profound importance to the business of making motion pictures. In 1938, the US government instituted the anti-trust suit that was eventually to compel the majors to separate their theatre-chains from studios and sales. Practices such as block booking (selling in one package a studio's projected output for an entire year) had ensured profitable operation, and the perceptive saw at once that the essential nature of the venture was imperilled. Other shifts of social taste and economic influence were to play their part in the ultimate toppling of the studios, but many commentators were unanimous in their belief that, whatever happened afterwards to postpone the evil day, 1938 was the beginning of the end.

9

The High Life

By the later years of the decade, Cary Grant was a leading member of the jet-set. Neither that mode of commercial flight nor, therefore, the term itself had then been invented, but he was one of that élite group upon whom the label, along with others such as 'the beautiful people', was to be appended by the 'sixties. The erstwhile promising newcomer at the Court of San Simeon had a much bigger part to play in a social set that had welcomed him with open arms.

Even today, television is the only rival of motion pictures in conferring instant and world-wide fame. Thirty or so years ago, television barely existed, but being a leading man in big Hollywood productions bestowed a status, familiarity and acceptability that were transcontinental and international. As Jerry Lewis once said, "When Cary Grant used to walk down a street in New York, the city was on fire with excitement."

In those days, 'the jet-set' would more accurately have been dubbed 'the luxury passenger-liner set'. Air travel was in its infancy, and though by the late 'forties Grant was an enthusiast, even then there were hardships to be endured such as erratic heating systems on transoceanic flights. Before he took to the air, however, it was significant that Grant, in common with many others, established the foundations of lasting relationships during the transatlantic crossings of the great steamships of the times. The surroundings were luxurious, the voyage was – by more modern standards – leisurely, and the vistas of sky, sea and unbounded horizons were conducive to romance as well as to the suspension of urgent but mundane concerns.

More than ever before, Grant was an eligible bachelor – among the world's most eligible. His taste for the high life had developed, and by 1940 or earlier he was an inveterate party-goer and singer of popular songs to revised, suggestive lyrics. His impudent wit was as much appreciated in private as in its public airings on the screen.

Whatever criticisms might have been levelled at the social world through which he moved with grace and ease, it exerted a powerful fascination, if not enchantment. Grant was to become a frequent guest at the home of the Cole Porters – concomitant with a somewhat strange chapter in his screen career in 1945. Among the actor's friends were David Niven, Noel Coward, Irene M. Selznick and playwright Frederick Lonsdale, with whom he enjoyed a particularly close alliance. Lonsdale, in Grant's own words, "spent years of his life crossing by ship between London and New York", and the maritime note resounds through Grant's own personal life. In 1938, he dined with Barbara Hutton on the *Normandie*, little realizing that the meal was a prelude to marriage with this heiress, granddaughter to the founder of the Woolworth Company, Frank Winfield. Nearly ten years later, on another ship, the *Queen Mary*, Merle Oberon was to introduce him to a young actress called Betsy Drake. History was about to repeat itself.

Tempora mutantur nos et mutamur in illis ... With the perspective of history, it is easy to ridicule the good life of the 'thirties. Already could be heard the gruesome tuning-up for the concert of atrocities that was the Second World War – an event that, it might be argued, left life more serious than it had been before, with a shifting social order in which the wealthy could enjoy themselves only with a sense of unease. The pre-war decade was perhaps the last great playtime, and not infrequently those who played hardest – like the stylish, witty, dazzlingly talented Cole Porter – were also those who worked hardest.

Grant's profession scarcely made him one of the idle rich. Nor was he ever so enamoured of high society as, for example, Douglas Fairbanks Jr, who, without quite the same enthusiasm for acting, grew more British than the British, was made an honorary Knight Commander of the British Empire in 1949, turned his back on his screen career and settled happily in fashionable Kensington, where he became a renowned host.

Grant's relish for the *haut monde* was not on the same scale, and yet, like Fairbanks, he ran foul of a certain section of the Press, who mainly because he shunned them, began to attack him as a social-climber and later a fortune-hunter. If there was any justice at all in these attacks, they missed the point. What Grant enjoyed was rubbing well-tailored shoulders with brilliant, colourful personalities – people who were helpful, from whom he could learn, who were, in his own words, "tolerant of [him]". Some of them were insincere, of course, and there were those who showed him unfriendliness. (He never mentions them.) But there were also those who had talent and respected it in others, who were charming and gay (in the days when the word could be used unthinkingly) and who enjoyed money as, in Orson Welles' words, "the sixth sense that enables us to enjoy the other five".

One such was Countess Dorothy di Frasso. The daughter of a New York millionaire, she lived on the income from a $1,000,000 trust fund left by her father. Marriage with an Italian aristocrat, Count Carlo di Frasso, bestowed her title. For many years, her escapades as the darling of the film colony and a prominent member of café society made headlines, but few were bigger than those devoted to her cruise to the tropics in September 1938. On board, besides friends from Hollywood, was Bugsy Siegel, the handsome mobster whose entry into society had been sponsored by the Countess. (Nine years afterwards, Siegel was the victim of a gangland slaying in Los Angeles.) The ship itself had a direct connection with the movies – a 150-foot schooner called the *Metha Nelson* that had been used in *Mutiny on the Bounty*.

Four months later, after a variety of misadventures that included a violent and disabling storm, the ship limped back to its home port, San Pedro, where a federal grand jury investigated charges of mutiny brought by the master against two crew members. The whole bunch, the captain alleged, had been dangerous thugs, difficult to subdue, and the Countess di Frasso had feared kidnapping, if not for her life. However, when the Countess and her friends denied the story, the charges were dropped.

It was a striking, even lurid, paragraph in her eventful life. At the Villa Madama in Rome, she would throw extravagant parties, and her house guests included (not necessarily at the same time) both Gary Cooper and Cary Grant, who was a good fifteen years her junior. In January 1954, she died of a heart attack at the age of sixty-six. She was on a train returning from Las Vegas, where she had been celebrating the New Year with Marlene Dietrich. The actor Clifton Webb, it was reported, found her lying fully clothed and wearing a diamond necklace worth $175,000. She was covered with a full-length mink, and her baggage contained another $100,000 of jewellery.

If ostentation appeared to be her forte, Grant valued her for her sense of fun, her "rare ability to laugh at herself". In her buoyant company, he could seldom maintain a fit of depression, and as a last tribute, he accompanied her body to New York for the funeral.

Such friends as Countess di Frasso, though, were complemented or even outnumbered by members of his own profession. From the beginning, Grant was never one to shun, as some other stars did and do, fellow performers. (After all, he was to marry three of them.) Among stars, Frederick Brisson, Randolph Scott, David Niven and Rosalind Russell were to be good friends, and Sir Alexander Korda, until his death in 1956, was an occasional visitor to Grant's Bel Air home, as was Korda's second wife, Merle Oberon. But such alliances were natural and inevitable. What was noteworthy was that as Grant increasingly moved in affluent and sophisticated circles, he retained and even intensified his enviable ability to be at ease in any company — always the natural and friendly man. In part at least, this gift was the heritage of those unsettled, almost nomadic years in his early twenties when he had learned to mix with all sorts and conditions of people, often with poverty as a common denominator.

While to some journalists intent on viewing it from only one angle, Grant's life in the late 'thirties began to look like a succession of glittering parties, he continued to work hard. True, his output had dropped since the hectic first years of his career, the statistics of which read: 1932, seven pictures; 1933, six; 1934, four. The difference was that he was no longer a victim of the familiar scatter-gun technique of the major studios — that prolific production of films that at once exploited a star's services to the maximum and bombarded the public in the hope that familiarity would be enduring and profitable.

Free of such pressures, Grant chose well for his three films in 1939. The first, *Gunga Din*, though technically almost impeccable, makes uncomfortable viewing today, when one is immediately aware of the picture's racism, colonial attitudes and generally patronizing treatment of Indians — all received ideas of the times. Predictably, Gunga Din himself, though played with great charm by Sam Jaffe and allowed a heroic deed at the film's climax, turned out to be a minor character, and Rudyard Kipling made a spurious appearance at the end to lend authority to the proceedings 'derived' (Ben Hecht and Charles MacArthur dreamed up the story) from his poem about the waterboy who yearned to be a soldier. Essentially *Gunga Din*, was *Boys' Own Paper* stuff — high jinks and derring-do featuring three sergeants (Grant, Victor McLaglen and Douglas Fairbanks Jr) involved in a not especially interesting plot.

For RKO, though, this was a most ambitious venture. It was

allocated the studio's biggest budget up to that time, and location-shooting took place in the Alabama Range, near Lone Pine, two hundred miles north of Los Angeles, where a large camp was set up. Three years earlier, Warners, also looking for a reasonable approximation of India's north-west frontier, had filmed *The Charge of the Light Brigade* there. For *Gunga Din*, six hundred people moved into the location-camp, elaborate sets were constructed, and nine hundred extras enacted the final battle on the slopes of Mount Whitney.

This and the other action sequences were brilliantly directed by George Stevens, who ensured that the film was, of its kind, first-rate entertainment. Grant and his two co-stars were splendidly, if rather simple-mindedly, funny, but they were not too plausible as characters, and their wholesale killing became sickening, defying any sensitive movie-goer to shrug off the carnage as just what might be expected in an adventure picture.

Such carping aside, *Gunga Din* was important for Grant in two ways. It was arguably his first action movie, and he coped admirably and athletically with its demands. Furthermore, George Stevens, realizing that he had struck gold, allowed his star to improvise in scene after scene, with a resulting freshness that was patent on the screen. Grant elected to appear in two more pictures directed by Stevens, who thus, in company with George Cukor and Leo McCarey, made a total of three films with the actor. As for *Gunga Din* itself, it was successful enough to inspire two inferior remakes: *Soldiers Three* in 1951, with Stewart Granger, David Niven and Robert Newton, and *Sergeants Three* in 1962, with Frank Sinatra, Dean Martin and Peter Lawford. (Kipling's own "Soldiers Three" had given Hecht and MacArthur notions for their original story.)

When Harry Cohn of Columbia Pictures wanted something for Grant and Jean Arthur at short notice, Howard Hawks rapidly dreamed up the plot of *Only Angels Have Wings*, which he also directed from Jules Furthman's screenplay. For an action picture, Hawks' second project with Grant was surprisingly static and talky — an uninspired tale about airmail-fliers in South America. This colony was dominated by Grant, and their exclusive set was disturbed by a provocative showgirl played by Jean Arthur. Her intrusion into a man's world — though it was not intentional, for she had been stranded — was predictably resented. Nobility of character was to be taken as Grant's justification for bullying her — it was the *macho* fantasy of many other better and worse Hollywood movies. After she had qualified by total acquiescence to its rules, she could be condescendingly admitted to the masculine domain. The film's fliers mocked her expressions of grief at the death of Joe, one of their number who had crashed in bad weather. Later, chastened and seeing the light, she declared, "I hadda behave like a sap." Grant asked her, "Grown up?" "Hope so," she replied. "Good girl," he said, approving her reformation and immediately testing it by inquiring, "Who's Joe?" Arthur came through with flying colours by announcing, "Never heard of him." She had accepted not only the code and stoicism of the fliers but also the fact that a woman's role in the world of *machismo* was by definition subordinate.

Despite such piffle, the picture was a great success in its time and is still venerated as a cult movie. Looking more handsome than ever, Grant handled his unsubtle part well, and Jean Arthur was excellent. But *The New Republic* saw through the high polish when it stated that it was "too bad [Hawks] and an above-average cast had to be wasted on the story of *Only Angels Have Wings*"!

Also well made but unworthy was Grant's third film of the year, *In Name Only*, a romantic-triangle drama directed for RKO by the great John Cromwell. Compared with Kay Francis and Carole Lombard, who performed excellently, the male star had little to do, and his somewhat passive presence recalled similar roles before he struck out as a free-lance actor. On 11th December, the three principals recreated their parts for a Lux Radio Theatre version of the film, and 1939, with Lux shows also of *Only Angels Have Wings* and *The Awful Truth*, was one of Grant's busiest years in radio.

Though professionally preoccupied, Grant along with other members of what was loosely called the English colony in Hollywood, observed the outbreak of hostilities between England and Germany in September of that year with feelings markedly different from those of most Americans, many of whom were passionately isolationist. His thoughts were radically different from those of, probably, the majority of workers in Hollywood, "whose political conscience was non-existent" (according to John Baxter's austere judgement in *The Hollywood Exiles*). Grant's feelings, however, were complicated by the fact that he had already begun the lengthy process of becoming an American citizen. Emotional ties to the land of his birth, to say nothing of his sympathies with the oppressed (soon to be expressed in tangible form), made it impossible for him to shrug off the war as merely one more of the world's regrettable calamities, and yet he was just as strongly bound, not least professionally, to another country whose president would not lead it into battle on the side of the British until December, 1941 – more than a year later. Grant had boyhood memories of the First World War and was steeped in the recent history of Great Britain. He could neither put his motherland's predicament out of his mind nor easily decide what, if anything, he ought to do. Though there were those who refused to recognize the fact, at least his situation was strikingly different from that of numerous British movie-makers who, before the war was much older, hurriedly accepted offers of work – hitherto not so tempting – that took them to the US and safety.

Meanwhile, Grant pursued a career that brought him, during the making of *His Girl Friday*, the friendship of both Frederick Brisson and Rosalind Russell, later to become husband and wife. At that time, Brisson was staying with Grant at his Santa Monica Beach home, and he was more than a little excited to discover that his host was engaged on a picture with the very star with whom he had recently fallen in love – at least on celluloid, having doted on her performance in *The Women*, which was shown on board ship during a transatlantic crossing. For her part, Rosalind Russell was by no means unaffected by the proximity of her co-star, then between marriages, not to say between girls. (Though this was a period during which he dated Mary Brian, Ginger Rogers and Phyllis Brooks, the young starlet with whom he made a number of broadcasts.) Russell and Grant dined and dated on several occasions, but towards completion of *His Girl Friday*, Grant repeatedly tried to arrange meetings between his leading lady and Frederick Brisson – vainly, since a woman in his company was hardly likely to become animated at the prospect of dating some other, anonymous male. Nevertheless, Brisson at last made efforts on his own behalf, and wooed and won Miss Russell. The Brissons retained the affection of Cary Grant, and since he became a frequent house guest of theirs, they were uniquely positioned to observe the problems that developed in Grant's second marriage.

Before those days, however, there occurred troubles as hilarious as any ever dreamed up for a Grant comedy. These took place at the Russell-Brisson wedding, at which Grant was to be best man. The bride, it was planned, should walk down the aisle accompanied by her brother while the groom and best man would enter from a side door and join her at the altar. What nobody had anticipated was that a monk at the mission chosen for the ceremony had decided to lock the side door so that fans could not intrude upon the nuptials. The wedding march announced the departure of Rosalind Russell down the aisle, and in a scene worthy of *The Awful Truth*, Brisson saw Grant desperately working the door handle like an actor frustrated by a recalcitrant prop. Fortunately for both men, the noise was audible both to the bride, who slowed her steps, and to the guests, one of whom was Arthur Hornblow Jr, who came to the rescue by turning the key, left in the lock on the other side of the door from the alarmed groom and his best man.[1]

But if that episode had its farcical element, it was nothing compared with the escapades depicted in *His Girl Friday*, which was released early in 1940. The film was based on Hecht and MacArthur's 1928 Broadway hit, *The Front Page*, which was largely concerned with the outrageous expedients employed by editor Walter Burns to thwart the threatened retirement of his ace reporter Hildy Johnson. The background and plot owed much of course to the authors' own experience as journalists. An earlier film-version of *The Front Page* had been directed by Lewis Milestone in 1931, and Howard Hawks, probably wishing to avoid direct comparisons, dreamed up a startling revision that both stimulatingly altered the nature of the original work and gave to Rosalind Russell a wonderful part. Turning Hildy Johnson into a woman resulted in a romantic storyline not dissimilar to that of *The Awful Truth*, in which Ralph Bellamy had played the role of patsy-in-the-middle just as he did in *His Girl Friday*. The later movie, however, was much tougher and harder, less reliant on visual comedy and bristling with pungent dialogue delivered at seemingly incredible speed. As Pauline Kael was to point out, "word-gags [took] the place of the sight-gags of silent comedy, as this vanished race of brittle, cynical, childish people [rushed] around on corrupt errands".

Since both Grant and Russell were great ad libbers, Hawks made the most of their shared propensity. (One of Grant's most interesting interpolations occurs when he retorts to a fellow player: "The last person to say that to me was Archie Leach just before he cut his throat.") Their delivery became so fast that their speeches overlapped, and Russell grew worried that audiences would be unable to follow them. Hawks reassured her: there would be changes of tempo, moments of relief; the audience would love the wild exchanges between the stars. In her autobiography, *Life Is a Banquet*, Russell tells how one day, inventing comic 'business', she threw her handbag at Grant and missed. Improvising, he countered, "You used to be better than that." Hawks was a clever enough director to leave this sort of thing in the final cut. When Grant shoved his co-star down hard on to a couch, Hawks exhorted him to do so even harder for the next take. Grant demurred that he didn't "want to kill the woman". Hawks thought that over for a moment before he said, "Try killin' 'er."

Seeking gratuitously to enhance the stature of a master director, film historians have claimed that Hawks *invented* overlapping dialogue in *His Girl Friday*. Neither he nor his actors did so, but merely took over a device that was already written into Hecht and MacArthur's play. Nor should Hawks' own story be taken too seriously of how he hit upon the idea of a girl playing Hildy by accident. He was the author of an anecdote that has unfortunately passed into history in which he asked a girl, just because she happened to be the only person available, to read Hildy's part while he, Hawks, read the editor. In the midst of the reading, he stopped, struck by the extraordinary effectiveness of the contrast of the sexes. As Pauline Kael has pointed out, the story is charming but not entirely convincing. There was a well-established tradition of 'screwball' romantic newspaper comedies, one of them, as Hawks no doubt knew well, having been *Wedding Present* starring Grant in 1936. Not only was the wisecracking girl-reporter a requirement for box-office success, she was also almost always modelled on Adela Rogers St Johns, the smart and attractive journalist who worked for the Hearst press. Hawks was aware of what he was doing: he was making a *romantic* comedy in which Hildy's change of sex was much more than a happy accident. Rosalind Russell, as Pauline Kael perceptively remarked, "was so obviously playing Adela Rogers St Johns that she was dressed in an imitation of the St Johns girl-reporter striped suit."

His Girl Friday was a great success, though some critics described the goings-on in it as tasteless. Today, both critics and audiences having much stronger stomachs, the essential situations would be called black comedy, and so it was scarcely surprising when in 1974 the film was remade yet again as *The Front Page* by Billy Wilder, who was no doubt attracted by the misanthropy and sour humour that have never been far from his best work. Jack Lemmon and Walter Matthau restored the original's single sex character.

10

They Also Serve ...

In 1939, Grant had passed the age of thirty-five and reached a watershed in his life, if not his career. Man may be alone among creatures in looking back on his younger self with distaste or even horror. In retrospect, Grant was to judge harshly his pre-1939 personality. Naturally, so precise an age as thirty-five indicated a fairly arbitrary choice in his character analysis, but the dividing line served its purpose. Before it, he had been 'impossible' – the least stringent of his verdicts upon himself. (If he qualified or softened the opinion, it was only by extending it to all other men, too.) After it, he made no arrogant claims to self-knowledge or special insight; he was still painfully groping his way towards understanding of himself and others.

Thus, pushing thirty-six and with, by any reckoning, half a dozen hit movies behind him, he had, he hoped, laid the foundations of a personal and professional stability upon which, luck and good management doing their part, he could build. Psychologically, there was little of Hamlet in him; he was not "a Peer Gynt-like searcher". But he had an awareness of himself, however inchoate, that at least suggested progress and bred confidence. As for his acting, knowing both what properties he wanted and that he could secure them was a stimulus in itself. He was eager to make pictures, and he did – "probably too many," as he said in the 'sixties, looking back. By and large, though, they were the right pictures, and if he made too many, so did most other comparable stars in the Hollywood of that era.

With war rumbling across the Atlantic, out of earshot but not out of his thoughts, Grant starred in two more films that were released in 1940 to general acclaim. After a serious car crash had put paid to his ideas of directing the picture, Leo McCarey produced *My Favourite Wife* for RKO from his own concept. Garson Kanin, who was later to describe the finished work as "mechanical", directed in McCarey's place, and while the mature Kanin might have had doubts about the result, most who saw *My Favourite Wife* or review it today found it and continue to find it a comedy of some freshness and charm. The plot concerned Grant's discovery, having just married for the second time, that his first wife, believed dead, was still living. Furthermore, for the preceding seven years, she had been marooned on a desert-island with attractive Randolph Scott. Irene Dunne played the first wife, and out of such froth, she, Grant, and the rest of the cast made an entertaining if not especially memorable offering that was to be remade in 1963 as *Move Over, Darling* with James Garner and Doris Day. *Time* magazine hinted that *My Favourite Wife* was not truly worthy of Grant and revealed that he had been paid a fee of $100,000.

He followed this insubstantial fare with *The Howards of Virginia* (a.k.a. *The Tree of Liberty*), worthy but somewhat dull, and a rare foray into the world of historical drama. At least this Revolutionary War story proved that Grant was one of a comparatively small number of male stars who could be at ease in costume roles, but *Newsweek* commented that he was "obviously miscast". Critics generally experienced problems in believing in Cary Grant as a rough-hewn frontiersman with democratic ideals, but if his performance left them unconvinced, all were impressed by the picture's aura of historical authenticity, largely obtained by shooting on location at Williamsburg.

That year, members of the British colony in Hollywood were increasingly disturbed by the problem of what they should do as the news of the war in Europe became ever more depressing. Although a course of action might be decided upon collectively, any decisions had essentially to be personal – since there was at that time and in those circumstances no question of a call-up. Having settled matters with his own conscience, he who wanted to stay out of the fighting could do so, even if at the risk of scurrilous gossip about his motives. Whatever the decision, life was not easy for the British expatriates who honestly pondered their obligations; the situation did not exactly call for the boy who replied, "I can" when duty whispered low, "Thou must".

Grant told Quentin Reynolds, "You feel so damn helpless here. I want to go back ... I could be an ARP warden. I could be a fire-fighter. I could do something." When it was rumoured that he might be donning a uniform, Elsie Leach made a mother's statement of the kind favoured by recruitment posters: "I see he says he intends to volunteer for service in the US Armed Forces. If he does, all well and good. I shall be proud ..."

David Niven's experience, however, was not untypical of the treatment meted out to patriotic English actors. Within days of England's declaring war on Germany, he tried to enlist in the Canadian Army, which had the merit of being relatively close and cheap to reach. Douglas Fairbanks Jr stood him a farewell party with many famous guests, Cary Grant among them. The Canadian divisions, though, turned out to be grossly oversubscribed, and so Niven, making his way to England by a circuitous route, attempted to join the RAF. Neither the newspapers nor the RAF were impressed. The actor had travelled seven thousand miles at his own expense merely to have it implied that he was a publicity seeker.

Others less patriotic simply remained in Hollywood and were attacked for so doing by the British Press. There was, however, a demand among the expatriates for the clarification of some sort of collective attitude, and in the summer of 1940 it resulted in Grant and Cedric Hardwicke, as representatives of the British colony in Hollywood, flying to Washington for a meeting with Lord Lothian, the British ambassador, to solicit his advice about how best to serve the war-effort, without necessarily returning to England. In effect and perhaps not surprisingly, the ambassador advised: "Stay put and carry on doing what you do best." Since most of them were actors – whether good, bad or indifferent – what they did best was to appear in front of motion-picture cameras. As far as Lord Lothian was concerned, there was nothing bogus, either, about their remaining in Hollywood. To the British government, he added a footnote: "It is quite unfair to condemn older actors who are simply obeying this ruling as 'deserters'." For the British cause, moreover, it was healthy to maintain an influential colony within Hollywood, which was seen as 'very volatile'. If propaganda films were to be made, the presence of English actors would help to ensure that such films were pro-British. In the event, history and pictures like *Mrs Miniver* (whether artistically good or bad) proved Lord Lothian's point. President Franklin D. Roosevelt told *Mrs Miniver's* director, William Wyler, that his movie had been instrumental in swinging public opinion away from isolationism and towards backing up Britain's fight.

Did Cary Grant qualify as an 'older actor'? Obviously not in the sense that Sir C. Aubrey Smith, Sir Cedric Hardwicke or Ronald Colman did. But if one took, as most people did, the age of forty as a rough dividing line, thirty-six was on the mature side. Furthermore, if Grant's position was not unique, it was undoubtedly special. His career in Hollywood might have begun a full ten years after that of Colman, but it was now just as firmly rooted – and so, arguably, was Grant himself. Colman had emigrated to the US in 1920 – the very same year in which the younger actor, though he did not realize it at the time, emigrated too. Finally, if human beings could be reduced to crudely mathematical propositions, Grant was three-fifths an American, the process of obtaining citizenship being well advanced by 1940.

He resumed his work in Hollywood, where he neither forgot England (How could he – with his mother and many other kin living in a city that seemed – and sadly proved – a logical target for enemy bombers?) nor missed opportunities to aid the war-effort. His next film was *The Philadelphia Story*, for which he was paid a salary of $125,000. Later, although this reported statistic was not flatly contradicted by the star, he strongly implied that the figure was exaggerated. Exaggerated or not, the entire sum was donated by Grant to British War Relief.

The Philadelphia Story, which was released in early 1941 to become one of his most fondly remembered pictures, had an interesting pre-history and owed its genesis entirely to Katharine Hepburn. In 1938, exhibitors had declared her 'box-office poison', and she had faced an obvious hiatus, if not worse, in her screen career. Even the possibility of playing Scarlett O'Hara in *Gone With the Wind*, a role that would surely have restored her fortunes, evaporated when David Selznick, perhaps never serious in considering her, chose Vivien Leigh at the end of his long quest. Hepburn needed something – and she needed it fast. Remembering Philip Barry, the author of *Holiday*, she approached him for a play, and he obliged with *The Philadelphia Story*, a work in which her part was tailored by the dramatist down to the minutest detail. If she had trouble with even one line, Barry revised until she could articulate it gracefully. In the Theatre Guild Production on Broadway, she enjoyed a great personal success, winning the New York Drama Critics Circle Award. *The Philadelphia Story*, it was clear, was a hot property that Hollywood would be eager to acquire. MGM rose to the bait. The studio soon discovered that the wily Miss Hepburn owned twenty-three per cent of the play's stock and had a contract deeply involving her in any film rights. To get the property, they *had* to take her – box-office poison or not. MGM reputedly paid $175,000 plus the star's fee of $75,000. The studio's insurance, however, was Cary Grant and James Stewart as leading men – more than enough, they surmised, to offset Hepburn's alleged lack of popularity. With Cukor directing, the production began to look like a reunion of old friends, and all was set for a notable triumph.

To secure Grant's services, MGM had to agree to give him top billing and to pay his salary to British War Relief. He was offered the choice of male leads: he could play either K.C. Dexter Haven, the playboy ex-husband, or Macaulay Connor, the newspaperman. Notwithstanding the fact that Stewart, in the second role, won an Academy Award, Grant was his characteristically astute self in picking K.C. Dexter Haven. It was purely and simply the better role. (Why Stewart in the one part won the award and Grant in the other did not was merely one more mystery in the string of enigmas that mark the history of the Academy Awards.)

The Philadelphia Story was typical Barry country – a sophisticated comedy of manners in which socialite Tracy Lord (Hepburn) discovered in the course of the day before her second marriage that she was still in love with her ex-husband, Dexter. The ramifications of the plot were witty and delightful, and the coruscating language on the surface, as usual with Barry, concealed emotions that were none the less moving for being understated.

Cukor demanded and got lengthy rehearsals that resulted in smooth shooting. The first big problem came with the final cut, which was thirty minutes too long. (Even as shown, the picture ran to 112 minutes – somewhat lengthy for that period.) There was rumoured bitterness among the players about what should be excised, each naturally wishing to protect his own performance.

Nevertheless, the success of *The Philadelphia Story* had rewards for everyone, though artistically that success was compromised by the script's prolixity – a plethora of talk that tended to weary audiences as well as critics. If the acting fell short of the level achieved in *Holiday*, its related work, the whole cast did well, Hepburn winning the 1940 New York Critics' Award. Curiously, though the general public liked her best in *The Philadelphia Story*, her steady admirers were less enthusiastic about the performance. Years later, Penelope Gilliat singled out for special praise Grant's beautifully developed "style of unwounding mockery" towards his screen ex-wife. With songs by Cole Porter, the picture was remade in 1956 as *High*

Society, with Grace Kelly, Bing Crosby and Frank Sinatra in the principal roles.

As for the original, *The Philadelphia Story* marked the end of Grant's fruitful professional association with Katharine Hepburn and George Cukor. More than three decades later, during interviews published in the 'seventies, Grant gave the lie to rumours that he and Hepburn had had serious disagreements during the filming of *Bringing Up Baby*. Although he had 'belted' her in one picture and she had done the same to him in another, the actor said, there had never been any problems.

Grant's next picture, for Columbia, was a weepy — superbly made and rising to great heights, as in the star's plea for permanent custody of his and Irene Dunne's adopted child. In synopsis, the plot revealed its crudity: infertile couple adopted child; child died; marriage tottered; couple acquired second child, its arrival saving marriage. Such cloying emotionalism cried out for directorial legerdemain and found it in George Stevens, who won over the most cynical movie-goers with taste, intelligence and wit — qualities that were already to be found in Morrie Ryskind's sound script, calculating though it was.

In sum, *Penny Serenade* was a wonderfully crafted, potent treatment of a bland, factitious story. Donald Richie has commented that in the film "hundreds are destroyed in an earthquake so that Irene Dunne's miscarriage may be successfully accomplished." Furthermore, children are *not* the cement that binds marriage, but so skilled was the implying of this 'message' that it slipped convincingly by. The picture was aided enormously by the fine playing of its principals, with Grant particularly good in his scene with a judge. He might have missed an Academy Award in *The Philadelphia Story*, but *Penny Serenade* at least brought him a nomination — his first.

For Grant, the film was memorable in one other, personal way. During its making, he met Stanley Fox, who later became his lawyer-manager and remained such for the next forty years, besides being possibly the star's closest friend. Without him, Grant once said, "I'd be adrift."

Captivatingly romantic on screen, Grant was also waxing romantic in his private life. After the *Normandie* encounter in 1938, Countess Dorothy di Frasso re-introduced the actor and Barbara Hutton when the two women returned from a trip to Honolulu. The acquaintance ripened into genuine mutual regard, and in August 1941, in a bid to elude journalists, Grant, Barbara Hutton and some friends travelled to

Mexico for a vacation. With two men companions, Grant drove there in the Hutton Cadillac. Barbara flew to San Antonio with a woman friend, and then all five went to Acapulco. Away from the glare of publicity, the star and the Woolworth heiress toured Mexico for some weeks.

They were almost invariably together that year when Grant was not filming, and at about this time sections of the Press critical of him as a fortune-hunter began to refer to the couple as "cash and Cary". Barbara Hutton had reputedly inherited $12 million at the age of seven — a sum that grew to $20 million by the time she was twenty-one, seven years before her intimate involvement with Grant. While such wealth undoubtedly dwarfed his own, he might, had he chosen to retort, having pointed out that his own personal fortune was by then probably $3 million.

A marked decrease during this period in the number of pictures he made could be attributed to his preoccupation with Barbara, but in the fall, *Suspicion*, Grant's first film with Alfred Hitchcock, was released. Its somewhat curious genesis had begun in 1939 when Boris Ingster and Nathanael West jointly adapted *Before The Fact* by Francis Iles (a pseudonym of Anthony Berkeley) as a vehicle for Laurence Olivier. Just before the property went into production, however, Hitchcock was said to have got wind of the project, liked it and acquired the rights. Though Hitch thought the original script was "absolutely beautiful", he none the less had Samson Raphaelson, Joan Harrison and Alma Reville prepare a different screenplay.

In the story as filmed, Lina MacKinlaw (Joan Fontaine), a repressed, unstylish girl, met Johnny Aysgarth (Grant), who was a pathological liar and spendthrift, and eventually married him. Though deeply in love with her husband, Lina came to believe that he intended to kill her. In fact, though she had been accurately alert to the flaws in Johnny's character, he had no such intention. Her suspicions had been delusions.

The film gripped and amused *despite* the plot and the essentially unconvincing characterization. It said much for Hitchcock's direction and Grant's acting that the ambiguities of Johnny Aysgarth's conduct and personality carried even surface persuasiveness. If the Johnny the audience saw, however, was to be taken as a figure born of Lina's fantasy, neither script nor direction found effective means of suggesting the subjectivity of her vision. As matters stood, with Lina's intuitions unfounded and her life in no danger, *Suspicion* was aptly titled and at the same time rather silly. To possess impact and conviction, the story *demanded* Johnny's intention to murder his wife.

In fairness to Hitchcock, it must be said that his plan was to end the story with Lina's murder (as *Before The Fact* had done), satisfying Hollywood morality by depicting Johnny, after poisoning his wife, cheerfully mailing to her mother Lina's last letter, in which she told all and explained that she loved Johnny so much that death had become preferable to living any longer.

It is hard to believe that Hitchcock seriously expected to be allowed to film that ending – not because it defied credulity (as it did), but because neither RKO nor any other studio was going to turn Cary Grant, a great popular star, into a callous murderer. For Hitch to present him as a petty swindler and chiseller was quite daring enough. As John Russell Taylor has pointed out: "We ... know that this is Cary Grant, so that however black the case may look against him, he cannot be a wife-murderer. The man he is playing might be, but he, Cary Grant, cannot be, because he never, ever, is. So Hitchcock's idea was to carry out the ultimate double-bluff, by making him turn out after all to be a wife-murderer, thereby administering a cosmic shock far beyond anything that the film story itself could be expected to give. Alas, this was going too far; the effect was too strong for the studio, who insisted that Grant must be exonerated at the end, as we knew all along he would be."[1]

RKO went further than that. After *Suspicion* was finished, Hitchcock, returning from two weeks in New York, discovered that a studio executive had taken out all the scenes implying that the male star might be a murderer, with the result that the cut version lasted a mere fifty-five minutes. As the effect was so plainly unsatisfactory, Hitch was allowed to restore the picture.

Grant's performance fascinated yet was as uneasy as the tale being told. Though the role as written was close to unplayable, he was impressively crude, bumptious and manic, and he cast enough psychological shadows to suggest that he *could* have played a murderer memorably. (Yet would he ever have agreed to? It seems unlikely. Weakening the force of the later comedy-thriller *Charade* was movie-goers' certainty that Grant, again in highly suspicious circumstances, simply could not be a villain and a killer.)

In the easier role, Joan Fontaine was her familiar charming, diffident and sensitive self, and she won the 1941 Academy Award for best actress. Of her co-star, with whom she had also acted two years earlier in *Gunga Din*, she had little good to say – one of a small number of fellow workers who have actively criticized Grant.

If Grant had had problems with an abortively conceived part in *Suspicion*, he was almost totally defeated by his role in his next picture, *Arsenic and Old Lace*, though it was hard to think of an actor who *could* have licked the difficulties posed by a script that called for exasperation, stupefaction and more exasperation – and very little else. Aside from his excursion to MGM for *The Philadelphia Story*, Grant had been alternating strictly between RKO and Columbia. At this stage, however, he moved over to Warners to join the small cast that Frank Capra had assembled for filming Joseph Kesselring's farce, which was already a hit on Broadway that year. Having volunteered for the US army signal corps, Capra selected *Arsenic and Old Lace* as a property that he could turn speedily into a film whose success would ensure the financial security of his family during his wartime absence. Jack Warner had agreed to a stipulation that the movie should not be released until after the Broadway run was over, but probably nobody at the time realized that Kesselring's play, which opened at the Fulton Theatre on 18th August 1941, would go on for three and a half years or well over thirteen hundred performances. The result was that the movie-version was not released until the fall of 1944.

The briskness with which the filming took place was attributable to more than Capra's pressing engagement with the US army. He wished to avail himself of the services of Josephine Hull and Jean Adair, who played the eccentric, not to say homicidal, old ladies who were central to the plot, but he could borrow both them and John Alexander from the Broadway production only during their four-week vacation. It was all very well to have a splendid cast of colourful characters in which the familiar faces of such screen-stalwarts as Edward Everett Horton and James Gleason could be seen as well as the less familiar features of the players from Broadway, but what *Arsenic and Old Lace* patently lacked was a big star-name to lure people into the cinemas. A name bigger than those of Raymond Massey and Peter Lorre, who would swell the homicidal crowd was needed for success. After Bob Hope had turned down the offer of the lead, so great was Capra's enthusiasm for the idea of using Cary Grant that Jack Warner was persuaded to pay the actor's $100,000 fee – though again the money reportedly went to War Relief. But the part for which the star was scheduled had not, originally, been a star part, but rather a comparatively minor role – a straight man to balance the play's superabundance of grotesques. Accordingly, the part was built up, creating serious imbalances in the dramatic structure.

This is not the context for a dissertation on differing media, but, to be crudely succinct, the ways of the cinema are not the ways of the theatre. Running for nearly two hours, *Arsenic and Old Lace* seemed overlong, slow and, being virtually a one-set picture, claustrophobic. Much of the farce was rudimentary slapstick, and Grant, supposedly playing the one sane person in a houseful of murderers, exhaustingly pulled faces, did takes and double-takes and maintained barely controlled hysteria for scene after scene. "Frank Capra," said Pauline Kael, "has Grant performing in such a frenzied, dithering manner that throughout much of the picture he seems crazier than anybody else." Though audiences didn't seem to mind when the film was at long last released, critical notices were mixed. "A fine actor merely mugs," the *New York Herald Tribune* reported, while the *Los Angeles Times*, though describing the movie as "a museum-piece", said of its star, "He is an expert" at farce.

If *Arsenic and Old Lace* was an uneven work, by the time it appeared on the nation's screens, its success was assured in advance. During its making, on 18th December 1941, Roosevelt delivered his declaration-of-war address to Congress, and thereafter a country preoccupied with fighting the Japanese and Nazi powers proved uncritically entertainment-hungry. Big names sold big but often inferior pictures, and with his enormous popularity, Grant could afford to appear in one or two of them without harming his reputation. Not that such appearances were deliberate. However, the standard set by *His Girl Friday, Penny Serenade* and *The Philadelphia Story* alone was so high that it was inevitable, no matter how carefully he endeavoured to select, that the actor would find himself involved in some productions of lesser merit. Even so, the general level of Cary Grant movies throughout the 'forties was nothing to be ashamed of.

It could be argued that rarely in his career did he agree to appear in a picture involving another male star of comparable stature. There were exceptions, however: Melvyn Douglas, Robert Mitchum, Frank Sinatra, even David Niven, perhaps. One of them was Ronald Colman, with whom Grant co-starred in *The Talk of the Town*. A slightly uneasy blend of comedy, drama and polemics, the film was kept together by the directorial talents of George Stevens and the

deftness of its leading players. It showed how an alleged murderer
(Grant) took refuge in the home of a mature jurist (Colman) and was
shielded by the jurist's housekeeper/landlady (Jean Arthur). Among
its incidental delights, the movie provided the joy of observing the
interplay set up by the screen's two most suave male stars. As Grant
enriched Colman's character by giving him an appreciation of the
spirit, not the letter, of the law and Colman steered Grant towards
sympathetic consideration of the legal apparatus, they met in
tolerance and understanding on a remarkable plateau in the art of
acting. Though a dramatic star, Colman also excelled in comedy; and
if he was arguably the world's best light comedian by this time, Grant,
though he rarely elected to appear in completely dramatic roles, had
an enviable range as a straight actor. It is a tribute to both to say that
in *The Talk of the Town* one could admire Colman's comic gifts as
much as Grant's serious playing, both actors being called upon to be
grave and gay in roughly equal measure.

The film won seven Oscar nominations but no outright awards. It
was happily difficult to label, and though it was both a critical and
commercial success, the reception was something short of ecstatic.
One big question – though hardly of great aesthetic moment – was:
who would get the delightful Jean Arthur in the end? In the picture's
closing moments, it appeared that Grant would be the loser. He kissed
her farewell and walked off. But wait! Back he came and embraced
her. In the last shot, they walked off together. There was something
quirky, puzzlingly arbitrary about this resolution, and *Newsweek*
revealed the truth: Stevens had filmed two endings, leaving it to the
voting of several preview audiences to decide who paired with whom.

Of much greater significance than such unadulteratedly commercial
caution was Grant's role and his performance in it. His powerful
acting in *Penny Serenade*, the unappealing recklessness and dissolute
character he created for Johnny Aysgarth in *Suspicion* and, third, the
excellence of his playing as the sometimes bitter, impatient Leopold
Dilg in *The Talk of the Town* appeared to pose a question: was he
essaying a transition to more dramatic, less predictable, more
obviously demanding parts? These pictures encouraged expectations
that he was to satisfy only fitfully. His 'deeper' acting (if it really was
deeper than his more usual performances in comedy) was almost
without exception parenthetical, a counterpoint to the avowedly
comic, and it occurred in unfailingly commercial contexts. Those who

asserted that great actors took risks and that Grant assiduously
avoided them were to find little to reverse or qualify their verdict in his
subsequent career.

As the war, scarcely begun for America in 1941, extended into
1942, Grant joined numerous Hollywood stars who in March toured
the US in a whistle-stop tour lasting three weeks. The aim was to sell
bonds to aid the war-effort. Bert Lahr had a renowned "Income Tax"
sketch in which he often used Grant as his 'feed'. The routine was for
the train to arrive in a given town in the morning and for a parade of
stars to take place. In the evening, there was usually some sort of
theatrical presentation.

It was a busy year. On 26th June Grant at last became an
American citizen and also legally changed his name from Archie
Leach to Cary Grant. Both acts seemed like nothing more than they
were – the formal endorsement of established fact.

Less than a month later, on 8th July, in a simple six-minute
ceremony at the Lake Arrowhead home of Frank Vincent, then his
manager, Grant married Barbara Hutton. There was a studied
avoidance of ostentation, and only those closest to the couple were
present to see them joined in matrimony by the Reverend H. Paul
Romeis of the English Lutheran Church in San Bernardino. RKO's
publicity staff took the only photographs and saw to it that the barest
facts were released to the newspapers.

Grant was in the middle of making *Once Upon a Honeymoon*.
Ironically, he and Barbara did not have one themselves. The groom
went straight back to work, though it was conceded that he might
report on set an hour later than usual on the day after his marriage.

11

Barbara Hutton

"Experience," Wilde cynically but ungrammatically observed, "is the name one gives to their mistakes"; and both Grant and Barbara Hutton were experienced. She had been married twice before and had twice divorced. He had the failure of his marriage with Virginia Cherrill to look back on. In his analyses of his dissolved partnerships there was always to be something at once perceptive and disarmingly charitable. Thus for what had happened he blamed not Virginia but himself. He had been possessive, he realized, too scared of losing her and, paradoxically, running that very risk because of his fear. Both had been victims – tense and too mistrustful of happiness that might have been theirs for the taking.

There are two contrasting views of marriage and its failure. One assigns blame and error, carefully shares out the guilt and is essentially puritanical. (A corollary is the belief in a winner and a loser; not for nothing did Rilke's mother describe the wedding ceremony as "prayer before battle".) The other, more pragmatic and more modern, sees marriage as a partnership that, like other partnerships, may run its course or, with the best will in the world, founder on previously unperceived difficulties – a tolerant view that takes account of mutability and eschews blame. His public utterances indicate that Grant has fairly consistently inclined towards the first view, and he has always been ready to shoulder at least his just share of any culpability.

If, however, one was to talk of mistakes in the partnership of Grant and Barbara Hutton, the first was the marriage itself. It held small promise of a happy future. As Grant came to realize, he and Barbara had little in common, being different in education, background and upbringing. Elegant living had brought them together, and as a shared interest, elegant living was not enough for partners in a marriage. He had grown to know himself a little, but in retrospect the process of self-understanding had, he was to see, only just begun. His bride was probably no more psychologically mature than he. Two marriages had given her experience but not happiness. She was barely thirty, but she looked like a woman of forty-five, and photographs captured an emptiness in her expression that suggested someone who had forgotten something but couldn't remember what.

It could hardly have been the admonition given her by a manservant at the age of eight: "You're fat and plain. When someone wants to marry you, it will be because you're rich. People will envy your possessions." In horror, she ran to her father, who — almost incredibly — confirmed the truth of the cynical analysis. Barbara never forgot the traumatic episode. Small wonder that she tended to treat her succession of husbands like servants. In turn, some of them confirmed the pessimistic prediction of her childhood by regarding her as just a source of funds.

If she had been born to money, she was in many ways brought up austerely — for example, permitted no meat or sugar. During vacations, she was left at her expensive boarding-schools.

However, she and Grant did have one key experience in common, as both were motherless from an early age. Barbara's mother died in mysterious circumstances (possibly suicide) when Barbara was only five. She saw little of her father, who was preoccupied with business. She therefore had usually only servants for company and was rather a solitary child. After Grant's mother disappeared when he was nine, he did not seem to be close to his father or grandmother and was also a somewhat lonely child. Nevertheless, while Barbara seemed to retreat into a dream-world, writing poetry, Grant, by contrast, was much more friendly and outgoing and capable of enjoying himself with friends of his own age.

On their wedding-day, Barbara Hutton's appearance juxtaposed oddly with Grant's aura of vitality and confidence. A rank outsider armed with the most superficial facts might have shaken his head over their prospects, and, curiously, dissolution was implicit even in the terms of the union. Before he married her, Grant silenced those who had accused him of fortune-hunting when he signed a waiver to any claim on her fortune or, in the event of a divorce, for alimony. His critics would henceforth have to content themselves with allegations that he was a social-climber; and there were always those ready to say that.

Almost immediately, Grant's career and his numerous visits to

With the ATS in Bristol in the 'forties

With Myrna Loy and Melvyn Douglas in *Mr. Blandings Builds His Dream House* (1948)

With Betsy Drake in *Every Girl Should Be Married* (1948)

With Betsy Drake and Franchot Tone in *Every Girl Should Be Married*

Action in The *Pride and the Passion* (1957)

With Ingrid Bergman at a Dorchester (London) reception in 1957

A great romantic partnership: Cary Grant and Grace Kelly

With Eva Marie Saint in *North By Northwest* (1959)

With Audrey Hepburn in *Charade* (1963)

(*this and facing page*) A star
matures—and his looks improve

That Touch of Mink (1962) with Doris Day

army camps and hospitals began to tug the couple apart, ensuring his repeated absence from the home on Amalfi Drive in Pacific Palisades that they had rented from Douglas Fairbanks Jr.

One of several ventures in which they *were* together was the financing of a clinic in San Francisco for wounded servicemen. It was during the Second World War that London's *Daily Mail* dubbed Grant "probably the most generous man in Hollywood", but whereas he was willing to make efforts in person, Barbara, just as well intentioned but less gregarious, tended to resort mainly to her cheque-book. Nor was Grant's striving automatically of the kind to grab headlines. One of his less publicized gestures was to serve on the Los Angeles committee of the British War Relief Society, which took the extremely practical measure of sending over four thousand packets of seeds to the National Allotments Society for distribution in Great Britain, where, throughout the war, the population remained enthusiastic about growing vegetables and "digging for victory".

The Talk of the Town was released a month or so after the wedding, and it was followed on 27th November by *Once upon a Honeymoon*, a sub-standard Leo McCarey comedy-thriller with an alarmingly misjudged sequence in which Grant and Ginger Rogers were rescued from a concentration camp. The style and the smoothness of playing might have been admired, but the picture was slight, its use of an about-to-erupt Europe as a backdrop against which the hero and heroine might enjoy adventures always verging on the offensive. Nevertheless, the teaming of Grant and Rogers was sufficiently attractive to create high expectations when it was announced ten years later that they would star in Hawks' *Monkey Business*.

Even less memorable was Grant's sole film of 1943, *Mr Lucky*, in which he played a draft-dodging gambler who was reformed by Laraine Day. In sharp contrast, *Destination Tokyo*, his first film of 1944 (it was actually released to coincide with New Year's Day), found him playing a submarine commander in the contemporary war. Though in many ways routine and propagandist, the picture was impressively authentic, and its thrills were well handled by Delmer Daves, directing for the first time after a successful career as a screenwriter. His debut was the result of intervention by the star, who used his right of director-approval to extend a chance to potential but yet untried talent. Grant's help was amply rewarded by the fine job Daves did in his new function. As for Grant's performance, it was refreshingly austere. Even so, the jettisoning of idiosyncratic touches of comedy did not leave the submarine commander devoid of humanity. He seemed the sort of man whom John Garfield and Alan Hale, as members of the crew, would trust as well as obey.

Nothing too surprising there. Grant could scarcely have been expected to play a US naval commander on active service as a bon vivant and dilettante. And yet there was an authority to his acting that pointed to possibilities that he might one day be disposed to explore in full.

That he scarcely did in *Once Upon a Time*; though for a fable about a dancing caterpillar, it proved tolerably engaging. Had it been made with Humphrey Bogart and Rita Hayworth as originally planned, it could hardly, one suspected, have possessed the warmth and humour infused into it by Grant, Ted Donaldson and Janet Blair, whose ensemble-playing was excellent. In essence, however, Grant was again appearing as the hustler who reformed – a role in which there was no challenge for him.

Yet he was seeking a challenge at that time – and a specific one. He had become keenly interested in playing Ernie Mott in *None but the Lonely Heart*, which was written and directed by Clifford Odets, who was to direct only one other film (*The Story on Page One* in 1959) and had previously been associated exclusively with the stage as actor, writer and director. In the mid-'thirties, Odets had been a founder-member of the enormously influential Group Theatre, along with such luminaries as Luther and Stella Adler, Morris Carnovsky and Elia Kazan. A later member was the legendary John Garfield, whose friend Odets became, and for whom he wrote the play *Golden Boy*. He had based the screenplay of *None but the Lonely Heart* on Richard Llewelyn's novel, which told the story of a young man growing up in the 'thirties in the poverty of London's East End, embittered by his father's death in the Great War and his mother's penury. The character of Ernie Mott was not 'a Cary Grant role'; it had complexity and depth. Beneath Ernie's sardonic, hostile exterior was not the cliché heart of gold but a smothered sensibility. Grant turned out to be masterly in capturing and conveying the antitheses of the hero's personality. As much as by the part, he had probably been drawn to the story, which had overtones reminiscent of the history of Archie Leach. True, Archie's mother, unlike Ernie Mott's, had not died of cancer in a prison ward, and Archie's father had not been killed in the war. Yet there were parallels in this tale of deprivation and loneliness that presupposed a strong personal identification in Grant, who, as James Agee put it "asked that [the picture] be made".

Agee called it "an unusually sincere, almost-good film" – an assessment indicating his awareness that *None but the Lonely Heart* was uneven and sometimes diffuse. Its strengths were of the cinema, and its weaknesses, not least some heavily static dialogue scenes, belonged to the theatre. It was a picture that divided critics, some of whom hated it to the extent of ridiculing it and saw in the hero only the familiar Cary Grant gloss. It was hard to deny that he looked too well nourished; his grooming was a shade neater than it should have been. Even Agee thought that the star was miscast.

The opinion was a minority one. A strong cast included Ethel Barrymore, June Duprez, Jane Wyatt, Barry Fitzgerald, George Coulouris and Roman Bohnen, but Grant none the less dominated the picture, which brought him his second Academy Award nomination as well as a more personal reward – the friendship of Odets, whose "stentorian convictions" he admired and whom he called "a stimulating, generous man".

Grant had never before played so *obviously* difficult and demanding a role, and the question again posed itself: was it his aim to find less light-weight parts in less commercial pictures? The clean answer, signalled by his next half-dozen movies, was an unequivocal no. Yet the paradox of his career was already forming itself. Grant's pictures might be resolutely commercial, without exception stylish entertainment – no more. But if he was 'only' a light romantic comedian, Grant's performances in those pictures had an emotive power that one might have sought in vain in more avowedly serious productions. The culture-vulture who, in Cyrano de Bergerac's words, found "True genius only among Geniuses" would continue to overlook Cary Grant's career. More sensitive souls would not.

So much for the career, then, as it scaled an artistic summit. But what of the man and the marriage that, among the cousins in Bristol, had given rise to the quip: "Now we can go into Woolworths and have anything we like – provided we pay for it!"?

In 1943, Grant, at the age of thirty-nine, had been rejected for the Army Air Corps. He did his bit, however, by bolstering the morale of at least two nations, and his war-effort was not confined to screen performances and financial donations. He toured service camps, talking to GI's, who discovered a sympathetic, unaffected presence. To the wounded, he gave a firm handshake and the unique warmth of his smile. To the fighting-fit, his celebrity gave a shot of adrenalin, and his humanity assured them that the rich and famous could care as much as the folk back home who had sons, brothers, husbands and sweethearts to lose. By definition, his concern was less personal, but it was no less genuine.

Rich and famous he certainly was, and yet even though he had no direct involvement, he was not beyond the effects of a civilian's war. His fears for the safety of Elsie Leach were to prove unnecessary, but the Blitz came to Bristol, and in one 'incident' three generations of Grant's family were wiped out. In January 1941, a blockbuster bomb struck a house in Dean Street in the St Paul's district (that same street in which was located the pub in which the curious had peeked at the young star a decade earlier), and in the basement died John Henry Leach, Grant's paternal uncle, the uncle's wife, their daughter and son-in-law and a young grandson.

But there were relatives who of course survived and kept an eye on Grant's mother. "Poor Auntie Elsie," one of them was to recall, "could not cope with rationing and was always popping in for tea, sugar, etcetera. Cary sent food-parcels when possible, and I remember one Christmas we had the luxury of some gorgeous crystallized fruits."[1]

There were many ways in which a star could help, some obvious, some not so obvious. In May 1944, Warner Brothers released a ten-minute short called *Road to Victory*. Grant was one of a star-studded cast, and the film was made to promote the Fifth War-Loan Drive. Such courses of action − propaganda films, private and public philanthropy, personal appearances − were positive, hopeful, optimistic. (And, for the star, occasionally unfortunate. An incident that occurred on one of his train journeys may long since have faded from his memory, but the woman who was seated at the same table in the dining-car will probably never forget it. She was flattered and delighted to find herself in the presence of the actor, with whom she was soon chatting affably. Her small son, however, sickened by travel and unimpressed by Grant, without warning threw up over the table and over their famous fellow diner, too.)

The relatively uncomplicated business of doing one's bit for the war was one thing. Grant's private life was another matter. In his marriage with Barbara Hutton, there were good times and bad times, but the bad began to predominate. Grant detested publicity, but he had to face the fact that his wife, whether by instinct or because of professional advice, courted it and thus involved him. The Cholly

Knickerbocker column was a constant thorn in his side. It was bad enough that it constantly referred to Barbara as 'The Huttontot', but he exploded after he himself had been repeatedly categorized as an ex-hotdog-salesman – an inaccurate allusion to his days as a Coney Island stilt-walker.

Publicity was even given to Grant's highly private wish to have a child – which, through no fault of her own, was not to be granted by Barbara. ("God knows I had her try everything," her doctor once commented.) Perhaps indiscreetly, Barbara spoke of her hopes for pregnancy to Hedda Hopper over lunch. Barbara thought her remarks were off the record; Hedda didn't. To Grant's disgust, the news was promptly relayed to Hopper's vast readership.

During the star's frequent absences from home, Barbara wrote the poetry she composed for much of her life, but her husband took little interest in it – and later rebuked himself for his lack of encouragement. The complete professional, he did not allow his marriage to cause neglect of his acting in any way.

The partners' interests seemed to be pulling them apart, not strengthening their intimacy. What could be done about that?

Well, Barbara could take an active interest in movie-making – or an *acting* interest. At the time *Mr Lucky* was being cast and knowing of her inclinations, thus far endorsed by Grant, a highly placed RKO executive believed that Mrs Grant would be ideal to play the heroine opposite her husband. The executive was perfectly sincere: the role suited Barbara and vice versa, she photographed well, and she had histrionic ability. But Grant, who had not been prepared to take her ambitions so seriously, was stubbornly against the proposal. Laraine Day was cast in the lead.

In the 'seventies, Grant uttered comments in an interview indicating a strong disbelief that women could be happy with showbiz careers. Either he was speaking with sad hindsight or this was a strange idea for a man who married no fewer than three actresses.

On 16th August 1944, he and Barbara separated, but by early October there was a public announcement of reconciliation. Signs of trouble had been evident to the couple's friends for some time. Intimates such as Rosalind Russell and Frederick Brisson would observe Grant depressed to the point of tears. After one separation, they brought Barbara and Cary, who were staying with them, together again. But the next morning Brisson found her alone in bed and Grant asleep on the floor of a bathroom.

Before much longer, the pattern of alienation and reconciliation was resolved. On 10th July 1945, Barbara Hutton filed suit. In the court hearing that ensued on 30th August she was represented by Jerry Giesler, the famous lawyer who spoke in marital matters for Ingrid Bergman, Marilyn Monroe, Shelley Winters and Lady Sylvia Ashley (Clark Gable's wife), as well as defended Errol Flynn against rape allegations and Robert Mitchum against charges of illegally possessing narcotics. No great strain was placed on the attorney's remarkable talents, and after brief proceedings Superior Judge Thurmond Clark granted a divorce.

In this civilized manner, Grant had thus become another chapter in Barbara Hutton's much publicized history of marriage and divorce. While one may take the perfectly tenable view that movie stars are the true royalty of the twentieth century, he was the first of her husbands not to lay claim to a title. He had been preceded by Alexis Mdivani, a Russian prince, and Count von Haugwitz-Reventlow, a Danish aristocrat who gave Hutton her one child, Lance Reventlow, who became a racing driver and was killed in an aeroplane-crash in 1972 at the age of thirty-six. Barbara Hutton was to be married seven times, Grant's successors being Prince Igor Troubetzkoy, the playboy Porfirio Rubirosa, the tennis star Baron Gottfried von Cramm and Prince Raymond Doan Vinh Na Champacak. In later years, she was to say, "All the unhappiness in my life has been caused by men. I think I am pretty timid about marriage, but I am also too timid to live alone, and life doesn't have any sense without a man."

Of her marriage with Grant, one of her most specific complaints was: "He did not like my friends." If they arrived while he was upstairs, she could read his displeasure in the expression on his face when he came down to join them. "He obviously did not look amused."

After the divorce, Grant ran true to what was clearly becoming his form. The nearest he came to criticism of his ex-wife, with whom he said he had enjoyed some very good times, was in his description of her as "a sort of guinea-pig for one surgeon after another". "Our interests were not the same," he announced. "I was more interested in my work than I should have been, I suppose." To that bald analysis, he added, "She's a wonderful woman. I have only the best wishes for her happiness." He remained on the friendliest of terms with Barbara and her son Lance, though in the 'seventies he admitted that he had not seen her for a long time. Part of the reason was that she had become an invalid, and she died in 1979 at the age of sixty-six.

Before that day arrived, though, Barbara Hutton spoke wistfully of Grant as the one man who had not been after her money: "Cary Grant had no title, and of my four husbands, he is the one I loved most. He was so sweet, so gentle. It didn't work out, but I loved him."

12

A Strong Flavour of Success

In the mid-'forties, people didn't talk about superstars. But they did make a distinction between minor or fleeting celestial bodies in the Hollywood firmament and tried and tested 'true' stars. In an interview with Ezra Goodman, Humphrey Bogart hit that distinction exactly right: "Movie stars? I don't like the name ... The words 'movie stars' are so misused they have no meaning. Any little pinhead who does one picture is a star. Gable is a star, Cooper is a star, Joan Crawford, as much as I dislike the lady, is a star. But I don't think the so-called others are. To be a star, you have to drag your weight into the box-office and be recognized wherever you go."

By that definition, Grant was undoubtedly a star – and one of the greatest. He was about to make a film (*Night and Day* – of which more later) that, however unworthy artistically, would turn out to be one of the biggest grossers in the history of motion pictures. The industry was in a healthy state – less restrainedly, business was booming. In 1946, weekly cinema attendance in the United States alone was ninety million. Grant's was among the biggest names.

He was a household word, a household image. Those who actually encountered him in the flesh seemed to doubt the evidence of their senses and wished to be reassured of his mythic qualities. "Say something" was a customary request, as though the familiar voice would dispel any fakery or illusion. Say what? Anything would do. Of course, "Judy, Judy ..." might have been deemed the magic words. Grant once commented, "I don't remember ever saying it in a movie, but now, every once in a while when I'm with friends, I say, 'Judeeee, Judeeee, Judeeee,' and everyone breaks up. Isn't that a good imitation of an imitation of an imitation?" As late as 1979, the impressionist Rich Little could get an enormous laugh at a Caesar's Palace celebration of Frank Sinatra's sixty-fifth birthday by approaching Grant, one of the guests, and saying – in a brilliant approximation of the star's own voice – "This man is far too young to be Cary Grant. I don't believe it. But, listen, if you really are Cary Grant – I'm a little sceptical – would you say something as Cary Grant for us?" Grant replied, "What would you like me to say?" Impressed, Little commented, "That was fair. Now could we hear your Burt Lancaster?"

Those who did not meet Grant in person missed a phenomenon that became almost as legendary as his screen *persona*. What the camera almost always failed to capture was the full force of his laughter, which was like an explosion of purest joy, his eyes welling with tears. Such uninhibited mirth, unrestrained enjoyment, deeply impressed those who had previously witnessed only his more controlled hilarity on film.

First and foremost a movie star, he had already clearly distinguished himself from his contemporaries. Cagney, for example, had had a great success in 1942 with *Yankee Doodle Dandy*, but the undulations of his career contrasted sharply with Grant's steady popularity and commercial success. Likewise, the career of his old rival, Gary Cooper, was about to enter a difficult period in which it would not so much peter out as undergo great vicissitudes. Spencer Tracy had much fine work ahead of him, but a good case could have been made that his most original performances had been filmed in the 'thirties. What these stars and others lacked was the control over material that Grant had won for himself by turning free-lance in the mid-'thirties.

At forty-two, he was beginning to display that invulnerability to age that was to be the marvel of the next three decades. On repeated occasions, he was to deny that he took special pains with his health, exercise or diet, attributing the reports of strict regimens to over-zealous newspapermen. The disclaimer has always seemed to carry a modicum of conviction. For example, there is no doubt that Grant's renowned tan, admired as much on film as in the flesh, is the result of his being a sun-worshipper rather than the product of self-conscious efforts to enhance his appearance. It is completely natural. After a number of years as Grant's butler-chauffeur, Anthony Faramus testified that he had never seen his employer resort to any artificial aid such as a sunlamp. Nevertheless, the tan did not just happen. It was produced and maintained by two or three hours each day under the California sun – a light and agreeable discipline, perhaps, but a discipline just the same.

Grant has consistently repudiated the notion that he is a fanatic about diet or the idea that he has regular workouts at swimming. For the second rumour, he can blame not only journalists but also colleagues such as David Niven, who stated that Grant had taken lessons in how to swim the crawl. Again, though he has been fond of listing horse riding as his interest in *Who's Who*, he would probably deny that he has laboured systematically at perfecting his horsemanship.

If he *had* been obsessive or even concerned about such matters as health, diet and exercise, why, unless he sought to minimize the effort involved, should he again and again contradict the reports? Grant himself has already given the answer, and it is one that concerns moderation. There is no great conscious programme to preserve physical well-being, to enhance good looks or to polish athletic skills. He has done what he wanted to do, what he enjoyed doing. Or, as he was to put it: "I like ME. Therefore I do only the things that are good for me." The comment implied diligent avoidance of any abuse or excess.

Instinctive restraint in one area was complemented by instinctive restraint in another. After fourteen years and forty-seven films in Hollywood, he continued to elude interviewers – not by actually giving them the slip but through the verbal dexterity with which he parried or evaded their questions about the real Cary Grant. To make his charming escapes even more galling, at least in retrospect, newspapermen realized that he enjoyed talking – but not about private matters. "I really don't like to speak about myself," he would declare, and the statement was no less than the truth. Perhaps this preference or reluctance was not unconnected with his association with Lady Elsie Mendl, who, from her seventies to her nineties, was a dear friend of his.

At an advanced age, she took up residence in Beverly Hills with her husband Sir Charles, a diplomat, and became a famed Hollywood hostess. In common with other celebrities of the period such as the Windsors, she scattered about her home silk cushions embroidered with philosophical advice, one such motto being, 'Never complain, never explain.' Grant was impressed by the message, the more so since Lady Elsie greeted the frailty and helplessness of her nineties with the same zest and stoicism she had exhibited during her previous years.

After two marriages and the modifications in life-style they inevitably produced, one more trait was beginning to manifest itself in the actor — a predilection for changing his houses with great frequency. There are those who believe that actors are drawn to their profession by the need to be loved, and this habit would not be without significance to a certain school of psychoanalysts who see in property a symbol of affection craved or denied. (One of their favourite case histories concerns the Empress Elizabeth, unhappily married to Franz Josef, who would tour Europe purchasing castle after castle, with the result that an imperial official was deputed to follow her, cancelling the deals she had made.) Much depends, it might be added, on whether one *changes* houses or accumulates them, but a more mundane, not to say more convincing, explanation of Grant's 'restlessness' over real estate probably lay in the tastes of his wives, his liking for mobility and his mistrust of stagnation.

In any case, he had a well-developed enjoyment of travel, as well as a keen interest in flying in all types of aircraft, very frequently alongside a great friend, the late Howard Hughes, whom he rated the finest pilot of them all. In his converted bomber, Hughes often flew the actor to Mexico, setting the 'plane down expertly in small fields that would have spelt disaster for a less gifted flier.

In early 1947, the Press, encouraged by airport officials at Dayton, Ohio, contrived to 'invent' that disaster. Piloted by Hughes and with Grant aboard, the war-surplus bomber had taken off for Amarillo, Texas, but after a single radio message placed the aircraft over Indianapolis, contact was lost, and the two men were officially declared missing. Some hours later, though, Noah Dietrich, president of the Hughes Tool Company and the millionaire's right-hand man, announced that Hughes and Grant were safe. The episode was typical of those that increasingly punctuated Howard Hughes' bizarre and ultimately tragic life, and one of its results was that Grant, like Mark Twain and Ernest Hemingway, enjoyed the dubious pleasure of reading his own obituary.

For all their fundamental differences, many of Grant's tastes and some of his friends (notably the Mendls) were shared by the composer Cole Porter, whom the star impersonated in his next film, *Night and Day*, which had the statistical distinction of being Grant's only picture of 1945, his first in colour and the one biographical movie of his career. In most other ways — aside from making a great deal of money — it was undistinguished. Apart from the musical numbers, one of which was "You're The Top" sung by the star, what took place on the screen was so factitious (not to say fictitious) and formula-ridden that it was far less interesting than either the truth about Porter's life or the circumstances in which the film came to be made. More than two hours long, this film was a travesty with scarcely a hint of authenticity in its inordinate length.

The idea for the work was born in 1943, when Irving Berlin suggested that Porter's life story, if filmed with emphasis on what the composer had achieved, despite the terrible injuries sustained in his riding accident, would encourage similarly crippled servicemen. Nobody at the time expected the war to be over so soon. (Germany surrendered in May 1945, and Japan in September.) Linda, Porter's wife, thought the idea appalling – perhaps because she, too, extolled as a virtue reticence of the 'never-complain-never-explain' variety. But Porter was enthusiastic, and in the end a deal was made with Warner Brothers with the stipulation that Porter should have script-approval and Linda be consulted about who should play her. From the start, there were script problems, and a whole string of writers worked on the project. Aside from his riding accident, ghastly though it was, Porter had been fortune's darling. Orson Welles, commenting on the lack of dramatic conflict, quipped, "What will they use for a climax? The only suspense is: will he or won't he accumulate ten million dollars?"

Amused by the contrived screenplay at last evolved and presented to him, Porter, after approving it, made the public pronouncement: "It ought to be good. None of it's true." Possibly much of his amusement derived from the fact that there was of course no suggestion of his homosexuality. Another irony inherent in the movie's genesis and simple-minded propositions was created by Porter's own conviction that he had not, in one sense, triumphed over his mishap, the central thesis of the movie – and that a decline in the quality of his music and lyrics dated from that terrible day when his horse had fallen on him, struggled to get up and then rolled on him yet again, crushing both his legs. But if Porter's work really had been impaired – and many would have denied the idea – his impish, courageous sense of humour was intact, and when Linda Porter requested that she should be impersonated on screen by Alexis Smith, Cole, his tongue lodged deeply in his cheek, suggested that he should be played by the celebrated heterosexual Cary Grant. Both proposals were accepted, Jack Warner opening negotiations with Harry Cohn of Columbia to borrow the male star for the picture.

Physically, the resemblance between the two men was minimal.

Porter was a dapper little man with the mischievous face and lively eyes of an elegant, slightly malicious monkey. If attractive, his looks were not those of a matinée-idol. Unsuited to the role or not, Grant tackled his task professionally, even to the length of dining repeatedly with Porter (no great hardship, perhaps, if one considered the composer's wit, his talent and his sophistication) in order to study, if not copy, his speech and mannerisms.

Porter prevailed upon Jack Warner to hire his great friend Monty Woolley as technical director, and plans were afoot to have the original stars of Porter's stage hits perform their numbers in the movie. However, when the accountants in the front-office considered costs, prominent among which were $150,000 to Grant and twice as much to Porter for the rights to the story and music, it was decided to trim a budget that shaped up as a then record of over $4,500,000. One of the results was the hiring of Ginny Sims as the singer who would represent in token such stars as Ethel Merman, though Mary Martin did appear as herself.

Night and Day had its première on 1st August 1946, but instead of attending the opening, Cole Porter gave a small dinner party, at which the guests included Cary Grant, George Cukor and Mrs Jack Warner. To Warner himself, who dropped by for a drink after the première, Porter said of the film, "It's a dream" – a probable allusion to *See America First*, his first Broadway show, which flopped after sixteen performances in 1916. He could not be drawn to specify the nature of that dream.

Though *Night and Day* might have been a travesty, and a routine travesty at that, Grant's casting was in one sense apposite – if ironically and unconsciously so. The true parallels between Cary Grant and Cole Porter included the facts that both enjoyed the reputation of exercising their respective crafts with ease, both had apparently achieved early success, and the 'ease' and the prematurity of their success were public-relations myths, diligently nurtured, that masked perfectionism, constant hard work and numerous failures. These were the types of truths, however, that could not be put over in a Hollywood musical that showed the composer at the piano composing "Night and Day" while being 'inspired' by Alexis Smith, a ticking clock and "the drip, drip, drip of the raindrops". (The number was actually written for Fred Astaire and the show *Gay Divorce*; but life can be as banal as any clichéd screenplay. The famous phrase in the lyric came to Porter during a meal with Mrs Vincent Astor during which rain spattered on to a porch roof and his hostess complained about the "drip, drip, drip".)

Something or rather somebody was bothering Grant during the film's making – its director Michael Curtiz. His record as a movie-maker was brilliant, but his reputation among actors was pungent. Errol Flynn, who made with him such famous pictures as *The Charge of the Light Brigade, The Sea Hawk* and *The Adventures of Robin Hood*, eventually refused to work with him ever again. He wrote of Curtiz: "He liked blood so much he insisted the tips be taken off the swords." Grant's impressions were equally unfavourable, but he made his decision much more rapidly. When shooting was over, he delivered a precise, pointed speech to the bullying director in which he swore that, short of penury or insanity, he would never make another movie with him. For that bit of eloquence, Grant became a hero among his fellow actors, and the story is not spoilt by the fact that Curtiz considered or pretended to consider the speech a joke. *Night and Day* made a staggering $4,000,000 in the US and Canada, but Grant did not go back on his word.

If *Notorious*, which was released in the summer of 1946, was not in the same commercial class as *Night and Day*, it was artistically and as entertainment vastly superior. Alfred Hitchcock's pictures have varied considerably according to his collaborators on any given project (*pace* François Truffaut and other *auteur* theorists), but *Notorious* had, besides first-rate direction, a clever and literate screenplay by Ben Hecht, memorable camerawork by Ted Tetzlaff and admirable playing by a distinguished cast. Although Grant found himself in the company of such accomplished scene stealers as Louis Calhern and Claude Rains, he was in no way overshadowed in his performance as a government agent after the outbreak of the Second World War who first of all enlisted Ingrid Bergman to infiltrate a group of Nazis in Rio de Janeiro and then, losing his professional detachment, fell in love with her, becoming bitter as, on orders, she first seduced one of the leading Nazis (Rains) and then became the man's wife. There was thin ice in the plot (with his feelings for Bergman, would Grant really have allowed her to go through with the dangerous masquerade?), and it fell to the male star to execute most of the graceful skating over it – a task that he carried off so well that there was little more than a whiff of psychological implausibility to his government agent. Grant's acting showed a new economy that was to become even more marked in the next two decades.

He was aided by one of the best 'entrances' in cinema – an early sequence in the film in which he was at first merely a vague presence, disembodied voice, at a drunken party. Almost by chance, it seemed, the camera would capture a glimpse of the back of his head or his crossed legs, perceived, so to speak, out of the corner of an eye. Thereafter, aided immeasurably by Ingrid Bergman, the anonymous personality of the Grant hero defined itself steadily into a three-dimensional characterization – a worldly man, committed to the whims of his government, but capable of great passion and resentment. Once more, a sophisticated veneer nevertheless permitted insights into inner depth, but this time they were more than glimpses. Grant's Devlin lowered his defences before the audience's gaze and became a vulnerable, tortured human being.

The picture was to be remembered – and exploited, in terms of publicity – for an extremely lengthy screen kiss, the sort of impudence Hitchcock has always loved to inject into his movies. In the days when film-makers actually timed kisses by the second in order to stay within the rules, a straight, sustained kiss would have provoked censorship. For a torrid love scene, Hitch dearly wanted to include a long, uninterrupted embrace between Grant and Bergman. But how? The director's solution was to make the osculation continual rather than continuous. The stars began their kiss on a balcony, they moved inside, they crossed the room so that Grant could answer an importunate telephone, and the resumed, never-truly-abandoned kiss punctuated the ensuing conversation: Talk, kiss, talk, kiss ... Ingrid Bergman summed up the device. "The censor couldn't cut it."

His record for this and the next two years made it look as though Grant was settling down to a steady two (released) pictures per year, but 1946 was complicated slightly by a third screen appearance in RKO's *Without Reservations*, starring Claudette Colbert and John Wayne. In a brief guest shot, Grant danced with Colbert, but his bit, like those of Jack Benny and Louella Parsons, was in the nature of a semi-private joke.

If one regarded Grant as a man of two countries, the ending of the war that had cut him off physically from one of them saw him re-establishing numerous links broken by the hostilities, though none stronger than the relationship between him and his mother – that rich and happy bond that must have come as a joyful surprise to both. In April 1946, he went to visit her at her home in Howard Road, Redland, after an enforced interval of eight years. "It is a long time since I saw him," Elsie Leach had said, "but he writes regularly, and I always see his films."

Grant found her as lively as ever, this small, active woman who was determined to live her own life, thrived on being busy and wanted no one to tell her what to do. Small wonder. Having 'lost' twenty precious years that should have been among the bravest and those most crammed with promise, Elsie had a lot of catching up to do, and she faced that challenge with zest and without a shred of self-pity. As if to compensate for what had been denied her, she was to live to a grand old age, her faculties scarcely diminished even near the end. Well into her seventies, May Kingdon recalled, Elsie would break off from casual conversation with an acquaintance on the street and dash off in sprightly fashion for a bus. She had a great sense of humour, and if she lived alone, she did not — with so many relatives close at hand — lack for companionship. Such propinquity, however, was not quite the same as the intimate sense of belonging, provided by marriage or a family dwelling beneath the same roof, and Ernest Kingdon told a revealing anecdote about her.

When he visited her one day, she asked, "What do you do, Ern? I mean, what do you do for fun?" He replied that he was fond of a game of darts at the local pub. He forgot about the incident, but the next time he called, she had a dartboard, hung behind a door. As the numerous marks on the door made by stray shots testified, she had been practising so that they could play darts together. The episode indicated her willingness to please and suggested that there were times when she must have been lonely.

After the war, Grant resumed regular visits, but that restoration of the pattern in the spring of 1946 was special in many ways, not least because Elsie, as full of ideas as ever (and not always practical ones), had a cocker spaniel that she wanted to put into movies with her son Cary Grant. (Could she have been remembering Asta's stunning performance in *The Awful Truth*?) The dog was well trained, she said, and a 'natural' for films. Furthermore, his name was Cary.

Grant probably roared with laughter at that. Any reunion with his mother was the signal for unlimited fun. They would talk and talk and joke together until the tears streamed down their cheeks. Once, in later years when grey had invaded her son's hair, he revealed: "She actually suggested that I should tint my hair because she said it made her feel old."

It made *her* feel old ... No mystery that he admired her spirit and still likes to talk of that "beautiful and wonderful lady".

Though Grant by then appeared to be a streamlined picture-making machine, he began 1947 with a smooth success and then, though the outcome was happy, went into his second film that year with an audible, uncomfortable changing of gear. *The Bachelor and the Bobbysoxer* (a.k.a. *Bachelor Knight*) was agreeably trivial, an unlikely comedy in which Shirley Temple and Myrna Loy, notwithstanding an age gap, played sisters. Temple was the eponymous bobbysoxer who fell for Grant's bachelor, and Loy was the judge who, after the bachelor had been compromised, sentenced him to keep her sister company until the crush abated. From such unpromising material, a gifted cast made an entertaining, if somewhat mindless joke, its humour deriving chiefly from the generation clash.

While the screen seems to be *par excellence* the medium for fantasy, comparatively few conscious excursions into that sphere have been successful. *The Bishop's Wife*, Grant's second release of the year, was possibly one of the exceptions – sentimental, unashamedly soft-centred, but also witty and stylish. The idea of Cary Grant as an angel called Dudley who materialized in order to help Bishop Brougham (David Niven) might have seemed excessively coy. In practice, it was played mainly for laughs – not cheap humour, but the wittier accomplishments of situation comedy. Flair and taste triumphed over potentially cloying material, so that, for example, the idea of Loretta Young as the bishop's wife falling for Dudley was faced up to and deflected – perhaps ducked – with a light touch that engaged and disarmed at one and the same time. Pure whimsy, one might have said; but *The Bishop's Wife* had technical and artistic merits that defied dismissal.

It was made, however, in far from happy circumstances and provided another chapter in the history of productions that gave, helped to give or should have given their participants many of the ills that flesh is heir to, from ulcers to strokes to coronaries. That *The Bishop's Wife* inflicted no observable damage to anyone was testimony to the durability and resilience of those involved. Though released by RKO, the picture was Sam Goldwyn's project. Robert E. Sherwood worked on the screenplay based on Robert Nathan's novel, but Sherwood, who was probably more at home with films like *The Best Years of Our Lives* (1946), for which he had written a remarkable script, was taken off and replaced by Eric Bercovici. From the start, Goldwyn wanted Grant to star, but when he contacted Jules

Styne of MCA, Styne said that his client was committed to four
pictures that would occupy him for the next four years. Goldwyn was
not to be deterred, and after six months of persistence, he struck
lucky: a project that had fallen through left a six-month gap in the
actor's schedule.

But did Grant himself really want to do the picture? It seemed not —
especially after shooting had begun and he knew exactly what he had
walked into. The roles of the two leading men had been conceived vice
versa — David Niven playing Dudley, the angel, and Grant playing
Bishop Brougham. The arrangement did not suit Grant, who insisted
that *he* should be the heavenly messenger. Even so, there was so little
to his liking that once the production was underway, he offered to give
back his salary in return for being released from the picture. The offer
was refused.

If an actor is too fastidious about the parts he plays, he soon finds
himself unemployed. Grant, however, could *afford* to be fastidious.
Or, to reverse the proposition, he could not afford to be anything else.
If not unique, his position was at least unusual. Whereas another star
might shrug off a failure with the excuse: "The studio made me do it",
Grant possessed rare powers of choice. *His* failures would require
more explaining.

William Seiter began directing, but after two weeks Goldwyn fired
him, junked the script and dismantled the sets — rumoured cost
$900,000. Seiter's replacement was Henry Koster, a UFA graduate,
best known in America for his films with Deanna Durbin, whom he
directed six times for Universal with great success.

To add to the catalogue of misery, this was hardly one of the
brightest times in David Niven's life, for earlier in the year he had lost
his first wife in tragic circumstances.

As *The Bishop's Wife* took shape, Goldwyn and Grant argued over
the star's interpretation. Nevertheless, Goldwyn was reasonably
happy about his picture until the preview. The following morning, he
called Billy Wilder, who was a friend, to tell him that he had a movie
on his hands that didn't make sense. Wilder and his then collaborator
Charles Brackett took a look at it and decided it needed three big
scenes. As a favour, they fixed the screenplay, working
uninterruptedly from Friday evening to late Sunday afternoon —
according to legend.

With the extra sequences, the film was cannily released in time for
Christmas, and if anything could have justified the sweat and tears of

its creation, then its reception at the box-office did so. Admirable playing from the rest of the cast made Grant's playing seem, by contrast, non-acting. The performance was carefully judged, but came over, deceptively, as little more than a benign presence and appropriately divine relaxation. The finishing touch to an entertainment of undeniable charm was provided by one of Hugo Friedhofer's finest scores.

The business side of Grant's profession was exerting a growing fascination that was to flower in the late 'fifties. At that time he went into active production on his own account, but among the preliminary throat clearings was a venture begun in April 1946, when he formed a company with Alexander Korda – as David Thomson was to dub him, "the self-styled khan of the British film industry". The idea was to film du Maurier's *The King's General*, but the project came to nothing.

So much for that. But the fizzling out of the one episode led, indirectly, to another of much greater moment. In the summer of 1947, Grant flew to London for abortive talks with Korda. That fall, he decided to return to the States on the *Queen Mary*, and during the voyage, a shipboard encounter opened one of the most significant chapters of his personal life, though it was also to affect his movie-making. He was attracted by Betsy Drake, a young actress who had lately enjoyed great success in the West End production of *Deep Are The Roots*. In the relatively confined life even of one of the world's largest ships, getting to know her posed no problem, but Grant felt shy about taking the first overt step. The great leading man of the screen would no doubt have devised some cunningly splendid way of 'meeting cute', but Grant recalled that he hid in a companion-way, nervous and lacking assurance, while his friend Merle Oberon invited Betsy on his behalf to join them for lunch.

His lack of confidence just might have stemmed from an awareness of the disparity in their ages. Born in 1923, Betsy Drake was nearly twenty years his junior. Yet she was immediately interested by this 'older man', and she was to prove one of the strong intellectual forces in his life, leading him to "better books, better concepts of living". "Betsy was good for me," the actor was fond of saying in later years, and it would not be an overstatement to say that her influence was educational. She was, for example, to introduce him to hypnosis and the controlled, scientific use of LSD – both of which expanded his awareness, the first possibly having detectable and fascinating effects upon his acting. (The relaxation of his performances in *I Was a Male War-bride, People Will Talk, To Catch a Thief* and later films was almost hypnotic in itself – appealing and enviable, and yet not precluding power and subtlety.)

Even to the Press, Betsy was to seem significantly different from the other women whom Grant had married or escorted for a time. To begin with, her appearance both delighted and disappointed newspapermen – the second probably more than the first. She used make-up sparingly and had little interest in clothes. To make her seem even more unworldly, she had walked out of a Hollywood contract and elected to act in the play in London.

The relationship between her and Grant developed with some speed, but the actor for a while did nothing to formalize it. Two previous marriages had at least taught him caution, and the age gap between him and Betsy was something to think about. For her part, she no doubt shared his caution, his reluctance to think prematurely of marriage, for her own parents had been divorced when she was a child. The truth was that, with *Deep Are The Roots* over in the West End, she had no home in any real sense to go to.

Grant's commitment, however, was strong, and he did involve himself in her professional life to the extent of suggesting that her career might profitably be continued on the West Coast, where, after she had followed his advice, he introduced her to movie moguls who were far from reluctant to do a favour for Cary Grant.

He did better than that, though: he co-starred with her in one of his own pictures the very next year.

Before it was made, though, he appeared with Myrna Loy and Melvyn Douglas in H.C. Potter's *Mr Blandings Builds His Dream House*, a witty, light-hearted comedy that explored the trials and worries of home-ownership. Since it was, in a sense, concerned with eternal verities (even if trivial ones), it has dated scarcely at all. As one half of a couple who had decided to build a house in rural Connecticut, Grant turned controlled frustration into a high comic art, his expressions perfect for a man to whom life had become a rope paying out too rapidly for him to retain his grasp on it. Loy and Douglas were at their best, and one would look in vain today for a trio of comparable stylists.

Nine months elapsed between the release of *Mr Blandings Builds His Dream House* and that of *Every Girl Should Be Married*, Grant's first film with Betsy Drake. It appeared in time for Christmas, 1948, and its slight plot related how a salesgirl in a department store (Betsy Drake) relentlessly pursued and won her selected male, a doctor played by Grant. Critically pawed over if not mauled, the picture was none the less well received by audiences, who responded as so often with Grant movies to the skilled treatment of insubstantial material. Of Betsy Drake, comments such as "gangling" and "effervescent" were used in an attempt to pin down an original screen presence that owed much to an air of perpetual expectation and a highly distinctive speaking-voice. *Time* magazine seized upon the comic moment at which Grant imitated her stance, inflection and mannerisms "cruelly and accurately". It was all in the mind. He mocked his future wife, all right; but it could be said that he did so affectionately, with tolerant exasperation.

By the time the picture was playing to Christmas audiences, its male star was actively involved in the making of *I Was a Male War-bride* (a.k.a. *You Can't Sleep Here*), a film that was to take ten months to complete and was to assume the aura of a jinxed production. Shooting began on location in Germany, and while they were at Bremerhaven, Grant and his co-star Ann Sheridan visited Orson Welles and Joseph Cotten, who were working on Carol Reed's *The Third Man* – the very film Grant had missed when a one-picture deal with Korda fell through. Thereafter, the *War-bride* unit moved to England, where troubles multiplied. While shooting was taking place at Shepperton Studios, Ann Sheridan was languishing at the Savoy with pleurisy. Then Grant contracted jaundice. According to which newspaper one read, delays were costing $3,000 or $4,000 per day. Grant was hospitalized for a time, and later, in August 1949, he spent ten days in Johns Hopkins Hospital in Baltimore for treatment of his illness. As a result of the difficulties with which it had been plagued, the production transferred to Hollywood, and half Shepperton Studios were left unused, with 150 or 450 lost jobs – the reports again varied wildly. There were mutterings in the Press about a vile American plot to destroy the British film industry, but the truth was less sinister: *force majeure* in the shape of Grant's sickness had led to the transfer.

After so much trouble, *I Was a Male War-bride* might well have turned out a flop, but it did nothing of the sort and was, on the contrary, one of the happiest of Grant's farces. Based on an autobiographical novel by Henri Rochard, the picture told how the author (Grant), a captain in the French Army in the Second World War, met and married an American lieutenant (Sheridan). Much of

the action concerned itself with the attempts of the newly-weds to
outwit red tape so that the captain could accompany his bride when
she left occupied Germany for the States. Among the ruses was
dressing up Rochard in feminine costume, complete with a wig
extemporized from the tail of a horse. "The transvestism," Andrew
Sarris has since commented, "is the last stroke of humiliation for
Hawks [the director], and the period of actual transvestism is
mercifully short." (Sarris had bracketed *I Was a Male War-bride*
with *Monkey Business* as "sagas of perpetual humiliation".) But just
as Grant had made himself a master of comic exasperation, so he had
also proved repeatedly that he could turn discomfort to advantage by
being extremely funny. Besides, *War-bride* was *not* exclusively
concerned with discomfort. The sexual antagonism that was a prelude
and counter-point to the military pair falling in love was deftly handled
– an apogee of romantic comedy, and their marital misadventures, if
hard on Grant, were inventive in poking fun at convention and
morality. The real strength of the film, though, was the interplay of
Grant and Sheridan, starring together for the first and last time, and
the sight on film of Sheridan convulsed with mirth at her co-star's
predicaments not only proved hard to resist but also stimulated
speculation about whether she was laughing at the character Henri
Rochard or the actor Cary Grant.

Probably the second. He was by this time a peerless comedian and
possibly the greatest ad-libber in the world. On location in Germany,
much that was improvised found its way on to film, with the finest
contributions, in the form of both ideas and dialogue, coming from
Grant.

I Was a Male War-bride was released on 2nd September 1949. On
Christmas Day, Grant married the person who had been in constant
attendance while he was suffering with jaundice in London. He and
Betsy Drake were flown by Howard Hughes, then boss of RKO, to a
small ranch-house near Scottsdale, Arizona. Hughes was best man at
the simple ceremony on what Grant later described as "an
extraordinary day" – not just because it was his wedding-day, but also
because its circumstances were subtly and thoughtfully engineered by
Hughes.

13

Not Out, but Retired Hurt

The marriage – Grant's third – lasted twelve years, longer than any of his other unions, and had a marked effect upon his life. Its rewards and riches were such that its eventual failure seemed to leave him bemused and incredulous. In the midst of it, he spoke like a man who had discovered undreamed-of contentment: "My marriage with Betsy has developed into a warm, relaxed companionship." When it was over, he commented, "Betsy and I are very close and talk often." He could not, he declared, recall why they had ended their partnership, though Betsy was to provide more than a hint when she said, "Cary's Mr Take-Charge. Mrs Cary Grant doesn't go into the kitchen, doesn't plan the meals. Everything a woman likes to do is done for her by the servants."

On their wedding-day, Grant was forty-five, and his bride was twenty-six. The juxtaposition suggested that he would educate her from his longer and wider experience of life, but if anything that proposition was inverted. Betsy was the one who demonstrated to him that there was more to living than he had so far discovered. He became converted to her faith in the powers of hypnosis, in which she became interested in typical fashion – by following a crash course of her own devising, a process that involved digesting twenty or thirty books on the subject. If the description sounds like a recipe for instant knowledge, it errs. Betsy sought not short cuts, but steadily illuminating studies that she pursued single-mindedly but patiently.

Perhaps with some scepticism, Grant, who had long been a thirty-a-day smoker, invited her one night to hypnotize him and plant a post-hypnotic suggestion that would help him give up nicotine. Betsy's technique was purely oral, and using soothing, rhythmic phrases and a calm voice, she hypnotized him while he was in bed and prepared for sleep. As he relaxed, she told him that smoking was bad for him and that he would thereafter have no craving for cigarettes. The next day, he quit – cold.

Possibly the experiment worked with the experimenter, too, because it was not long before Betsy also gave up smoking.

Equally spectacular was her prescription for spirits – or proscription of them. After his severe dose of jaundice, Grant had been medically advised to abstain from hard liquor – especially whiskey, bourbon and brandy. Again post-hypnotic suggestion worked its wonders, and the desired effect was achieved. As first-aid, too, hypnosis proved remarkably successful when one afternoon Grant badly scalded himself after knocking over some boiling coffee. Not only did Betsy manage to banish the pain, she also ensured that no blisters formed.

But Grant valued neither hypnosis nor his wife for feats or flashy stunts. Hypnosis was, he realized, the key to a tranquillity he had long sought, and among its practical uses, it could be employed for learning lines, inducing sleep or, above all, attaining remarkable relaxation of mind and body. As for Betsy, though her talents with hypnosis were not to be minimized, she gave him insights and stimulation, to say nothing of love and companionship, that were even more valuable.

The changes in him became clear to others, who also witnessed some of the hypnotic episodes. While she was filming *An Affair to Remember* with Grant, Deborah Kerr spent some weekends with him and Betsy in their Palm Springs home. "She was very 'in' to hypnotism," Miss Kerr said, "and I actually saw and heard her put him fast asleep. He awoke refreshed and full of energy. She also stopped him smoking. I remember him arriving on the set one morning at about 10 a.m., busily consuming his lunch [He always brought his own health-food lunch – carrot juice, soybean crackers, and so on], and he said to me, 'That damn Betsy – she's stopped me smoking, and now I am so hungry I am *already* eating my lunch!' "[1]

If Betsy could be serious, she was never pious. In yachting circles, there is a much-told story about her and the arch-humorist Art Buchwald, who was placed next to her at a dinner when she was Mrs Cary Grant. Possibly Buchwald had expected to encounter a flashy showbiz wife, because Betsy impressed him as a formal, aloof person, and thinking to disturb her composure, Buchwald told her of a recent visit to Aristotle Onassis' yacht *Christina* which had among its treasures barstools covered with the foreskin of a whale's penis. For a moment, it looked as though Buchwald's conversational torpedo had missed its mark. Then Betsy cried, "Oh – Moby's dick." Collapse of Art Buchwald.

After their marriage, Grant and Betsy began a life together that was arguably much less public than any of the other Grant matrimonial careers. Long before it became the fashion for movie stars to do so, the actor cherished his privacy, but the truth was that while he and Betsy might be seen at parties and previews, they mainly led a quiet existence at Grant's Brentwood house, the external events less significant than an unspectacularly nourishing, domestic contentment. "Betsy is the first wife I've had who is also a friend," her husband said, and as friends did, they enjoyed sharing their interests and enthusiasms, which, for Grant and Betsy, tended to be sudden and demanding.

The morning after the wedding, though they would both be reunited before long on celluloid, they were back in Hollywood engaged in separate productions — Betsy in *Pretty Baby* and Grant in *Crisis*, which was released in July 1950. Though few realized the fact at the time, Grant had begun the last segment of his film career, which, though it actually finished in 1966, might easily have terminated with *Dream Wife* in 1953. *Every Girl Should be Married* had turned out to be his last picture for RKO, and *I Was a Male War-bride* was the first of a new era in which he was, by anybody's definition, a free-lance. He was attached to no studio, making his own deals, more independent than he had ever been before, even during the ten years or so of his non-exclusive contract with RKO and Columbia. For the latter he would work only once more — curiously enough, in *Walk, Don't Run* (1966), his very last film. (Even then, "work for" was a loose term, in the sense that Columbia was the distributing company, while the producing company was Granley — as the name indicated, the star's own company.)

I Was a Male War-bride was a 20th Century-Fox picture and provided an auspicious beginning to the new stage in Grant's career, for it was listed by *Variety* as a top grosser. However, the year of *Crisis* (1950), yielded an omen of a less favourable kind. Having been 90 million in 1946, US weekly cinema-attendance sank by 1950 to 50 million per week. Movie-goers would no longer turn out to see their favourite star regardless of what picture he was in, and the cinema had already crossed the threshold into the age of uncertainty, with the industry generally in the doldrums.

But not, it had to be conceded, MGM, for whom Grant made *Crisis*. The studio's net profit that year actually rose by a million dollars. Once more, the Grant luck — or astuteness — was revealing itself. (If, only three years later, he was shabbily served by MGM, it was as a victim of economies during a period of slump.)

With *Crisis*, Grant gave Richard Brooks his directorial debut. Having begun on such unpromising material as *White Savage* and *Cobra Woman* (both Maria Montez vehicles), Brooks had established himself as a first-rate screen-writer on *Brute Force* and *Crossfire*, the second of which he had adapted from his own novel, *The Brick Foxhole*. Grant saw no reason why Brooks should not direct *Crisis*, which also had literary antecedents, being based on George Tabori's short story, and gently insisted that the screen-writer be given his chance to make the transition to director. The gesture might have seemed trifling, but it was not. Times were increasingly difficult, a star of Grant's magnitude had much to lose, and a bumbling tyro could have compromised the reputation that had taken most of twenty years to build up.

In the event, Grant's faith was amply justified. The picture was produced, improbably, by Arthur Freed, who ran MGM's legendary unit making musicals, but it was a thriller about an American brain surgeon (Grant) in an unspecified Latin American country where he and his wife were kidnapped and the surgeon, brought to the presidential palace, was ordered to operate on the ailing dictator (Jose Ferrer). The star's performance clearly reflected his belief in the story, and his acting, sardonic but never flippant, had a seriousness that gave the film credibility and the brain surgeon a strong aura of authenticity. If *Crisis* was never more than melodrama, it none the less exerted a powerful fascination.

For some areas, it was *too* powerful and credible and achieved the distinction of getting itself banned in Mexico, South and Central America and even Italy, where memories were comparatively fresh after the demise of Mussolini.

Like many other big stars, Grant assiduously avoided television as the great enemy of the larger screen that it undoubtedly was, but in 1950, as a gesture of affection towards one of his favourite TV shows, he made an uncredited guest appearance on "Dave and Charlie", the Los Angeles local television programme in which Cliff Arquette and David Willock regularly played. Grant popped up one night as a hobo wandering past the house of Charlie (Arquette). The idea for the surprise guest shot seemed to be entirely the star's own and was never repeated, but it was the sort of celebrity's whim that must have thrilled and delighted the audience immeasurably.

For his next film, released in September, 1951, Grant moved over to Fox. *People Will Talk* was another movie brought into being by a writer-director, this time Joseph Mankiewicz, who had freely adapted the successful German play by Curt Goetz, *Dr Praetorius*. The story told how the mysterious Noah Praetorius, working in a hospital and teaching in a university, fell foul of bigotry and gossip and was at length vindicated in an investigation. The film was idiosyncratic and unusual, full of wayward excursions and eccentric scenes, some of them remarkable for the – unemancipated – times. For example, Grant fell in love with and married Jeanne Crain, who had attempted suicide and was now an expectant but single mother. Crain's heroine was vulnerable and of delicate sensibility – a fine performance from the actress who had previously acquitted herself so well in Mankiewicz's *A Letter to Three Wives*. She responded admirably to Grant, whose acting had echoes of his portrayal in *Crisis* and created a doctor full of professionalism and compassion. His economy and relaxation were notable.

Among the scenes that lingered in the memory was a beautifully observed sequence in which three grown men – Grant, Sidney Blackmer and Walter Slezak – heatedly accused one another of the error that led to the derailment of model trains. But the film's climax, one that epitomized affirmation and reconciliation, was a sequence never to be forgotten by admirers of the star. His troubles over, his reputation unblemished and enhanced, Noah Praetorius conducted a student choir and orchestra in the Brahms Academic Festival Overture. As the music swelled into the composer's glorious orchestration of "Gaudeamus Igitur", a smile encompassed every feature of the actor's face, and his eyes glistened moistly in a moment of pure joy – as inspiring a coda as ever graced a motion picture.

It was an unashamedly emotional and emotive scene, but there can be no better way of remembering Cary Grant than in the crowning moment of *People Will Talk*.

When the picture was shown at Grauman's Chinese Theatre in Los Angeles, the chance was seized for carrying out one of Hollywood's most famous rituals. On a visit to Southern California, Georgia Douglas and her husband "noticed a crowd gathering to await the arrival of a motion-picture star who was scheduled to leave an identifying mark in the square of wet cement. In a short time, a big black car drove up and Cary Grant emerged. He was most gracious to the public, shaking hands, joking and standing still while we snapped pictures with our tourist-type cameras. A platform about three inches high had been placed near the wet cement, and he knelt on it, leaned over and left an impression of his hands. An attendant stood by with a basin of water and towel, and after cleaning his hands, he again talked and laughed with the people.

"A short time before this, we had occasion to see another popular star, but his attitude was so cold and unfriendly we never again went to see a movie in which he played an important part.

"Mr Grant was so congenial and friendly we felt we were lucky to have had the pleasure of watching and talking to him."

In like manner, the Press seemed to believe they were fortunate to have the pleasure of seeing *People Will Talk*. The *New York Times* spoke of the "delightful and good sense" of all the acting, and Ann Helming was exact in her analysis when she used the phrase "supremely noble and unpompous" to describe Grant's Dr Praetorius. *Newsweek* was pleased by an unusually adult and literate movie, and it praised Grant for turning in "one of the most intelligent performances of his nineteen-year Hollywood career".

Before that career was twenty years old, he appeared for the second time with Betsy Drake, on this occasion in *Room For One More*, which was released in early 1952. If *Every Girl Should be Married* had been insubstantial, *Room For One More*, a slight story about a couple who adopted first an unwanted child and then a cripple, turned out to be positively flimsy. The picture proved only what had been clearly established – for example, that Grant and Drake were an excellent comedy team and that Grant could breathe life and magic into a merely passable script. Nevertheless, if somewhat empty-headed on the subject of child-rearing, the film had its heart in the right place and possessed a certain sociological curiosity value in that Betsy Drake, as the mother, was the figure of authority while Grant, as the father, was the amiable butt of most of the family jokes.

Sadly, Betsy never made another film with her husband, her screen-career declining spectacularly in the years that followed.

Monkey Business, Grant's second film of 1952, was the picture that Andrew Sarris was to bracket with *I Was a Male War-bride* as Hawks' 'sagas of perpetual humiliation'. To which could be added the observation that the director's later movie was both less charming and less funny. In a variation of his role in *Bringing Up Baby*, Grant played an absent-minded scientist trying to invent a rejuvenating drug that was accidentally concocted for him by a chimpanzee and then

unknowingly taken by Grant and his wife (Ginger Rogers), who
mentally and psychologically reverted to infantile status. (Ten years
earlier, Rogers had appealingly performed a similar feat of acting in
Billy Wilder's *The Major and the Minor*.) Much of the fun was crude
and cruel, and audiences laughed even though they were aware that
they should not have been doing so – some sort of tribute to the
unsubtle but basic gags and direction that had the whole cast plunging
with abandon into the absurd antics. The fact was that the characters,
while they were under the influence of the drug and yet retained their
adult physical attributes, were being systematically degraded, and thus
all but the most unreflective laughter had an uneasy, almost guilt-
ridden ring. In the name of farce, one might have accepted most of
Grant's discomforts in *I Was a Male War-bride*, but *Monkey
Business* was indeed a saga of humiliation, from which the male star
did not emerge unscathed, even though he was extremely funny in a
bravura display of his comic technique.

In the fall of 1953, shooting began on *A Star is Born*, a production
in which Cary Grant, not James Mason, had originally been intended
to play Norman Maine, Judy Garland's dipsomaniac screen-husband.
Grant was approached and an offer made. Garland and Sid Luft, then
her husband, thought the star would be perfect for Norman Maine, his
alcoholism all the more horrifying as a descent from Grant's usual
elegance and aplomb. Since they both followed the horses, Luft took
to working on his quarry at the Hollywood Park Racetrack. Grant
was worried that audiences might come up with a stock response to a
drunk – laughter; and not the sort of laughter that he, playing a
serious role, would enjoy hearing. Legend has it that Betsy settled the
matter. Late one night, still dressed for the tennis game after which she
and Grant had agreed that he could no longer torture himself with his
problem, she turned up at the Lufts' house and cried, "Lay off Cary!
You must let him go. You're driving him out of his mind."

The male role in *A Star is Born* was something of a hot potato.
Henry Fonda and Brando also rejected the offer, and it was decided
that Bogart, though in many other ways ideal, was too old for the
part.

Aware that his popularity was not all that it had once been, Grant
looked to safer territory. He had wanted to film Terence Rattigan's
Love In Idleness with Deborah Kerr as his leading lady, but the
project never came to fruition. He was, however, to co-star with the
British actress in three pictures, the first being *Dream Wife*, which was

released in 1953. In intention at least, the film was a polished romantic comedy of the type for which Grant was famous and in which he had not appeared for two or three years. The wisp of a story, directed by one of its authors, Sidney Sheldon, concerned a triangle formed by Grant, his emancipated fiancée (Deborah Kerr) and an Eastern princess who offered all the traditional virtues of unemancipated womanhood (Betta St John). Both stars were in sparkling form and did much to impart a sheen to the production, as did the sets and wardrobe. Though its trappings demanded colour, *Dream Wife* was filmed in black and white by MGM, who released it during the slack season and gave it scant support by way of publicity and Press showings. The picture was, in Miss Kerr's words, "a much underrated and amusing little comedy", but it did business that was less than spectacular.

How much MGM had been influenced by Grant's declining status at the box-office is a moot point. There was evidence that the influential fan-magazines were turning against him. With the war's end, the *automatic* popularity of a film in which he or any other star of his stature appeared had been no longer assured, and his most recent pictures had left even well-disposed audiences slightly disappointed. Howard Hawks confessed that he had expected too much of the public's response to the over-extended farce of *Monkey Business*, and films like *Room For One More*, however amiable, inspired a slightly frustrated sense of *déjà vu*.

In mid-1952, MGM had made economy-cuts all around, not least in production costs, in order to check the downward trend of profits. *Dream Wife* had undoubtedly been a casualty of the campaign for thrift.

In any case, the year of its release, 1953, was not a good year for stars (though Deborah Kerr scored a notable success in *From Here to Eternity*, and *Shane* came near to immortalizing Alan Ladd). As television's threat grew larger, the cinema's big hits were novelties and ephemeral enticements such as *Bwana Devil*, the first three-dimensional feature movie – with little else to distinguish it. As the first picture released in CinemaScope, *The Robe* drew crowds to the theatres, not with its stars, Richard Burton and Jean Simmons, but with its gimmickry. Novelty thus had its uses, but not even novelty would provide a lasting cure for an ailing industry.

Where, in the midst of all this, was Cary Grant? It might have seemed impossible to contemplate, but the situation was that MGM and the fan-magazines had come close to setting the seal of doom on one of the most dazzling careers in the history of motion pictures. For Grant, whose price per picture had risen to $300,000 and who had again and again been in the list of top ten box-office draws in the 'forties, an ignominious fading-away was unthinkable.

If the time was out of joint, so much the worse for the time. In late 1953, Grant announced his decision to retire and cruise with Betsy. He explained afterwards, "It was the period of the blue jeans, the dope addicts, the Method, and nobody cared about comedy at all."

14

Second Innings – and Sophia

If the decision to retire had turned out to be irrevocable, the loss to the cinema, as we now know, would have been great, and the truncated career would have been shorn of two or three of the finest acting performances on celluloid. Think of what Cary Grant would *not* have appeared in: two of the best Hitchcock films (*To Catch a Thief, North by Northwest*), a last glow of the talents of Leo McCarey (*An Affair to Remember*); a brilliant example of the comedy-thriller (*Charade*); and an unclassifiable comedy (*Father Goose*) that probably would never even have been conceived without its star's utterly central performance. Anyone who believes that three first-rate thrillers and two memorable comedies can lightly be written off should stick with Ingmar Bergman, Godard and Joseph Losey.

Asked about his plans during this period of lying fallow, Grant made some shrewd observations about the current state of the cinema: "Actually, I'd love to get back to those comedies I used to do. But where can I find one? Writers take themselves too seriously these days. Also, really polished dialogue is hard to write. It's much easier to create crude, everyday speech, and writers make a lot of money doing it." He had no plans for an immediate return to the screen.

People who had closely followed Grant's career saw his decision as inevitable or at least understandable. Others were shocked. And yet others (though perhaps the majority), since his return to filming was relatively swift, never even realized that there *was* a retirement.

It was terminated after two years by *To Catch a Thief*, released in September 1955. The prospect of working again with Hitchcock on what Grant called "a bright, literate script" by John Michael Hayes tempted him to try to recapture his former popularity in a comedy-thriller about a retired cat burglar pressured to help trap a thief who was aping his style and bringing him under suspicion for a daring series of jewel robberies. (Hence the title – an allusion to "Set a thief to catch a thief" from H.G. Bohn's 1855 *A Handbook of Proverbs*.) For those alive to it, the story thus possessed in its theme of re-emergence from retirement a parallel with the star's own history. The parent novel had been standard fare, but using little more than its narrative, Hayes provided a witty and stylish screenplay that was laced with double entendres. There were several telling character sketches, and perhaps the main strand of interest was provided by a burgeoning love-affair between Grant and Grace Kelly that was contrapuntal in intention, but not in fact, to the story of how Grant set out to trap his imitator. One of the results was that the thriller aspect of the picture was somewhat neglected, its secondary place in the screenplay finding secondary attention in the director. Though audiences might have been slightly disappointed by the result, *To Catch a Thief* was relaxed, polished, civilized and stylish entertainment. In short, it possessed all the attributes for which Grant had been famous at the height of his popularity.

Opposite was the type of leading lady he preferred playing a heroine whom Hitchcock described as "the drawing-room type, the real ladies who become whores once they're in the bedroom". The director had used Grace Kelly twice before, in *Dial M for Murder* and *Rear Window*, but this was perhaps her finest performance for him, moving subtly from glacial reticence to a sexual efflorescence in the arms of Grant that took a pyrotechnical display in the night-sky above Monte Carlo to symbolize on screen. Before that, clad in a low-cut gown and apparently profferring her jewels, she uttered one of the film's memorable double entendres: "Here, hold them ... They're the most beautiful thing in the world, and the one thing you can't resist." In a picnic scene, she had been equally provocative over serving a chicken: "Will you have a breast or a leg?" (A line that was lifted for a later John Ford movie, *The Horse Soldiers*.)

For audiences, seeing Grant again was like renewing acquaintance with an old friend who had not so much improved during the period of his absence as impudently defied time. Observing him for the first occasion in the film, the superb Jessie Royce Landis, playing the refreshingly down-to-earth, *nouveau riche* widowed mother of Grace Kelly, murmured, "Mmm, handsome ... I wouldn't mind buying that for you." Her reaction might have been slightly different from that of women movie-goers, who wouldn't have minded buying him for *themselves*. Even for a *retired* cat-burglar, Grant was impressively sleek, lithe and agile. He looked as tanned as though he had spent his whole life on the Riviera, and he even appeared to have grown younger since *Dream Wife*. Inspecting Kelly at her mother's behest, he commented, "Very pretty. Quietly attractive." But his eyes added copious footnotes. To draw attention to himself at the Monte Carlo gambling tables, he deliberately allowed a chip to fall down a French woman's *décolletage*. When, embarrassed, she tried to ignore the 'accident', he protested impishly, with all his old master's timing, "But, madam! That was a ten-thousand-franc plaque!" As a lover, he was cool, assured, with an aloofness that provoked the passion it appeared to withhold.

For a finale that generated some typical Hitchcockian tension, Grant had to perch on and scamper over some high rooftops, thus initiating, he claimed, a decisive cure for acrophobia. He forced himself to work without a net, and after he had conquered his fears atop four-storied French Riviera villas, he was to submit himself to another dose of the same medicine at the hands of Alfred Hitchcock in *North by Northwest*. (On that occasion, Grant and Eva Marie Saint were working on a set, crawling over a simulated Mount Rushmore; but it was the tallest set in Hollywood.)

Ravishingly photographed in colour (Robert Burks won an Academy Award that year), *To Catch a Thief* was a predictable success, and it was chosen for the annual British Royal Film Performance in preference to the much fancied *Richard III* by Olivier – perhaps because the selection committee thought that Olivier's production might be striking the same sensitive royal nerves after the controversial showing of *Beau Brummell* the previous year.

To complete the regal associations, *To Catch a Thief* was the film that turned Grace Kelly into the future Princess of Monaco, for during the making of it she met Prince Rainier. News of that romance undoubtedly helped the film to become sensational box-office – together with four other Kelly pictures that year.

Grant had not chosen the easiest time for a return to movie-making. In 1955, weekly attendance in the US sank to an ominous 45.8 million – well over four million down in five years. But he was not the man to rush from a triumphant return to ill-considered films that might well founder during a time when people were increasingly uncertain of what would be good box-office. He was in no hurry. He read scripts, missed at least one hit (he turned down *The Bridge on the River Kwai* during this period), and travelled with Betsy, visiting places as far afield as Bristol and Hong Kong. (He was there with Betsy for Chinese

New Year in 1953, when he posed agreeably for the picture in this book, joking to photographer Joe Cocks, "You'll have to pay me ten cents for each shot.") The years of travel were interrupted first by *To Catch a Thief* and only after a long interval by *The Pride and the Passion*, which was not released until the summer of 1957.

What took place during its filming was interesting enough to make the dull proceedings on screen seem even drabber than they were.

"Windmillville" was Frank Sinatra's name for the location in Spain where *The Pride and the Passion* was shot. In this story of a mighty cannon and the Peninsular War in 1810, he was starring with Grant and Sophia Loren – two men in love with the same girl, at least on the screen. Brando had been announced for Sinatra's role, but, then, Brando, it sometimes seemed, was announced for every big role, and the practice continues today. Even close to the charms of Miss Loren, who was playing his tempestuous peasant mistress (and also falling for the British officer played by Grant), Sinatra could not control his impatience with the tedium of movie-making and the relentless heat, and he departed prematurely, without finishing his final scenes.

For years, friends and acquaintances had spread the story that Grant possessed a convenient knack of developing romantic feelings towards his leading ladies – and then, usually, relinquishing those emotions with the end of the shooting on the films in which they were involved. The star's impulsive affection, it was implied, was merely another device of his formidable technique. If so, the customary process went wrong with Sophia Loren and *The Pride and the Passion*. What flared between the actor and his co-star was both more urgent and less susceptible of convenient termination.

In later years, Grant, ever one to deflect personal questions with deceptive banter, made light of the matter. "Wherever did all those rumours start?" he would say rhetorically, expecting no one to retort, "In reality." Or there was the disarming observation: "If I remember correctly, [Sophia] was in love with Frank Sinatra." (True, but disingenuous: she was – in the film.) Most newspapermen were unwilling to correct or argue with the star who had once told Hedda Hopper that his private life was none of her goddamned business. To a British journalist who in 1971 brought up the delicate subject of leading ladies and amorous alliances, Grant revealed teasingly, "I know of only one with whom I had an affair." *He* knew, but for the rest of the world, her identity remained anybody's guess.

Rumours about Grant and Loren, however, persisted both at the time and for years afterwards, until they were eventually given the stamp of authenticity by Sophia Loren's best-selling autobiography (co-authored with A.E. Hotchner), *Living and Loving*, which devoted several pages to the affair. Grant's passion, the book asserted, had been genuine, and she had cherished it, if not responded to it.

The relationship began in jokes and banter. He called her "Miss Brigloren" or "Miss Lowbrigid". She was twenty-three, and he was fifty-two – almost ten years the senior of Carlo Ponti, who had turned Sofia Scicolone into Sophia Loren and masterminded her career. She had met him when she was sixteen (fourteen, according to some versions), and she had lived with him for most of the last four years. But Ponti was married, and a divorce did not seem imminent. Where did that leave Sophia?

She was not unimpressed by Grant's attentions. "I knew he loved me," she commented, "and that, if I chose to, I could marry him."

On paper, *The Pride and the Passion* represented her great bid for Hollywood stardom. Replacing Ava Gardner in a supposedly plum role that the American star had rejected, she was to be paid $25,000, and Ponti was negotiating a profitable deal with Paramount. In matrimonial terms and considering her career, she had a great deal on her mind, not least the question of how she and Ponti would make their relationship acceptable to the more reactionary segment of the American public. (The legal complications of divorce in Italy were staggering.)

To ingratiate himself with Sophia, Grant, whose attitude to autograph hunters was contemptuous and unyielding, cultivated a more indulgent response to his fans. But while she 'taught' him respect, he talked persistently to her of marriage. Grant was scheduled to leave for Los Angeles and work on *An Affair to Remember*, and Sophia was due to report for location-shooting in Greece on *Boy on a Dolphin*. With Sinatra's hasty departure, filming on *The Pride and the Passion* finished in some confusion, but Sophia at least welcomed the break for the opportunity it gave her to mull over her feelings and make up her mind calmly about Cary Grant.

In Hollywood, where Sinatra and the other principals worked on pickup-shots, there was further emotional confusion. Grant looked more attractive than ever, and though he was a married man, he was 'free' in a way that Ponti, separated from his wife but seeking annulment in a sternly Catholic country, seemed to have no hope of being. Sophia talked matters over with Ponti, who in any case could see for himself what was happening. Once filming the extra scenes for *The Pride and the Passion* was over, even though Ponti was present, Grant called her every day and sent her flowers.

To join her again on film, he returned to his Alma Mater, Paramount, for *Houseboat*, released in late 1958, by which time Grant's domestic circumstances had altered radically. As a British stuffed shirt, he had been glum in *The Pride and the Passion*, while Loren had been grotesquely inhibited by her lack of fluency in English. But much of the old sparkle of the Grant *persona* was again evident in the later film, and his co-star also mustered some complementary gaiety.

Though not without merit, *Houseboat* was little more than an agreeable reshuffling of ingredients that were already familiar via previous Grant comedies such as *Room for One More*. Smooth but forgettable, *Houseboat*, like *The Pride and the Passion* before it, was notable less for its essential qualities than for the peripheral drama contemporary with its making. Rumour had it that Grant proposed to Sophia just before the big love scene was shot and she turned him down. In her autobiography, she was somewhat more detailed and precise in her account of what took place. The situation came to a head towards the end of filming. With the three-cornered predicament seemingly unresolved, she and Ponti were staying in a bungalow in the grounds of the Bel Air Hotel when she read in her breakfast newspaper through Louella Parsons that one legal knot had been cut and another tied. In Juarez, Ponti had at last obtained a divorce and almost simultaneously married Sophia, two Mexican lawyers standing in for the principals at the proxy ceremony. Sophia was thus presented with a *fait accompli*. As a start to a marriage, her casual discovery of the truth would have been hard to rival. Had the Press beaten Ponti to the punch or had he reasoned that seeing the facts in cold print might bring Sophia to her senses?

How she *might* have reacted is purely hypothetical. The fact is that she accepted the accomplishment of what she had long desired – her yearning clouded in later days by Grant's interest in her. If she had regrets, they were not to amount to a rejection of her new status. The following morning, the shooting of *Houseboat*'s wedding scene took place – a nicely ironic piece of timing. Having read the Louella Parsons column, Grant offered Sophia his good wishes. He was greatly upset, nevertheless.

There were numerous sequels to the story of *The Pride and the Passion* and *Houseboat* and how Grant, by acting as Sophia's mentor and dragoman in Hollywood, had come close to supplanting Carlo Ponti. Among the less serious tales was one that Grant had been quick to console himself with a somewhat more generously built facsimile of the Italian star − a Yugoslavian basketball player called Luba. (The anecdote is related by David Niven in *Bring on the Empty Horses*.) It was certainly true, though, that it was Grant who told Sophia on 9th April 1962, that she had been awarded the Academy Award for her part in *Two Women*.

In 1980, after the recent publication of *Living and Loving*, public interest in the Grant-Loren liaison was still very much alive, and a three-hour television film based on the autobiography was announced. While a search was instituted for actors to play Ponti and Grant, it was stated that Miss Loren would play her mother and herself after the age of twenty-five. Mel Stuart would direct the project, which was to be shot in Hollywood, Switzerland and Italy.

Soon after the announcement, Grant reportedly threatened a lawsuit to prevent the film's making. Silent about the earlier disclosures in the Loren autobiography, he nevertheless protested over the planned production: "I cannot believe that anyone would exploit an old friendship like this."

The lives and loves of celebrities are subjects for gloating and glee among that huge section of the public that finds them stimulating − even though they often deny their addiction. For those involved, however, the reality is usually far removed from the soap operas that reach the media − both in essence and in the tangential events that may prove much more serious than the main incidents.

One person thus far omitted from the account of those events in the mid-'fifties is Betsy Drake, the woman with whom Grant had for so long enjoyed "a warm, relaxed companionship". What Betsy saw or sensed or, indeed, what her husband told her when she visited the unit on location for *The Pride and the Passion* must remain in the realm of surmise and speculation. What happened to her on her return trip is better documented.

On 25th July 1956, she was a passenger on the *Andrea Doria* when it collided at night with the Swedish *Stockholm* off Nantucket. Betsy was physically unharmed, but the *Andrea Doria* sank with the loss of fifty-one lives. Having been rescued, Betsy cabled her husband: ABOARD ILE DE FRANCE. ALL IS WELL. NOT A SCRATCH. Since he knew nothing, as it turned out, of the events preceding the wire, Grant was at first mystified and then, once inquiries had revealed the sinking of the *Andrea Doria*, frantic with concern for his wife and what she might have been through.

After the ordeal, in which she lost jewels and the manuscript of a book she was writing, Betsy sought treatment with Dr Mortimer Hartman, whose therapy included doses of LSD. Grant decided to use the drug, too.

He had long been interested in ways of expanding and exploring the mind, of commanding a greater awareness and understanding of his own psychology, and he had already, under Betsy's influence, realized the benefits of hypnosis and become proficient at self-hypnosis. This latter fact was attested to by journalist Peter Shield,[1] who revealed that Grant's body had been covered with knife scars received during the filming of a fight in *The Pride and the Passion* (on screen a tame affair) and that the scars had later mysteriously disappeared. When the star stepped from a shower, Shield, seeing no sign of them, asked what had happened. Grant explained that, to the astonishment of the unit's doctors, they had healed and vanished within two days after he had practised self-hypnosis. The power to anaesthetize at will any part of his body had made trips to the dentist, if not pleasurable, at least completely painless, but practical though such applications were, Grant valued hypnosis less for its 'stunts' than as an adjunct to peace of mind. "Hypnotism is complete relaxation," he told Shield. "And relaxation is the secret of everything – from golf to acting to lovemaking."

First, Betsy had introduced him to the rewards of hypnosis. Now she encouraged him to partake in medically controlled experiments with LSD. 'Acid' has had a bad Press, and it was, indirectly, to give Grant himself a bad Press in the 'sixties. But Grant discovered that, properly used, this hallucinogenic was remarkable as a psychological catalyst, that it opened up his thoughts and feelings to him, thus bestowing something like omniscience – or at least the *sensation* of omniscience. This self-exploration was guided at every stage by a doctor who would carefully prepare Grant for the next phase. Sceptics might raise their eyebrows, but the empirical truth was that Grant, after having used the drug known as LSD 25 a hundred times, gained immeasurably in confidence and serenity. For him, the proof lay in his acceptance of his early years and his parents, his ability to reconcile himself to the events of his existence, to "let fact be fact, and life the thing it can". Others, including interviewers, observed a change in him best summed up as a new accessibility and an outgoing interest in other people.

Anxious to minimize any risks in so controversial a process, Grant emphasized that he had used the drug "only with the direct inspection and care of a qualified doctor". But probably his last word on the subject was when he said, "My intention in taking LSD was to make myself happy. A man would be a fool to take something that *didn't* make him happy."

If the drug helped him accept facts, one of those that he had to face was that his marriage with Betsy was definitely in trouble. For a while the two of them stayed together, their nearness no doubt strengthened – if only temporarily – by her brush with death. But Grant was no stranger to dissolution, and the signs were clear. Though he might have felt guilty (his old habit), with experience he had come to realize more of human fallibility and to know that when a couple stayed together as a moral feat, the continuation of their marriage was not admirable. After he and Barbara Hutton had divorced, he observed, "Sometimes I think people expect too much from a marriage. They expect a paradise on earth." To the suggestion once offered that most folk getting married anticipated that they would be together always, he retorted hotly, "Yes – and kill each other." If his paradise with Betsy was lost, it was better to face the fact.

She was yet again, however, to be his support and comfort.

While he was making *An Affair to Remember*, the cameraman Milton Krasner commented on the bump on Grant's forehead that was making close-ups a problem to light. The 'bump' was a benign lipoma or thickening of tissue. A relic of the star's USO tours during the war, it had begun with the compulsory wearing of a steel helmet that had irritated a spot on his brow. He had never liked hats anyway, but after he had removed the helmet, he would rub the slightly inflamed area, making it worse and thus, in time, producing the lump.

He was about to begin filming on *Kiss Them for Me* when medical opinion ordered the excision of the growth, to the consternation of Stanley Donen, the director, and the Fox executives, who envisaged an expensive production held up while its star languished in hospital. Grant explained to Peter Shield what happened: "I'd taken advice about [the tumour] once from the great British plastic surgeon, Sir Archibald MacIndoe. He told me it would take about a month to remove. I couldn't afford the time. I had Betsy hypnotize me before the operation. She emphasized that I had to stay calm and even enjoy the operation. I did just that. The surgeon used a local anaesthetic. He might have been cutting my hair for all I cared. It will heal without a scar."

So it did. Hypnosis and the surgery carried out at Cedars of Lebanon Hospital "resulted in an incredibly quick healing," Deborah Kerr reported, "and no mark whatsoever of where [the growth] had been."[2]

On 9th October of the following year, 1958, the Grants split after nine years together. Having an innate predilection for privacy, Grant had come to value reticence just as much. (When Barbara Hutton married Rubirosa and the actor's opinion was solicited, he replied, "With so many people talking, I think this is a fine time to keep my mouth shut.") Nevertheless, it was obvious to both him and Betsy that they would have to say something to the Press. The joint statement they eventually prepared was a model of dignity and restraint: "After careful consideration and long discussion, we have decided to live apart. We have had and shall always have a deep love for each other, but, also, our marriage has not brought us the happiness we fully expected and mutually desired. So since we have no children needful of our attention, it is consequently best that we separate for a while ... We ask our friends to be patient with, and understanding of, our decision."

It was not the end, but it was the beginning of the end. They continued to see each other regularly, sometimes covering great distances to do so. At last, on 13th August 1962, Betsy divorced Grant in Santa Monica for mental cruelty. The recital of complaints became a familiar litany: he was bored with her, he disliked the institution of marriage, her friends bored him (shades of Barbara Hutton?).

Against the list had to be set the fact that, as she admitted later, she still loved him and that they remained friends.

As usual, Grant had no reply to make to the charges levelled against him – neither repudiation nor unkind words.

If failed marriages need epitaphs, Grant coined half of one with daunting simplicity when he said, "Betsy was good for me."

Probably he for her, too.

15

Always Leave them Wanting More

The Pride and the Passion had been the sort of movie that enhanced nobody's reputation, but Grant afterwards went straight into *An Affair to Remember*, a much better picture that was actually released a few days ahead of his earlier film. Though not without its longueurs and disappointments, *An Affair to Remember*, Leo McCarey's remake of his 1939 *Love Affair*, was well received and is still valued today, if largely for the playing of Deborah Kerr and Grant in roles originally created by Irene Dunne and Charles Boyer. The restraint, charm and deftness of touch in the later partnership was noteworthy, and Deborah Kerr had commented: "It was our most successful work together and, to this day, is shown over and over again in the States and in England and on the continent, as well as Australia ... and hundreds and hundreds of people tell me how *many* times they have seen the movie, and how they wept at every viewing."[1]

The last remark provides a strong clue to the film's potency. Unashamedly sentimental, it embraced emotionalism but nevertheless explored it with a taste seldom encountered in the 'woman's picture' (a derogatory term, but familiar and accurate enough). The story concerned Nickie Ferrante (Grant), a dilettante artist and man about town, who entered into a shipboard romance with Terry McKay (Deborah Kerr), a former nightclub singer. The two agreed to meet again six months later, after they had tidied up their lives, but an accident cruelly intervened before they discovered each other once more, their love undiminished by misunderstanding.

There was something anachronistic but more than slightly appealing about *An Affair to Remember*. Its morality — the idea of the lovers 'purifying' themselves before ultimate dedication — was easy to laugh at, but as David Ehrenstein said in a view much respected by Deborah Kerr, "If we reject what *An Affair to Remember* REALLY says about moral character and self-esteem, then it's not a measure of how far we've come but how much we've lost." (His comments were published in the *Los Angeles Examiner* apropos of a season of Cary Grant films screened in tribute at the Los Angeles County Museum of Art.)

Since *The Awful Truth*, a great deal had happened to Leo McCarey — much of it bad. Before he died in 1969 of emphysema, he had survived a near-fatal car accident and the ravages of drink and drugs. His talent had fluctuated alarmingly, and after the rabid anti-communism of *My Son John* in 1952, *An Affair to Remember* indicated a welcome revitalization of his gifts. Nevertheless, his control of this romantic comedy was uneven and at times flaccid. The humour of the early scenes was well handled, but McCarey's touch grew leaden in the later stages as factitious events led to near-tragedy. Even so, he made just four pictures in the 'fifties and 'sixties, of which only *An Affair to Remember*, whatever its artistic shortcomings, was a commercial success.

Much of its strength derived from the partnership of Cary Grant and Deborah Kerr. To his role of faintly disreputable bon vivant, Grant brought irony, a sense of the ridiculousness of passion, as well as the conviction that made irony merely one ingredient of a complicated experience. The picture profited greatly, in Miss Kerr's words, from "Cary's ability to play it 'straight' and move one enormously, a facet of his talent that he was not always given credit for." She herself complemented his sincerity with playing of rare delicacy and restraint, perhaps stopping short of irony, but never devoid of humour. There was a scene in a New York theatre in which Terry and Nickie, their affair apparently ended, met by chance after she, unknown to him, had been crippled in a street accident. Not willing or able to explain her changed circumstances, Terry sat waiting for the theatre to empty so that her escort could wheel her out. With a minimum of 'technique', the actress conveyed beautifully the character's uncertainty, her expectations and her vulnerability to the sardonic undertones of Nickie's formal greeting. Small wonder that audiences responded so favourably to a partnership of such rapport.

Grant, as Deborah Kerr found out during the shooting of this, their second film together, had "an eye for detail in every aspect of the movie being made, not just *his* particular part. I remember very well in the scene in *An Affair to Remember* when the ship is docking in New York and Nickie and Terry are ostentatiously keeping apart at the ship's rails, how he spotted one of the 'extras' (a woman 'passenger') resting her bright red beauty-case on the rails. He at once had the case removed because, in colour, on the screen, everyone's eye would automatically jump to the red case and be distracted from what was going on between the principal artists. *I* would never have thought of that – nor did anyone else – and I have never forgotten it, and in subsequent movies I have always watched out for the colour RED. It's a small thing, I know, but I think it illustrates his utter concentration on detail. He was not only the king of the 'double-take', but a superb 'ad libber'. In fact, a couple of scenes in *An Affair to Remember* we just ad libbed (mainly because either he or I had forgotten the line we were supposed to say) and our director, dear Leo McCarey, kept them in the finished product."[2]

While dancing in the film, Cary Grant and Deborah Kerr sang several bars of Harry Warren's title song, and it was announced that on an album they would record a full duet version. But though the album materialized, no duet by the stars was included, Vic Damone instead sang the number.

(If, on screen, the co-stars were a notable partnership, they had much in common in their own lives, for both, curiously enough, had been Bristolians. In early adolescence, Deborah Kerr had lived with her maternal grandmother at Weston-super-Mare, twenty miles from the city, and she was privately educated in Bristol at Northumberland House School in the 'thirties. Her younger brother worked as a reporter for the *Bristol Evening World* and was later head of newscasting in Bristol for TWW, the television network. The young Deborah did some early work in radio from the local studios, reading children's stories, and one of her first [amateur] stage appearances was in Archie Leach's home-town.)

Hollywood has always revelled in bizarre genesis, and Grant, pausing only for the minor surgery discussed earlier, moved swiftly into the odd and unsatisfactory *Kiss Them for Me* (1957), which Julius J. Epstein based on a Second World War novel by Frederic Wakeman and the none-too-successful play derived from it by Luther Davis. *Shore Leave*, the title of the book, summed up this story of three supposedly battle-weary fliers who, during furlough, became nauseated by the profiteering and cupidity of the civilians for whom they were fighting. The hero fliers were a juvenile lot reminiscent of the soldiers in *Gunga Din*, and the film's sole distinction was occasional lines of corrosive dialogue, leapt upon like hungry men by Grant and his fellow actors. The star has always expressed his preference for leading ladies who look like thoroughbreds and behave with instinctive good breeding. In *Kiss Them for Me*, he had one in Suzy Parker, one of America's top models. Unfortunately, in this, her screen début, she revealed minimal acting skill.

The film was directed by Stanley Donen, an arresting talent, who, though twenty years Grant's junior, had already secured his place in cinema history with the daring dance routines, innovatively filmed, in such musicals as *Singin' in the Rain* and *Seven Brides for Seven Brothers*. Before joining MGM as a choreographer, he had begun his career as a dancer in New York, and though arguably no more than one of his non-musical films could be considered to be imperishable cinema, any account of MGM or the musical would have to include him as a key-figure.

Though Donen and Grant were to differ over many points in movie-making, they greatly respected each other's gifts – sufficiently, in fact, to make four pictures together and to form the Grandon Company, which produced *Indiscreet* and *The Grass is Greener*.

The first of these, released in 1958, again teamed Grant with Ingrid Bergman, this time in a light romantic – not to say insubstantial – farce. (The progression from *Notorious* to *Indiscreet* seemed witty in itself.) Though the picture was set in London and appeared to have been conceived and made in the grip of galloping anglophilia, it had its irresistible moments, such as Grant's wild dancing of a highland fling at a military ball. The playing of the two principals was predictably smooth and engaging, especially once both dialogue and situations had acquired the bite of irony with Bergman's realization that throughout their affair Grant had been lying when he claimed himself unable to marry her because of his inability to obtain a divorce. At any rate, audiences much preferred this rather routine fare to the uneasy concoctions of *Kiss Them for Me*.

After the forgettable *Houseboat*, Grant made one of his finest pictures and his best for Hitchcock. *North by Northwest* (1959) had perhaps the choicest ingredients of any Hitchcock collaboration: the director himself at the top of his form, a polished and witty script by Ernest Lehman, magnificent cinematography by Robert Burks, a dazzling cast headed by Grant and, last but by no means least potent, a classic film score from Bernard Herrmann, whose brilliant orchestral fandango behind the main titles announced the chase that was to follow and tightened the tension even before the action had begun.

North By Northwest was a phenomenon: an immensely popular

movie that yet made no concessions to a mass audience. Hitchcock has ever attracted *outré* analyses from intellectual critics, and those who enjoy, for whatever reason, the solemn exegesis of such writers will not be disappointed by their utterances about *North By Northwest*, of which the following is a stimulating recent example: "Ostensibly a playful spy-thriller, [the film] is the American dream at twenty-four frames per second: Madison Avenue, Plaza Hotel, United Nations, Chicago, The Plains, Mount Rushmore. Its geographical and spiritual trajectory – with Cary Grant at its centre, the shallow man of admass who breaks a spy-ring for the CIA – is a return to critical and cultural imperatives."*

Possibly. It is also masterly movie-making and superb entertainment, the sheer magic of which dissolves upon analysis but is none the less there, gloriously mocking attempts to pin it down precisely. The script may be tight and inventive, for example, but how many other pictures have skated so brilliantly over thin, not to say cracking, ice? (A tribute to Hitchcock's directorial skill and cutter George Tomasini's feeling for tempo.) When Roger Thornhill, the character played by the star, is asked for a simple yes or no to the demand that he produce secret information, he replies, "A simple no. For the simple reason I simply don't know what you're talking about." Hitchcock has said that the line came directly from Grant, who failed to comprehend the movie's convoluted plot. (Don Siegel had a parallel experience with another star, Walter Matthau, on *Charley Varrick*.) One can understand Grant's bafflement: anyone who tried to take seriously Lehman's inspired nonsense would get into similar difficulties. But Lehman himself tipped us the wink with his title – a reference to Hamlet's: "I am but mad north-northwest: when the wind is southerly, I know a hawk from a handsaw." The improbable plot is the writer's insolently clever pretext for the fun dreamed up around it. And what fun. There are obvious delights such as Grant's deliberate disruption of an auction or the eerily inconsequential crop-dusting sequence – sure nominations for almost anybody's anthology of favourite movie scenes. But what could be more amusing than one of James Mason's speeches, as the spy Vandamm, to Grant (who is an actor playing a businessman who is not a spy but whom Vandamm believes to be a CIA agent who actually does not exist)? Mason declares: "Seems to me you fellows could stand a little less training

* From a British National Film Theatre Programme, April 1980.

from the FBI and a little more from the Actors' Studio." Or when
Grant defines advertising as "the art of expedient exaggeration"? Or
when he sceptically points out what the initial letters of his name —
Roger O. Thornhill — add up to?

Pauline Kael wrote: "Cary Grant is the perfect actor for the part
(he incarnates the directional confusion of the title — he seems to have
gotten younger and better looking, yet he's probably older than Jessie
Royce Landis, who plays his mother)." (Landis was Grant's exact
contemporary, and in *To Catch a Thief*, she had, of course, played
Grace Kelly's mother and therefore the male star's potential mother-
in-law.) Miss Kael was right. Grant was better than ever — seemingly
effortless and yet incomparably combining the wit, exasperation,
inventiveness, disillusionment and even wounded passion of Roger
Thornhill.

When one looks back over the seventy-two films of Grant's career,
they are memorable less for the effectiveness of his on screen
juxtaposition with actors like Melvyn Douglas in *Mr Blandings* and
Tony Curtis in *Operation Petticoat* than for the exquisite interplay
and sexual tension of his partnerships with his leading ladies. Though
he was to make only the one picture with her, Eva Marie Saint proved
a stunningly complementary co-star in *North By Northwest*, her
acting as economical as Grant's own. Their scenes on the train were
remarkable not only for their droll handling of dry conversation and
wet glasses but also for the counterpoint of vocal inflections and
rather naked glances (Eva Marie Saint's slid sideways in uncannily
seductive fashion) in such exchanges as:

GRANT: Oh, you're that type ... Honest.
SAINT: Not really.
G: Good — because honest women frighten me.
S: Why?
G: I don't know. Somehow they seem to put me at a disadvantage.
S: Is it because you're not honest with them?
G: Exactly ... What I mean is the moment I meet an attractive
woman, I have to pretend I've no desire to make love to her.
S: What makes you think you have to conceal it?
G: She might find the idea objectionable.
S: Then again she might not.
G: Think how lucky I am to have been seated here.
S: Luck had nothing to do with it.

G: Fate?

S: I tipped the steward five dollars to seat you here if you should come in.

G: Is that a proposition?

S: I never discuss love on an empty stomach.

G: You've already eaten.

S: But you haven't.

G: Don't you think it's time we were introduced?

S: I'm Eve Kendall, I'm twenty-six and unmarried. Now you know everything.

G: Tell me, what do you do besides lure men to their doom on the Twentieth Century Limited?

North by Northwest was originally to have been made by Paramount, but MGM gave it their best high production gloss and some notable sets, not least for the climax on Mount Rushmore. (Hitchcock, though he didn't have his way, had wanted to put Grant in Lincoln's nostril and give him a sneezing fit.) Ernest Lehman had written a screen-original – rare for the times, when almost all films were derived from successful and therefore previously tested books, plays and even films, and the freshness of his screenplay owed little to prior models. Though the picture was over two hours long (again unusual for 1959), audiences didn't mind a bit. Hitch had chosen Grant for his role because he believed they would identify with him, and identify with him they did in this classic example of one of Hitchcock's favourite cinematic themes – that of the pursued man.

Since *North by Northwest* was a record-breaker at the box-office, it seemed unlikely that its star would top its success – certainly not in the near future. Yet he immediately did so with *Operation Petticoat*, his second film of 1959, produced by his own Granart Company and commercially the biggest hit Grant would ever make. This service-comedy about a disabled submarine in the Second World War was directed by Blake Edwards – yet another example of Grant providing an important break for a promising talent. Edwards had originally been an actor and then a writer, and the impetus provided by the success of *Operation Petticoat* helped his career to flourish with such movies as *Breakfast at Tiffany*'s, *Days of Wine and Roses* and *The Great Race*. Edwards had a sound sense of construction and character and kept a firm grip on a film that might easily have been episodic and diffuse, but it had to be said that Grant, as the purposeful captain about whom all the fun revolved, scored yet another acting triumph in *Operation Petticoat*. With grey in his hair and restraint uppermost in his style, he was the elder statesman keeping alive a sense of purpose and determination. Since reviewers throughout his career had been fond of dubbing him 'slick', it was instructive to contrast his slickness with that of Tony Curtis – a much flashier, cockier brand from an actor famous for doing Cary Grant impersonations.

Grant took a year off before he joined Deborah Kerr again in Stanley Donen's *The Grass is Greener*. This light-weight comedy was an adaptation of a play by Hugh and Margaret Williams, who had enjoyed great success on the English stage with a series of vapid, typically British drawing-room pieces. If those who made *Indiscreet* had seemed to be suffering from anglophilia, it was a required condition of audiences seeking to appreciate *The Grass is Greener*, in which Grant was an earl who opened his stately home to a Texas millionaire (Robert Mitchum) who became romantically involved with the earl's wife (Deborah Kerr). This fatuous exercise left one sympathizing with the plight of a gifted quartet of actors attempting the impossible feat of sustaining comedy without a script. Nevertheless, some of their own enthusiasm for an unenviable task communicated itself. (Deborah Kerr has said, "*The Grass is Greener* ... was a joy to work in, in that the cast included my other most favourite actor, Robert Mitchum, and my very good friend Jean Simmons, whom I have known since she was a very young girl in *Black Narcissus*.'³) The film was made in England.

Though *The Grass is Greener* was not, predictably, to feature in the list of Grant's top dozen grossers, the star's career had reached a commercial apogee with *Operation Petticoat*, and he was to select four more extraordinarily profitable properties with which to round off his thirty-four years in movies. The first – and runner-up to *Operation Petticoat* – was *That Touch of Mink* (1962), in which Grant co-starred with the enormously popular Doris Day. Not the most sparkling of comedies, the film featured its principals in what *Variety* aptly called "the old cat-and-mouse game" between the sexes, its momentum nicely maintained by the inventive gags of the Stanley Shapiro-Nate Monaster screenplay. *That Touch of Mink* was funny enough to please critics and public alike, and nobody objected to yet another display of the utterly familiar yet wholly admirable Grant comic genius.

Another smash-hit, rivalling *North by Northwest* at the box-office
was *Charade* (1963), Grant's last film with Stanley Donen. It did not
seriously compete with Hitchcock and was perhaps not trying to. This
comedy-thriller set in Paris was deft, amusing and exciting and yet,
unpredictably, a touching parable about instinctive trust – those
reasons of the heart, to paraphrase Pascal, that the head knows not of.

Stanley Donen had been uncommonly persuasive. Paris in the
winter, when he could have been enjoying the warmth of his Palm
Springs home, was not the perpetually tanned Grant's idea of fun.
Moreover, much as he wanted to film opposite Audrey Hepburn, he
was seriously concerned at the obvious age disparity between him and
his co-star. It was screen-writer Peter Stone's task to find a solution to
the problem, and he did so, in a clever and witty script, by facing it
boldly and having the characters freely discuss their difference in
years. (In the midst of giving incomparable new life to old gags such
as: "Would you like to see where I was tattooed? Okay, we'll drive
round that way." – Grant occasionally uttered a line like: "At my age
who wants to hear the word 'serious'?" when Hepburn grew
romantic.) The strongest feature of this story of murder and the quest
for the proceeds of an ancient robbery was charm, though the picture
was not short of thrills and plot twists either. In one curious aspect,
Charade evoked memories of *Suspicion*: Grant had several baffling
shifts of identity, but at one stage everything pointed to his being the
killer. It was a measure of Peter Stone's talent that audiences probably
considered the possibility more seriously than they had in the earlier
film.

(Besides providing Grant with five separate identities in *Charade*,
the ingenious Stone has a predilection for surrounding himself with
mystery. The film's companion pieces, *Mirage* and *Arabesque*, are full
of puzzles and enigmas, but none is more provocative than the
mysteries the author creates about himself. Nearly half the time, he
uses pseudonyms, and even some of his collaborations suggest Peter
Stone working with Peter Stone. *Skin Game* has a script by Stone and
David Giler, but the film itself credits 'Pierre Marton', a pseudonym
he used on *Arabesque*. As Richard Corliss has pointed out, "Marton
is the surname of Stone's stepfather; Pierre is French for 'Peter' and
also the French word for 'Stone'." To compound the intricacies, Stone
also writes as Quentin Werty. There is a fascinating discussion of
these matters in *Talking Pictures: Screen writers of Hollywood* by
Richard Corliss, to whom the author is indebted.)

Charade had good direction and an exceptionally fine cast, and it was distributed by Universal, with whom Grant was associated for five films in a row, before releasing his last Granley production through Columbia.

Since Peter Stone had served him so well, nobody was too surprised when Grant next appeared in *Father Goose* (1964) from a screenplay by Stone and Frank Tarloff, in which the star played (in his own words) "an unshaven old grey-haired sot in sloppy denims" forced to act as a look-out in the Pacific in the Second World War and eventually, after reluctantly heroic adventures, winning the hand of the reforming French girl (Leslie Caron) he had fallen foul of. (There were parallels here with Huston's *The African Queen*, made more than ten years earlier.)

Audiences found much to admire in a film that had its full share of comic situations and biting lines; but no feature was more admirable than Grant's performance as Walter Eckland. Without systematically destroying a *persona* he had built up over years, he allowed himself to be convincingly slovenly, engagingly craven and surprisingly desperate before he was inevitably spruced up and transformed if not transmogrified for the picture's finale. If these were the liberties that could be taken by a superstar, they none the less had an element of risk and daring. It was an extremely funny performance, with added piquancy for a public who had rarely seen its idol dishevelled – only, say, as Leopold Dilg in *The Talk of the Town*.

Commercially, *Father Goose* was almost as successful as *Charade*, and accepting an Academy Award for his work, Peter Stone said at the ceremony, "My thanks to Cary Grant, who keeps winning these things for other people."

There were rumours that the star might retire. To Roderick Mann (*Sunday Express*, 7th June 1964), Grant had confided, "I am getting to the stage where I have to be very careful about love-scenes with young actresses. The public doesn't like to see an older man making love to a young girl. It offends them ... I am well aware that I can't go on playing romantic parts much longer. After all, I am quite an old fellow to some young people. But to be honest with you, I don't know what I will do. Maybe I will quit."

Again Grant waited a year before he starred in *Walk, Don't Run* (1966), in which he played Sir William Rutland, an English manufacturer visiting the 1964 Olympic Games in Tokyo and finding accommodation only by persuading a young girl (Samantha Eggar) to share her apartment with him. The film, which would turn out to be his last, had him in an avuncular or fatherly role. Though he looked improbably unchanged, his voice on sound-tracks had for some time been exhibiting signs of advancing age. Vocal deterioration is almost impossible to disguise, and while huskiness and gravelly qualities may suit a character actor, they detract from the performances of romantic leading men in a way fatal to their careers. Wisely, Grant allowed a young man (Jim Hutton) to woo the heroine. Though it had its points, the picture was a tame remake of *The More the Merrier*, the 1943 comedy in which Charles Coburn has had Grant's part. (A curious coincidence: Joel McCrea, unhappy with his role as the hero in the original, had actually suggested Grant as a substitute.)

By contrast with his startling Walter Eckland, Grant's Sir William was a deceptively muted impersonation – deceptively, because it was the star, in this peripheral part, who kept a flimsy house of cards from collapsing and provided humour and charm from next to nothing. *Newsweek* commented that he "could not be unfunny if he tried". Shrewdly, however, *Newsweek* also diagnosed Grant trying to prevent single-handed the decline of Hollywood comedy. It could not be done.

After *Walk, Don't Run*, Grant retired – finally and irrevocably.

Not for him the steady deterioration of some of his contemporaries – signposted by compromise, the coarsening of talent, self-parody and inferior roles in inferior pictures. Not for him the melancholy transition from romantic comedian and leading man to scene-stealing character actor.

His resignation was glorious in its finality. At the summit, his lustre undimmed, a great star walked away without a backward glance.

His decision was not beyond prediction: he had talked for years of giving up, and it was significant that in his last film he had not got the girl. Even so, public bewilderment posed the question: Why?

There was a multiplicity of reasons. Though healthily commercial, *Walk, Don't Run* had enjoyed nothing like the success of *Father Goose* or *Charade* and was in fact at the bottom of the twelve great Grant grossers, on a par with *Night and Day*, made twenty years earlier. "I said I would give myself a few years to see if a film-career paid off," Grant once remarked. "If it did, I'd give myself forty years, God willing, and then I'd leave." He was somewhat short of his forty years, but he was in a sense alienated by changes in the industry. The new realism, not to say sordid authenticity, of the cinema, along with violence, was repellent to the star who believed that motion pictures ought to have room for "laughs and the Plaza, too". It was no longer *his* world if there was no place for "high comedy and polished words". Though he never said so, if the world could get along without Cary Grant, then so much the worse for the world.

There were other reasons. After thirty-four years and seventy-two movies, no matter how indestructible he appeared to be or impervious to his age, his voice, among the most precious of an actor's assets, at last suggested fatigue. He *chose* to give up, thus preserving the Grant legend intact. He had no compulsion neurotically to hang on, to continue acting on any terms, no matter how disadvantageous. "I'm too old to get the girl," he said afterwards, just as he later commented, "It was time to climb off the celluloid and join the real world."

However, an event early in 1966 (of which more later) was doubtless not unconnected with his decision. At sixty-two, Cary Grant had become a father.

16

The Legacy

The pictures of his later years — when, as actor-producer, he had no
financial problems and selected his own properties and collaborators —
might have disappointed at least faintly. It was argued by some that
such pre-eminence carried with it not only uncommon privileges but
also the obligation to take great artistic risks. It was hardly surprising,
though, that Grant elected to do what he did best, in a sense reprising
his previous career.

For all its inequalities, that career had been undeniably a glittering
one. Disingenuously, Grant has claimed that he merely played
himself, but even he agreed that Cary Grant had first to be invented.
The answer to the question: What made him run? might well have
been the impulse to escape from Archie Leach ("I doubt if I was a
happy child"), genteel poverty and obscurity in Bristol. Little in his
background and early years suggested the star who moved in high
society with the same grace and confidence that he showed in the best
and worst of his films. Incalculable luck and hard work did much for
unique gifts, the greatest being that natural vitality and youthfulness of
spirit that left him all but unaware of the age disparities between him
and his wives. In any case, a charmer on the screen, he has
undoubtedly been a charmer off it, no matter what ugly labels might
appear in the divorce court obituaries of his marriages.

Genius thrives on controversy and dissent, and opinion about Cary
Grant is far from unanimous. John Kobal said, "Grant had a limited
range of acting-ability — it was nicely and accurately sent up by Tony
Curtis in *Some Like it Hot*." "He delights with his finesse," Pauline
Kael stated, and added acutely, "Everybody thinks of him
affectionately, because he embodies what seems a happier time." Then
there was Andrew Sarris and his apotheosis: "the most gifted light
comedian in the history of the cinema" — almost grudging compared
with David Thomson's: "He is the best and most important actor in

the history of the cinema." Set those judgements against the view of David Shipman: "His range must be the most limited of all the great matinée idols."

One might expect "the best and most important actor in the history of the cinema" to provoke and dismay as much as to delight and inspire, but Richard Corliss has surely spotted what has often led even alert critics to underrate his gifts: "Because Cary Grant is never called on to play Hamlet, except indirectly, applause and Oscars have eluded him. 'He's *only* a movie star.' And yet the range of his roles – manic managing editor in *His Girl Friday*, desperate adoptive father in *Penny Serenade*, vulnerable charmer in *North by Northwest* – and the breadth he effortlessly brings to these roles suggest an acting-ability as large as it is self-effacing."

Cary Grant was everybody's perfect house guest. Directors and screen-writers have always taken pains (until recently, when they have stood the principle on its head) to give their leading men impeccable manners. But Grant's, one sensed, had nothing to do with stage directions. Furthermore, his courtesy seemed to be a "courtesy of the heart" – to borrow Scott Fitzgerald's memorable phrase about Dick Diver, the hero of *Tender Is The Night*, whom David Selznick envisaged played by Grant in a long-planned film version.

Exuding relaxation, Grant made himself comfortable in his roles in such a way that, even when the pictures were inferior, his parts in them seemed superior to their context. In the ordinary sense, this accomplishment was not a trick – not, for example, simply attributable, greatly though they helped, to the bits of business he invented, the grunts, the tentative, almost animal noises, the angle of his head as he spoke, the impaling stare on which he skewered hypocrisy and pretentiousness. No, there was more to his practised ease than this veritable battery of trademarks, and that more was not so readily definable. He took his parts for what they were, never striving turgidly for effect, and his ready acceptance of the human qualities he found there created the impression that he was wearing those roles as handsomely and assuredly as he wore a well-tailored suit. Probably nobody else has ever seemed quite so relaxed before the camera.

His career had, if not a sense of waste, an aura of unrealized potential, so that sadness was bound up with its glory. The nature of the business, the perilousness of taking risks, the limited acceptance of audiences, the style of the vehicles that he sought and that were tailored for him — all these combined and overlapped to ensure that the upper and lower reaches of his talent remained relatively unexplored. His bitterness at Eva Maria Saint's betrayal and debased use of sex in *North by Northwest* has tragic hues. In *An Affair to Remember*, his anguish at discovering that his lost love, Deborah Kerr, and the unseen crippled girl who has bought his painting are one and the same gives a resonant depth to that uneasy picture. Anguish may be the basic emotion, but he eloquently suggests self-accusation, too — the bitterness of a man who has discovered that he is flawed, vanity-ridden. *The Talk of the Town* has him run through an entire gamut of uncharacteristic emotions — rebelliousness, self-pity, arrogance and solemnity. Hitchcock, though he hedged his bet, perceived the dark side of his nature, which emerged to masterly effect in *Suspicion*, as though if Hitch would not shrink from presenting genuine nastiness, then he, Grant, would willingly provide that nastiness. Much more subtly and perhaps more disturbingly, since it is a better film, the shadows are there in *Notorious*, in which the star brings to the character Devlin authentic vengefulness and sexual obsession — not the most attractive elements of human nature but traits that, in Grant's performance, bestow an impressive dimension on the drama. *Father Goose* is memorable not merely because Grant dons what Richard Corliss, surveying the many masquerades in pictures scripted by Peter Stone, called "the most audacious disguise of all: that of a grizzled old beach bum". It also contains a noteworthy piece of acting from its star — predictably superb in its comedy, naturally, but so convincing, too, in its demonstration of inebriated exasperation and misanthropy that it more than proves how well Grant could have played, say, Don Birnam in *The Lost Weekend*. Again, the climax of *Charade*, a 'mere' comedy-thriller, provides Grant with the chance to put on a rare display of what might be called philosophical fervour, as, in the person of Peter Joshua, he calls upon Reggie (Audrey Hepburn) blindly and intuitively to trust love alone and thus, without rational justification, place her life in his hands rather than those of the more plausible villain. Grant's plea has the worried, desperate eloquence of a powerful and disciplined actor. Almost always, though, these facets of the Grant *persona* were contrapuntal — they had to be, as it were, sneaked in, dexterously passed off on a mass public who wanted their idol manly or comic or dashing or suavely romantic, but showed scant liking for seeing him pitifully human, despicable, tragically weak or downright sinister.

His appeal to women was obvious – dark good looks, a soothing voice, attentive manners, a bearable intensity that was continually being lightened by comedy. Men saw him as wholly masculine, on occasion handy with his fists, never a patsy for either man or woman, capable of subduing a situation by his demeanour only. Furthermore, his nature came over as essentially optimistic, not to say exuberant. He was seldom brash, but his spirit was such that it verged upon impudence. If, usually, he was far from sadism, masochism was nowhere to be detected in him. Yet his vulnerability, while never masochistically exploited (he left that to Gary Cooper), is fascinatingly to be glimpsed beneath the handsome surfaces of the characters he plays in *An Affair to Remember, Holiday* and other films. It is the obverse of his zest for living – this innocent capacity to be hurt.

Never obsessed with greatness in the most obvious sense of big parts in big pictures, he sought, perhaps more cunningly, the *best* parts in the *best* pictures of their kind. Thus his humanity did not emerge in the great gestures and grandiloquent roles of a Charlton Heston. Rather, in the midst of the trivial and the ordinary, he revealed the eccentricity, the lovableness, the strength and occasionally the depth of human psychology. He long ago made the minor keys his study – muted anguish, understated ridicule, underplayed moral denunciation signalled by a raised eyebrow or a sceptical smile. He habitually limned or etched in the subtlest shades.

The gaps in his career were significant. He made a careful choice of limitations (no Westerns, for instance), and conventional 'men's pictures' seldom presented him at his best. His action pictures were traditional (*Gunga Din*), static and loquacious (*Only Angels Have Wings*) or stiffly historical (*The Howards of Virginia, The Pride and the Passion*). But his poor choices were few. As a free-lance, Grant shaped his career in masterly fashion. His courage in separating from Paramount was noteworthy. His acumen in picking the directors and scripts he needed was equally remarkable. If that freedom was, in the 'thirties, a unique privilege, it was also a demanding responsibility.

More accurately than any of his critics, Grant knew what he did best. Typically, Grant on film was a hero in a lounge suit, surviving on his wits, extemporizing brilliantly – and almost always with humour. For the most part, he spurned heroics with uniforms and weapons. In a thriller like *Notorious*, it was significant that he carried off the climax without a gun. Economy was his trademark as much as any other quality. Always, however, he returned to farce and comedy. Those were the genres in which his audience loved him, and he assiduously wooed that audience.

Journalists have complained affectionately that Grant gives interviews that reveal, once the newspapermen inspect their notes away from the magic of his charm, that he has eluded his interviewers like a butterfly. That is to be expected. The heroes he played were always vague in class and background – like Grant himself. After all, he *invented* Cary Grant – an eloquent evasion rather than a clearly defined character. The evasion has not concerned us too much, but the eloquence has unfailingly diverted us and sometimes moved us deeply.

Finally, one is left with the judgement of his fellow professionals, to whom he was the consummate artist and technician, a perfectionist who brought sound ideas as well as undimmed enthusiasm to each picture he made. "One doesn't direct Cary Grant," Hitchcock told Peter Bogdanovich, "one simply puts him in front of the camera." Bogdanovich himself called Grant "the ideal leading man, the perfect zany, the most admirable dandy and the most charming rogue". Ann Sheridan thought him an extremely clever actor, full of stimulating ideas, and she wondered why he never tried to direct. (He probably did – in his way.) It was not merely for what is today referred to as 'bankability' that directors sought his services. He was that rare animal – a truly creative actor who could bring a character to life even when, on paper, there was little to help him. Other actors spotted that gift instantly. As Tony Curtis said, "You learn more by watching a professional like Cary drink a cup of coffee than by spending six months with the Method boys."

Perhaps a last word should go to Deborah Kerr, with whom Grant made some magic moments in cinema and who knows well not merely his professional qualities but also his human ones: "He is one of the outstanding personalities in the history of the movies. His extraordinary good looks, his elegance, his graceful way of moving, his expertise in getting a laugh (sometimes out of *nothing*) have not been paralleled ... He is also an extremely astute businessman, which is a rare combination in the acting-world. Of course, I do not know any specific details of his shrewdness, but it is well known that his business acumen made him an extremely wealthy man. But he has never lived ostentatiously, indeed quite the contrary. An extremely private person, he never gossiped or indulged in commenting unfavourably on *anyone*. His private life was, and is, his private life.

"Working with him was such a joy. Each day was full of humour and fun, as well as demanding work. What more could one ask for, and what more can I say of a superb comedian and straight actor? I am so grateful to have worked with him and only wish he would work again and that we could do so together."[1]

17

Dyan, Bristol and After

Just before he went to Paris for the shooting of *Charade*, Grant visited Philadelphia to see a young actress called Dyan Cannon in the trial run of a play called *The Fun Couple*, which also starred Jane Fonda, Bradford Dillman and Ben Piazza — an ill-fated production that survived only three Broadway performances in October 1962.

To Grant-watchers professional and amateur, his presence in Philadelphia was of more than passing interest. Almost as soon as he had divorced Betsy Drake and at the age of fifty-seven, he had begun to date Dyan Cannon, who was twenty-two at the time. His predilection for youth was running true to form — and with no concessions to his own advancing years, with the result that the disparity of age was greater than ever. If, however, one presumed that Grant's intentions were serious — and the rumours to that effect grew louder — Dyan was in one respect quite different from the previous women who had become Grant's wives: she had yet to attain the fame of a Virginia Cherrill or a Betsy Drake — hardly surprising, in view of her youth. Thus Grant was courting potential rather than achievement, though he had never been a snob about such matters. In a familiar phrase, Dyan was a "promising newcomer".

How the two met depended on which account one believed. According to one, Grant spotted Dyan in a television show. Another was more specific: a cheesecake publicity shot promoting the television series "The Aquanuts" drew his attention to her. Yet another reported that she was tested, unsuccessfully, for a part in a film that Grant was making.

She was born in Washington as Samille Diane Friesen, the unusual first name coming from her grandfather Sam. She was raised in Seattle and trained as a model. After Jerry Wald had spotted her in a restaurant, he changed her name to Cannon but did little else for her in the way of a career in movies. However, she eventually took a job with MGM touring as one of a team of three girls in Australia, Hawaii and South America in order to promote the studio's *Les Girls*. The job over, Dyan took drama coaching as a preliminary step in her by then determined pursuit of work as an actress. Her first breaks came in television, and these led to indifferent film roles, including a part in *The Rise and Fall of Legs Diamond* (1959). She was a small, pert blonde with looks that Pauline Kael was to describe memorably as "comic-pornographic" – a quality that perhaps brought her a succession of movie roles as sexpots.

To Dyan, young and doubtless impatient, Grant's courtship, which was to last for approximately four years, must have seemed interminable. But he observably made great efforts to please her, mainly by becoming much less of a recluse, and there was a suggestion of mentor and disciple in their relationship, made sharper by both Grant's age and his pre-eminence. In most senses of the word, Dyan was a beginner. Grant sought to minimize that suggestion: "I'm aware of the difference in our ages and the talk about it. But it's Dyan I'm interested in, not her age. She has brains, maturity and wit. What more would you want in a woman?" One realistic answer might have been: "Compatability". But he was to find out the hard way about the disparity in their interests.

Cary and Dyan became, in the parlance of the gossip column, a steady 'item'. With only *Father Goose* and *Walk, Don't Run* left to round off his film career, his schedule was much more relaxed than it had ever been, and while in the 'seventies, after *Bob and Carol and Ted and Alice* (1969), Dyan would make a whole string of pictures, she had scarcely begun her own career in movies. The two were seen together continually if not constantly, and 1964 was not an untypical year. True, when Grant visited Elsie Leach in Bristol for two weeks in February, he did so alone, and it was the same in April, when he went to Bristol for forty-eight hours. But on 8th November Grant and Dyan together were much in evidence at the wedding of Cheryl Holdridge and Lance Reventlow (Barbara Hutton's son from her second marriage), with whom the actor had remained on almost fatherly terms. (In the 'fifties, long after his mother had divorced Grant, Lance still called him "The General", and the actor would introduce Hutton's son to starlets and eligible young ladies.) While Lance was getting married, Barbara Hutton lay severely ill in Paris.

Dyan Cannon toured America in the national production of *How To Succeed In Business Without Really Trying*, which would eventually need a new leading lady to replace her. The tour included a stop in Las Vegas, Nevada, and it was in that state, in 1965, that Dyan obtained a marriage licence at a place called Goldfield, a small desert town 185 miles north-west of Las Vegas. The name she gave for her intended husband was "C. Grant".

That the four-year courtship was about to end in matrimony was not particularly surprising. Even given Cary Grant's instincts for privacy, however, a fourth marriage that would elude the world's Press and hoodwink even the gossip columnists would be a considerable *coup*. How could it be done?

Surprisingly simply. A Las Vegas Justice of the Peace, James Prennen, conducted the ceremony on 22nd July at an hotel and promised to preserve confidentiality for thirty days. He was as good as his word; it was to be Grant himself who broke the news – and before a month was up. "We kept it secret," the actor said afterwards, "because marriage is a very private affair, and I prefer to do things quietly, without fanfare or intrusion."

But he was about to have his preferences brushed cynically aside.

By the end of July, Mr and Mrs Grant had checked into the Royal Hotel in Bristol, where the star had formerly stayed on several occasions in the Churchill Suite. There he was interviewed for the *Sunday Graphic* by Roderick Mann, whom Grant once described as "a valued friend". (In the same breath, he mentioned Joe Hyams of the New York Herald Tribune Syndicate as a journalist with whom he shared intimate thoughts.) To Mann, he revealed the truth about his marital status, adding, "I'm only telling you now because you asked me. So many people have been hinting that we were thinking about marrying, were about to marry or were actually married – but nobody actually came right out and asked."

The Graphic printed the story, and all hell broke loose in Bristol.

"You can't go home again," wrote Thomas Wolfe – a truism that few have been able to respect either before or since he gave it expression in 1940 (the year in which his novel of that title was published). In the period following the Second World War, Grant made numerous visits to Bristol, but he was not, whatever his thoughts on the subject, going home. To begin with, his trips had a specific purpose – to see his mother, with whom he had, in a very real sense, begun a new relationship as Cary Grant. And it was as the movie star that he returned, not as Archie Leach, however accurately he recalled the people who had been a part of Archie's life.

In the 'thirties, Bob Bennett noticed no significant change when he met him again: "I found him *not* the big filmstar. He was the bloke I used to know – a friendly chap, no 'side' at all."[1]

Ernest Kingdon, however, intuitively realized that a wealth of experience sundered Cary Grant from Archie Leach, that he was no longer 'one of the family' and that perhaps he did not wish to be. (But, then, was such a reintegration possible? You *can't* go home again.) "Cary never said too much," Ernest Kingdon commented (even his use of the *star's* name being significant). "I was talking not to a cousin but to a film star. Of course, he knew the Leaches better than the Kingdons, whom he had to discover in later life."[2]

Nevertheless, Cary Grant had been known to make impressive use of Archie Leach's memory and thus to create the illusion that no radical changes in his existence had distanced him from boyhood friends. After they had renewed their acquaintance following a lapse of several years, Bob Bennett, his old pal of scouting-days, issued an invitation: "We were about to have a scout reunion-camp near Pensford, and I said, 'Why don't you come along?' Cary said, 'I would if I could, but I've got to fly over to Paris for the weekend. I'll send you a wire, though.' I didn't imagine he'd remember to do so, but he did. It was full of names of people in the troop. 'Remember me to Vic Smith' and so on. This long telegram ... Several names that were mentioned, along with little remarks, showed that he remembered certain incidents."[3]

In effect, Grant had sent along a document to prove that he still recalled vividly those whom he had known as Archie Leach, not merely the names of the boys but also their characteristics and idiosyncrasies. The gesture was greatly appreciated.

Once, Grant said, "I'm like the salmon – or is it the elephant? I always come back to the spawning ground. I love Bristol and always have done." But he would have found it impossible to live there. His work was elsewhere, the greater part of his life was elsewhere, and as an addict of the California sun he could never contemplate permanently residing in the British climate. Accordingly, he made the most of his numerous visits to Elsie and his favourite relatives Eric and Margaret Leach.

One of the measures he eventually took to safeguard his mother's privacy was to arrange informally with Bristol newspapermen that if they would leave her undisturbed, he would inform them whenever he arrived in the city. Occasionally, though, if he wished to be specially unobtrusive, Grant would go to nearby Weston-super-Mare, where he several times stayed at the Grand Atlantic, a large hotel on the sea-front to which he once brought his daughter Jennifer while she was still under twelve months old.

The star's bid for anonymity seemed to work well enough. One night, the star and Eddie Tinker, then the Grand Atlantic's manager, walked into the hotel lounge and caught the closing moments of a Cary Grant film on television. When it was over, the residents grouped about the set broke up, some drifting away towards the bar. Nobody recognized the man standing with Tinker as the actor they had just been watching on film, and Tinker, sworn to silence, had to restrain his urge to tell them that the star was in their midst.[4]

If there was no slot into which Grant would neatly fit in Bristol, he did at least play beautifully his role of the famous son returning. Indeed, this was not a pose or an act, as the word might suggest. He accepted Bristolians as he found them and behaved with his customary naturalness, tacitly acknowledging that his status both conferred privileges and exacted obligations.

If the local Press demanded pictures, Grant in his later years used to ask that Jack Garland (now retired) of Bristol United Press, whom he valued for his straightforward approach, should take them. Garland never asked for silly poses. While he discovered that Grant enjoyed remaining anonymous as he had done at the Grand Atlantic, he also observed that the star was "very friendly and very much liked his local connection". Grant indulged in "no-nonsense relationships", and he welcomed Garland as a fellow abstainer. When others were imbibing, he would announce, "Jack and I drink only orange-squash."[5]

(Grant probably had his share of missionary zeal. After he stopped smoking, he would barely tolerate those who had the habit – a natural trait of non-smokers and reformed smokers. Not too seriously, Polly Bergan, who herself found no cure for nicotine addiction in Grant's recommended hypnosis, referred to him as "one of those obnoxious converts".)

On one post-war visit to Bristol, the former Archie Leach, then in his sixties, returned yet again to his old school. It was, admittedly, a publicity stunt, and Bob Bennett and Jack Garland, both at the time active in the local Press, went along with him – Garland to take pictures and Bennett as a former school chum (slightly spurious, because, it will be recalled, Bennett had no memories of Archie Leach at Fairfield School, vividly though he remembered him in the 1st Bristol [YMCA] Scouts).

Grant being met by Virginia Cherrill as he arrives in London in 1933

Grant with Barbara
Hutton in 1944

With Betsy Drake

With Betsy at London Airport in 1961

A shower on the
honeymoon: Grant with
Dyan Cannon at Bristol
Zoo

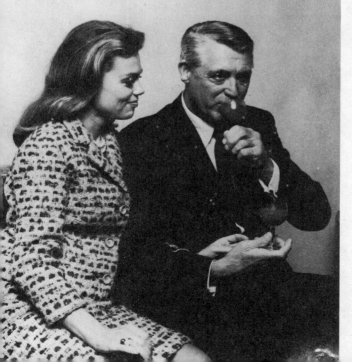

With Dyan in London
to promote *Walk Don't
Run* in 1966

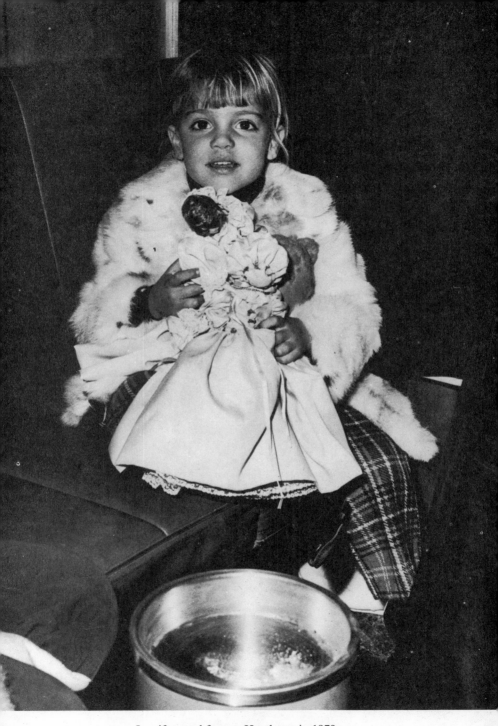

Jennifer aged four at Heathrow in 1970

With Barbara Harris in 1979

Encounter in Hong Kong: Grant with Hilde Cocks

At a Bristol bus stop in the 'fifties   At the Avon Gorge Hotel, Bristol

Cary Grant with Jack Garland (with camera), Bob Bennett and
Roger Bennett; (*overleaf*) Happy retirement: the mature goodwill-
ambassador

School was actually in session when the trio, without pre-arrangement, invaded it. "We went up to Fairfield," Bob Bennett reminisced, "messed around in the playground and took one or two photographs, and then we went inside the school through the back door, which happened to be open. All the tables were waiting to be set for school-dinner. Jack Garland said, 'Let's lay the table, Cary.' Cary said, 'That's an idea.' So he and I got a pile of plates, and we were distributing them around the tables for a photograph."

Conceivably, any pupils who spotted the illustrious old boy of Fairfield Secondary (by that time a grammar school) did not know who he was, but "there were one or two teachers sitting there, and one of them, a woman, came gushing up and said, 'I've just heard who you are. Do you know, I've never met a film star before?' Cary said, 'Oh, haven't you? Come over to Hollywood. They're two a penny there.' "

Without anyone thinking to ask whether he spoke in jest, he also remarked at one stage, "I was chucked out of this school – goodness knows why."

The whole jaunt was unsanctioned and unofficial, but newspaper-pictures soon made it highly public. "Later on," Bob Bennett said, "I heard that the head asked, 'Who gave you permission for this to be done?' "[6] But nobody seriously minded.

It was always the same in Bristol. Grant was treated like royalty and yet at the same time without adulation – certainly not the hysterical kind. He had charmed local newspapermen so that they handled him and Elsie Leach with kid gloves or at least with a deference that might have served as a model for the rest of the world. Hotel staff would jealously guard his privacy. Not long before he divorced Betsy, he had driven with his mother, his wife and Eric and Margaret Leach around the haunts of his youth that had remained unchanged. No jostling mobs assembled. There were no ugly scenes. People who could not have named six of his films worshipped him, and yet he could walk along the Bristol streets without fear of being mobbed or pestered by autograph-hunters.

"You say people like me," Grant remarked to John Coe of the *Bristol Post* in July 1963. "But I like them. We stretch out to each other." He probably had his fellow Bristolians specifically in mind. Even if the city could no longer be called his home, they made him feel at home – perhaps not one of the family exactly, but an honoured and respected guest.

It was always the same in Bristol – until, that was, he arrived there in the summer of 1965 with Dyan and the news broke that she was his bride of a few days.

When they checked into the Royal Hotel on Friday 30th July on arrival from California, Grant took the Churchill Suite as usual, but Dyan had a separate room further down the hall – at least for the sake of appearances. If appearances counted so much, then, the newly-weds could have had no clear intention of soon revealing their recently acquired status, and exactly why Grant chose to impart red-hot information to Roderick Mann remains conjectural. He could have acted spontaneously, on an impulse; or Dyan and he might have talked the matter over, reaching the conclusion that Bristol, England, was the best place in the world to break the news.

In that case, they were wrong.

To newspapermen, Grant had always been of prime interest – the sort of subject out of whom, with or without an interview, they could get a good deal of mileage or, to change the metaphor, a great many column inches. But now, after four years in which he and Dyan had progressively stimulated public interest, the star had married an attractive girl who was much his junior, in the memorial phrase 'young enough to be his daughter', decidedly a product of the 'swinging' 'sixties and a movie actress to boot (the last word, as shall be seen, an appropriate if involuntary pun). Visions of their publicity prospects at fever pitch, the world's media men descended on Bristol in droves. There were photographers who would have sold their souls (or some other marketable portion of their make up) for a shot of Grant and his new wife together. Grant was aware of the fact, even if only because he had overheard one of them state that out of such a picture he could make enough to get a new car. If anyone got a new car, the star swore, it would be him.

Though he scarcely needed one. CG1, one of Grant's two Rolls-Royces, was in the city – a truth of which the newspapermen were more than mindful. (In the circumstances, its registration was hardly restrained, but even had the number been less self-explanatory, Anthony Faramus, Grant's chauffeur, was being observed by hundreds of eyes.)

The Royal Hotel was under siege, its entrances and exits watched at all times by the Press. Even when the worst of the mêlée was over, one Bristol reporter, realizing that his quarries were in an elevator, charged up the hotel staircase in the hope of beating it to its destination and thus waylaying Grant and Dyan.

With or without the added inducement of their having turned out to be married, the couple would almost certainly have been tracked down in Bristol and there become the target of the world's Press. For Grant had probably done little for their hopes of anonymity or privacy by advertising in the personal column of *The Times*, using his own name, for a house to rent in or near Bristol. Ironically, rented accommodation was to become a bone of contention between him and Dyan, but in any event, evading the Press on her honeymoon was not his bride's idea of fun.

Local newspapers, which had by and large dealt fairly with Grant over the years, were not free from blame in the undignified scramble to beat the competition and report his activities and the new Mrs Grant's in the summer of 1965. The *Western Daily Press*, a morning paper, "embarked on a news campaign and literally hounded the Grants by sending reporters wherever they went and daily reporting their stories".[7]

For one Bristolian, this sustained impertinence was too much, and H.R.C. Buston wrote to the paper concerned:

We all appreciate that Mr C. Grant is a Bristolian and that to a certain extent he owes his popularity to public demand in general, but surely this continual hounding of a man who is trying to spend a while in this city for the purpose of visiting his ageing mother is carrying reporting too far ... On your reporter's own admission, only one other reporter was trying to pry into his personal affairs, and how degrading to read that your man bounded up the stairs of the hotel in an effort to beat the lift. From this I can assume that he must be extremely fit or rather young in age and the heyday of Cary Grant is something that his parents related to him with a certain amount of pride.

You have had your story that he is here in Bristol. Now forget it. The public would certainly like to. How nice it would be if he was allowed to walk through the town and acknowledge the nods and smiles of admiring people without the fear of molestation from over-zealous reporters. Let him, his wife and family try to live a normal life for a little while.

Whether the *Western Daily Press* modified its coverage or not, it did, to its credit, publish the Buston letter in full, one of the results

being that on 13th August its author received the following
telegram:

THANK YOU, MR BUSTON. APPRECIATIVELY – DIANE (sic) AND
CARY GRANT.

(There was a happy sequel for H.R.C. Buston. In the 'seventies, he
spotted Grant alone in Marks and Spencer's Bristol store – "looking
as debonair as ever". With customary Bristol politeness, he
approached the star and made himself known. Grant well remembered
the occasion of the telegram, they shook hands and he again
thanked his defender.)

To suggest that the pressure on Grant and Dyan during that
memorable honeymoon visit never relaxed would be inaccurate. In
conditions of privacy, Dyan met her mother-in-law again. (She had
been introduced to Elsie the previous Christmas at the Chesterfield
Nursing Home in Clifton.) Unmolested and with relative casualness,
the Grants visited Bristol Zoo one Saturday afternoon for three-
quarters of an hour, during which Grant realized that there had thus
far been nothing that might have been described as a honeymoon
picture – or not an 'official' one. Accordingly, he *asked* for Jack
Garland to join him and Dyan at the zoo, where they managed to look
happy and natural, though caught by a shower of rain, for a shot that
was later included in the British Press Pictures of the Year Award
exhibition.

The most lurid or at any rate most publicized episode in Grant's
long association with his home town ended when he and his bride
decided that they would have to escape from the city. Anthony
Faramus, who had hitherto been almost as elusive as his employer,
was used as a decoy. The first stage in the Grants' 'disappearance'
was when the news was relayed to the sceptical journalists of half a
dozen countries that they had checked out of the Royal Hotel. The
information was hard to believe, the more so since reporters had been
standing sentinel on all the doors, and it set up an uproar that the
Bristol police, stolid and imperturbable, had to contain. Presumably
summoned by the management, they restored order in the hotel lobby
despite the fact that there were more clamouring newspapermen than
there were constables. The way in which the uniformed officers
handled the provocative, angry journalists was an outstanding
example of British cool.

As if on cue, Faramus then made an appearance in the hotel bar,
which was in fact, if not officially, the Press headquarters of the

visiting members of the fourth estate. He proved surprisingly approachable and answered many questions, turning coy, however, as if well schooled, whenever the inquiries about his master became too prying or intimate. In the midst of this completely unexpected and not entirely trusted break for the Press, Faramus was paged with a telegram. Surprise, surprise ... Not only did Faramus open it then and there, but he also showed no disinclination to share its contents with the agitated reporters. It turned out – and Faramus presented the telegram for corroborative scrutiny – that it had come from Cary Grant in London and it provided succinct instructions for the chauffeur to pack everything into the black and gold Rolls and take his time about driving to the capital.

What could have been more decisive? As the trail had gone cold in Bristol, where they had never found the glorious stories or photographs they sought, most of the members of the foreign Press resigned themselves to leaving in frustration. It was mainly the British and Americans who remained sceptical enough to linger and maintain the vigil at the Royal Hotel.

Giving them more food for thought, Faramus left within the hour, and with his departure there ended the great siege at Bristol and a possibly ill-advised honeymoon trip.

What had happened to Grant and Dyan? To make their escape, they climbed out of one of the Royal's back windows, and they then found refuge in the West Country with friends, with whom they stayed for two weeks.

The marriage had begun with something like a farce, and it continued in an atmosphere of tension and misunderstanding. The older husband who had been so indulgent and proud of his wife before he wed her afterwards proved critical and much less tolerant. "I've hurt everyone I ever loved before," he had said. "But there's a new Cary Grant, who won't hurt again."

He had been married to younger women before, but they had been young in a way that he understood and sympathized with. Dyan, on the other hand, was the child of rapid, accelerating change, and the cultural gap between them was daunting. (One had merely to recall Grant's defeated comment after the *Dream Wife* fiasco to guess at how much provoked and irritated him in the 'permissive era': "It was the period of the blue jeans, the dope addicts, the Method ...") Furthermore, whereas once he had blamed himself for neglecting Barbara Hutton in favour of his career, in the 'sixties his movie-making was less demanding, and thus he spent more time with his partner and, in all probability, expected more of her during their hours together.

Rumours of their disagreements and conflict began to leak out. Grant hated Dyan's mini skirts and boots, once reprimanding her for meeting him at an airport in the fashionable footwear. Dinner in bed at eight followed by television-watching were much to his taste, but such tame evenings did not please his wife at all. The Grants accepted few invitations, however, and became notorious for arriving late and leaving early.

Grant had always shown a predilection for renting houses rather than buying them, and during his fourth marriage, he rented Gordon and Sheila MacRae's home in the San Fernando Valley. Perhaps it was a house of ill omen, for the MacRaes had separated. It was said that the biggest bone of contention between Grant and Dyan was his refusal to buy her a house.

By the fall, though, prospects looked much brighter with the sort of development that traditionalists deemed the greatest force for matrimonial stability and health. On 14th October it was announced that Dyan was expecting a baby in May, when the prospective father would be sixty-two and she would be twenty-eight. One newspaper spoke memorably for all when the *New York Journal* put its exhilaration into the headline: CARY'S FOURTH EXPECTS FIRST.

These were heady times for Grant. No matter what temperamental clashes existed between him and his young wife, she was about to present him with a child — and for that he could be nothing but grateful. Eleventh-hour fatherhood must have looked like a miracle, but better than that, it was a *desired* miracle. "I feel like becoming a father," Grant had said earlier. "I've never had any children, and I would like to more than anything else in the world."

Meanwhile, he had the making of *Walk, Don't Run* to keep him busy and stave off all the fears that one who had "waited all [his] life hoping for children" was legitimately entitled to. For the next six months, he would control his anticipation but naturally "hope like mad" that all would go well.

All did go reasonably well, but not according to expectation. A daughter, Jennifer, was born two months prematurely on 26th February 1966, at St Joseph's Hospital, Burbank. The baby weighed four pounds, eight ounces.

At eighty-eight, Elsie Leach had become a grandmother, and she first saw the new grandchild in June in a picture received over the wire-service by the *Bristol Post*. "She's lovely," Elsie Leach declared, "and she looks just like Cary."

In August, Grant was in London with Dyan in order to promote *Walk, Don't Run*. The two of them also visited Bristol, where they saw Grant's mother and attended celebrations to mark the opening of extensions to a local firm's premises. A Bristolian who encountered Grant window-shopping discovered that he seemed to bear no ill-will after his and Dyan's experiences the previous year. She found him as approachable as ever – genial and faintly teasing. Since he was a new father and she a new grandmother, they compared notes. Afterwards, she asked whether he would mind if she celebrated the thrill of a lifetime by shaking his hand. "Not at all, not at all," he said repeatedly as he pumped her hand up and down. With consideration on the one side and affability on the other, the meeting epitomized Grant's relationship with the people of Bristol.[8]

As if the two events might be connected in his mind, fatherhood and retirement, *Walk, Don't Run* was to turn out to be his last picture. As for parenthood, it appeared to do little to slow down the disintegration of Grant's fourth marriage. It struggled on to the end of the year, but on 28th December he and Dyan separated.

In an attempt to shore up the marriage, Grant, who had an interest in an original property, *The Old Man and Me* by Isobel Lennart, had said that he would agree to make the picture only if Dyan co-starred and that she must be hired without a screen test. The second stipulation was too much. Even Cary Grant's word that Dyan would perform well was no guarantee, and in the end nothing came of the project.

"Some men cannot be married," Dyan once said, "and Cary is one of them." Certainly it sometimes seemed as though he was the sort of romantic who doubly valued what was lost or unattainable, for though the signs were that greater bitterness existed between him and Dyan than any that had sundered him from previous wives, he continued to see her after the separation. For example, he was with her in November 1967, when she was starring in *The Ninety-Day Mistress* at the Biltmore Theatre. If such reunions kept alive hopes among Grant-watchers, sentimental expectations were to be dashed.

After the separation, Grant went to live with Johnny Maschio, an agent friend, and Connie Moore, Maschio's actress-wife, in their apartment in Westwood. Across the continent in New York, he lived

in public relations consultant Bob Taplinger's town house, Dyan
having objected to his proximity in the Crydon Hotel, where she had
taken up residence with the baby. On 22nd August 1967, she began a
preliminary divorce action against Grant for treating her in a 'cruel
and inhuman manner'.

After that lurid beginning, nothing much happened until 12th
March of the following year, when it was reported that Grant had
been seriously injured in a traffic accident on the Long Island
Expressway. Though the injuries were bad enough, the reports erred,
perhaps bolstered in their exaggeration by pictures taken of the actor
soon after the crash and by his own fears. (Initially, he was having
trouble with his breathing.) On the way to Kennedy Airport, Grant's
chauffeur-driven car was hit head-on by a tractor trailer that, having
been struck from behind by another truck, had jumped the highway-
divider in heavy rain at night. X-rays revealed that Grant's suspected
broken nose had no fracture, but his passenger, Baroness Gratia von
Furstenberg, a second cousin of Betsy, had a fractured leg and collar-
bone.

That Grant's injuries were not trivial was illustrated by the fact that
he was still in hospital eight days later when Dyan, with unfortunate
timing, had her day in court on March 20th.

Dyan's allegations did not pull their punches. She told the New
York court that Grant was an "apostle of LSD" who had attempted to
prevail on her "to use the drug many times. [She] did use it once
before [their] marriage, but never after." Her husband had had
"yelling and screaming" episodes and had beaten her. As an example
of his conduct, she related an incident in which Grant had frustrated
her attempt to have an evening out by confiscating the keys of their
three cars and bolting the gates of the estate. He then locked himself in
her dressing-room, where he began reading poetry. Later, he began to
hit her. "He was laughing," Dyan claimed, "and screamed for the help
to come and see what he was doing. I was frightened and went to call
the police." At that, he had begged her not to, because of the likely
attendant publicity, and she had relented.

There was more in the same vein. As Grant watched the Academy
Awards ceremony on television, "he became violent and out of
control. He jumped up on the bed and carried on. He yelled that
everyone on the show had their faces lifted. He was spilling wine on
the bed." On another occasion when they were planning a trip to
England with Jennifer, Grant refused to allow Dyan to take along with

her a supply of baby food because "the cows in England are as good as they are in this country".

If the last anecdote was amusing, the rest was strong stuff – even if true, the sort of testimony that should never be aired in the all-too-public context of a divorce court. Perhaps the most damaging assertions, however, concerned Grant's alleged determination to 'break' Dyan as the necessary preliminary to transforming her, through psychotherapy and LSD, into the sort of wife he wanted.

On 21st March, Judge Robert A. Wenke granted the uncontested decree, but modified alimony to $50,000 a year in support payments. Dyan lost her plea that Grant's visits to Jennifer should be limited to daylight hours and that he should not visit her overnight or without a nurse being present. It was said that the money granted was considerably less than Grant's first offer, and the judge, believing evidence that he had not used LSD for more than a year, gave him two months a year visiting rights without restrictions.

The financial award could scarcely have troubled Grant: it was estimated that he was worth more than ten million dollars. And as it turned out, he had no cause to fear what had inevitably threatened to be bad publicity. Spectacular disclosures, allegations of the star's "cruel and inhuman" manner, left the world unimpressed. Memories of the Grant magic were too strong or awareness of the expedients of divorce was too great, or perhaps both.

Nevertheless, four divorces had left their mark, had given him cause to look back with a certain bleakness. He once gave a collective epitaph on his marriages thus: "It has taken me many years to learn that I was playing a different game entirely. My wives and I were never one. We were competing."

New York became his base – specifically, an apartment at the Hotel Warwick on West 54th Street, but he had homes as well in Beverly Hills, Malibu, Palm Springs and the Bahamas. The public aftermath of the divorce was a series of legal wrangles between him and Dyan of which their clash in court in May 1975, was fairly typical. Dyan asked Judge Jack Swink to order Grant to move out of his Malibu Beach home, three doors away from hers. She did not like being stared at by her ex-husband. The judge refused, but ordered both not to molest, annoy or harass each other. There was Dyan's annual battle over Jennifer's holiday arrangements. The judge ruled that Dyan could take the child with her in the last half of June, while she was filming. Jennifer would spend July with her father and August with her mother, but Judge Swink refused to allow Dyan to take Jennifer on vacation in Tunisia. Dyan said, "I feel so good. It's the first time in three years I haven't lost."

The repeated court appearances seemed, even so, a sad way of settling the differences between former husband and wife.

Coming to fatherhood so late, Grant manifested a near-obsession for Jennifer's safety and well-being. For example, it had been decreed in court, at his insistence, that her face should never be photographed because of his fear of kidnappers. Typical of him was the story that Dyan, leaving Hollywood with baby Jennifer to rehearse a new play in New York, was surprised to discover that her husband was at the airport and had a seat on the same flight. He was going along to ensure that the baby was all right – scarcely a compliment to Dyan's maturity and sense of responsibility.

There was, however, another and less publicized side, it was said, to their post-divorce tug of war over Jennifer. Whatever the legal stipulations, Grant and Dyan, the argument runs, have managed to achieve a modicum of give and take, more flexible and amicable arrangements for the access of each to their daughter. "We had to work out something," Dyan explained, "for the sake of this little girl of ours." Nobody, though, could say that the working out came easily or that it was attained without frequent judicial intervention.

So much bitterness ... And yet so much happiness. For Cary Grant, the birth of Jennifer was a new and radiant chapter in his life that even the end of his marriage to Dyan could not mar, except temporarily. Like a man converted, he was to say, "It took me a long time to learn a simple lesson. My marriage record is nothing to be proud of. I've had four wives and one daughter. Just think how much better it would have been if I'd had one wife and four daughters. If I'd known then what I know now ..."

Looking back, though, was not his forte. Even in his sixties, there was so much living to do, so much affection to lavish on Jennifer, so much enjoyment to be derived from her.

Repeatedly, he called her "my only ticket to eternity" – more meaningful and more enduring than all his films put together. "I will do what I can for her," he promised. "I want Jennifer to give one man love and confidence and help."

One man, it had to be presumed, besides Cary Grant, the proudest father in the land.

18

Leftover Life to Live

One day in the 'sixties, Grant surprised Jack Garland by asking him what he thought about cosmetics for men. The question was not idle, but Garland, his mind on a photograph of the star playing with a passing dog at Ashton Court, a Bristol beauty-spot, probably murmured a non-committal reply to the effect that beyond the usual bottle of after-shave lotion given him for Christmas, he had not pondered the matter of men's cosmetics. Grant himself was far more positive. "There's a big future in this," he insisted, as though disappointed that the photographer showed no great inclination to debate the topic.[1]

Grant had done some careful thinking – just how seriously Garland realized in 1968, when, on 22nd May it was announced that the star was joining the board of Rayette-Fabergé. His salary was to be $15,000 per year, with $200 extra for directors' meetings. George Barrie of Fabergé, who had also recruited song-writer Sammy Cahn as a consultant, had probably done much of the persuading.

Four years later, Grant was to describe his post, that of a "travelling businessman", as his "most successful role ever". "I took the job," he said, "when I left Hollywood because when it was offered to me they threw in the odd bit of travel and a roof over my head." There were other fringe benefits. He could use whenever he wished a house in London's Mayfair on which Fabergé spent a million pounds in renovations in the early 'seventies, and he also had the firm's executive jet at his disposal.

With the passing years, his love of flying had clearly not palled, and in the 'seventies he also accepted a directorship with Western Airways – a fairly well guarded secret until, in 1971, there was some commotion about his being given a free first-class seat on a London to New York flight ("one of the perks of the job").

Was this, then, the new Cary Grant – a tycoon wheeling and

dealing, negotiating important deals? Not exactly. He was quick to point out that the two directorships with private travel thrown in were hard to resist. He was a sort of good-will ambassador, occupied in the stimulating process of meeting people and talking to them. Not, then, a tycoon — "I regard myself as more of a public-relations man. Most company-presidents are men who've seen my movies, so it's easy to establish a liaison. Seriously, though, I don't have to work for any other reason except that I like it."[2]

After *Walk, Don't Run*, he did not issue a formal statement of his intention to retire permanently, but as the years went by, his absence from the screen spoke for itself. Inevitably, there was the occasional announcement hinting at his return to films — but not from Grant himself. For example, it was rumoured that he would take part in a project of Mervyn LeRoy (a good friend), *Cowboys and Indians*, or, much later, that he would play God (sic) in *Heaven Can Wait*, Warren Beatty's remake of *Here Comes Mr Jordan*. Nothing came of the talk. Nor did he succumb to television — that rest-home for retired actors. He was, however, seen briefly in MGM's *Elvis — That's the Way it is* in 1970 — one of the notables attending a Presley concert in Las Vegas and caught by the documentary movie-makers. ("Are you on?" Grant genially asked the cameraman and scarcely stayed for an answer.) Again at Vegas, nearly ten years later, he had a more willing part in the showbiz tribute to Frank Sinatra on his sixty-fifth birthday — a televised event at Caesar's Palace with a thousand guests. No one was more affectionately received than Grant, who, although in his mid-seventies, looked little older than Sinatra himself. "Frank," he said to the guest of honour, "you may not believe this, but I can't sing as well as you" — before leading everyone, the guests at Vegas and the viewers at home, in the singing of "Happy Birthday".

Such appearances, though, were extremely rare.

Anyone could have been forgiven for thinking that to the 'new' Cary Grant work was play, and he has certainly spent the fifteen years since his retirement from films enjoying himself. (But, then, he always did; he worked hard and he played hard. We should not forget Cole Porter's: "I must play to work, and I must work to play. It's all bound up together.") What Grant had more than before was freedom. He put it this way: "I get up in the morning, go to bed at night and occupy myself as best I can inbetween. I do what I want, when I want."

To those who suggested that being a businessman was quite a

switch from being in the movies, he pointed out that he had always been a businessman on a large scale: "Do you know of any other business where a man can earn a million dollars in ten weeks?"

Naturally, he was much missed. In an age when superstars could not handle compliments, however sincere, when they simultaneously courted and fended off publicity, it was easy to think nostalgically of Cary Grant with his aura of worldliness and disciplined suavity.

Grant himself, though, had no nostalgia for his past. He had never been one to utter the conventionally virile throat-clearings of *macho* idols like Flynn and Gable and, later, Newman and Redford – all about how unmanly acting was, what a bogus business it was to be a star. His filming days were over, and movies were no longer a part of his life. Except financially. The negatives of all his films for Universal, beginning with *Operation Petticoat*, were to revert to him, and he owned the negative of *Penny Serenade* – all of which, sold to television or re-released, would make vast sums for him. Even so, he was to comment in the 'seventies, "I sold all the negatives of the last ten pictures I owned. I not only refuse to view any of my own pictures, I rarely go to any movie unless it's a Disney film that my daughter Jennifer wants to see. We all have our evolutions."

Unlike the terminations of the relationships with his wives, this divorce was final.

There was, however, a loose end that was to be tied off on Tuesday, 7th April 1970, when the Academy of Motion Picture Arts and Sciences, as if unbearably guilty about its previous oversights, gave to the star four years after his career had finished a special award carrying the inscription:

> TO CARY GRANT
> for his unique mastery
> of the art of screen acting
> with the respect and affection
> of his colleagues

Frank Sinatra, Grant's near-neighbour in Palm Springs, presented the award, remarking, "It was made for sheer brilliance of acting ... No one has brought more pleasure to more people for many years than Cary has, and nobody has done so many things so well ... Cary has so much skill that he makes it all look easy."

It was an emotional moment. Those sceptics who had laid bets that

Grant would not even turn up for the ceremony were confounded. With his dove-grey hair and the signs of age showing around his eyes, Grant responded to a thunderous standing ovation, struggling with tears and laughter, as handsome as ever. To the audience at Music Center, Los Angeles, who had watched a montage of clips from his movies, he said, "Probably no greater honour can come to a man than the respect of his colleagues." True to his word, he named some of them, especially writers and directors he had worked with. "Why not?" he asked. "This is a collaborative medium. We all need each other."

Fred Allen's assessment of the film colony still haunts us: "You could take all the sincerity in Hollywood and stuff it into a gnat's navel — and still have enough room left for an agent's heart." But on that night in April, the emotion was understandable and sincere, for all its showbiz schmaltz. The Academy had at last made amends.

With relish, the star settled back into being plain Mr Grant — roving businessman and citizen of the world, around which he jetted to visit old friends such as the Rainiers in Monaco, the Pontis in Rome, Ingrid Bergman in Paris and, of course, his mother in Bristol, soon to be over ninety. His work was not arduous, but it kept busy a man who had never been a slacker, just as it kept mobile one who had always loved travel.

Some of those friends he dropped in on were closer than others. In March 1957, it had not been without significance when he accepted on her behalf Ingrid Bergman's Academy Award for *Anastasia*. Grant's feelings for her were partly professional. Once, talking of those names the mere mention of which could induce backers of movies to part with their money, he remarked with justifiable hyperbole, "The only woman on the list is Ingrid Bergman." But he also had great personal affection for her. In 1950, when she gave birth to a son by Roberto Rossellini just before her divorce from Peter Lindstrom, Grant was one of a number of firm friends who offered her good wishes: "Ingrid dearest: It would not be possible in a single cablegram to tell you of all your friends who send you love and affection."

Such people were rare, and Bergman, for so long a victim of the world's respectability, knew it. "For years, [Cary] was the only one in Hollywood who even contacted me," she said. "I had done no wrong in his eyes." Knowing well that among those who criticized Bergman's conduct were many who had done much worse, Grant stated simply, "I can't stand hypocrisy."

Just before she started work in London on *Indiscreet*, Bergman announced her separation from Rossellini and was pursued by Europe's Press to London's Heathrow Airport. Grant went with her Press-agent to meet her, was waiting when her flight unloaded and adroitly deflected questions on her behalf while she smiled for the photographers.

He could be the same tower of strength for others; nor were his good works performed with what was once described as "thunderous stealth". Both Grant and Betsy Drake were among those who rallied round when Patricia Neal suffered a series of near-fatal strokes in early 1965. Somewhat euphorically, Grant has made light of his reputation as a good friend in foul weather: "I have always found that the nicer you are to people, the nicer they are to you. So I'm receiving as much as I'm giving. If I make someone happy, I'm making myself happy, too. It's all very simple. I guess I just love my fellow-man — and woman."

With or without photograph, his name popped up here and there. In February 1970, he visited Elsie Leach with Jennifer. He also attended a charity gala that year in London to aid the World Wildlife Fund. He went backstage after a performance of *Sleuth* in April, 1971, and it was later reported that he would appear in the movie version. He never did so: "I decided it would be too much work." Though the film would have reunited him with Joseph Mankiewicz, with whom he had made *People Will Talk*, his decision was wise: *Sleuth* was a creaky theatrical entertainment with little to recommend it. In 1972, Grant became an adviser to a company developing a multi-million-dollar seven-hundred-room resort near Shannon in Ireland. He reserved a three-acre plot for Jennifer — somewhere for her to take her friends when she was a teenager. The present, however, had its problems. Although Dyan had been forbidden to remove her daughter to Europe, where she was making *The Last of Sheila*, Grant took Jennifer to the location unit on the French Riviera anyway, since she was pining for her mother.

One of his many interests was an engagingly frivolous cause — the preservation of the English muffin. Grant had discovered to his cost that American hotels and restaurants were wont to advertise 'English muffins' for breakfast and then serve a frustrating $1\frac{1}{2}$-muffin order. Outraged by what he saw as the dishonest use of a plural, he decided to form an organization of English muffin-lovers. *Sans* dues, officers, meetings or by-laws, the organization had just one rule: any member

ordering muffins had to insist that at least two were served to him.³
(Ironically, the average Englishman would not know a muffin if he
were engulfed by a cascade of them.)

Back in Bristol, Elsie Leach was still a grand old lady, but it had
become clear years earlier that she could no longer live on her own.
"She was alone in the house," as one relative put it, "and we used to
be very concerned about the electric fire. She had a habit of putting
one on the table by her bed ... She had a dizzy spell ..."⁴ After one or
two scares of that nature, Grant had arranged for her to move into the
Chesterfield Nursing Home in Clifton, the best establishment of its
kind in the area.

In the summer of 1972 he stayed in Bristol for three days, when he
was seen and photographed in the company of Eric and Margaret
Leach and also Sue Mooney, a young girl from Cornwall. ("We're just
good friends," Grant said flippantly. "I've known her family for
thousands of years.") On 13th June, he visited the Hippodrome,
another backstage occasion, and chatted with the performers in an
ice-spectacular. He also, and perhaps most importantly, spent time
with his mother.

Even a grand old lady, from whom her son surely inherited his
durability, could not last forever, and when Grant next came to
Bristol, in January 1973, it was for her funeral. To live until her mid-
nineties and to enjoy far more than solace from her rediscovered son
had given to Elsie Leach's life a satisfying balance – compensation, if
such there could be, for her lost years in the mental hospital. In a
curious way, there was already a parallel in Grant's own life. No
shadow as dark as the one that had threatened his mother had been
cast on *his* earlier years, admittedly, but Jennifer, the unexpected but
not unhoped-for bonus, was proving the joy of his declining years.

But 'declining', with its suggestion of limitations and diminution of
energies, was scarcely a word to apply to the actor as he neared
seventy. He worked and played with relish: the two activities
overlapped; one led to the other.

There were still those who found it hard to believe that he was
finished with pictures. In the early 'seventies, he sold seven of his
movies to television for nearly two million dollars. But would he make
more? Patiently, Grant answered that question: "I've always been a
good businessman, and I got very bored with movie-making. It's a
funny thing. At one time, it was a fabulous industry. But now I feel
that the public has grown up too much to believe in films any more.

Their own lives nowadays are as interesting as anything they are likely to see on the screen ... I get scripts sent to me all the time, but I regard that part of my life as being in the past."

In 1974, the year of his disputed seventieth birthday, Grant was as active as ever. Among his more interesting engagements was one to unveil a plaque that fall at the United Nations Building recording the opening of a new landscaped area on New York's East Side. It was called the Bristol Basin – appropriately, because it was built over tons of Second World War blitz-rubble shipped over from Bristol in the form of ballast. After a taxing flight from Los Angeles, Grant looked astonishingly fresh as he performed the ceremony. He was "incredibly bronzed – a charming, natural man".[5]

The middle 'seventies found his name persistently and romantically linked with that of Maureen Donaldson, with whom his first encounter occurred in August 1973, at Sun Valley, Idaho, whither she had been sent to cover a film festival for the Hollywood magazine run by Rona Barett. Maureen was twenty-six, the daughter of a retired fireman from Muswell Hill, London. She had trained as a nanny and was married for a time to a rock singer, Dee Donaldson, from whom she was divorced soon after she met Grant.

Was marriage a possibility? Grant was quite definite: "The answer is no. I've been married four times. I'm obviously a failure at marriage. What went wrong? Who knows? ... Anyway, I'm not going to try again."

One of society's biggest taboos is reserved for relationships between old men and young women, but while the world was far from indifferent to the Grant-Donaldson link, it waived its prejudices, as it had done so many times before, for Cary Grant. His predilection for youth was as well known as his apparent imperviousness to old age, and only a few columnists wrote unpleasant comments or made ugly insinuations. Public acceptance of the friendship with Maureen Donaldson – and others – might have had much to do with Grant's sense of privacy. He was not 'discreet' – a word too often used to describe those with something shameful to hide. But he simply never flaunted his young companions; they were not 'toys' or 'props' with whom he allowed himself to be seen in order to make others gasp with envy or admiration.

Nevertheless, he could not expect such alliances to go unnoted by the media, nor did they. In February 1977, a story broke with the trappings of drama and intrigue when an early-morning fire caused the evacuation of the Avon Gorge Hotel at Clifton, Bristol. Among the residents were several famous names, including Jacques Cousteau, David Attenborough of the BBC, and Cary Grant, who was not to be found in his room or in any of the public rooms, since he had not yet returned from a night out with his female companion, who was also staying at the Avon Gorge. Eventually, they showed up in the midst of the excitement and spent ninety minutes in the street with other guests while firemen did their work. When it was over, Grant stood the whole crew drinks.

The woman with him remained unidentified and was inevitably referred to by the media as "his mystery companion". If there was an enigma, it was not one upon which much light would be shed by a restrained hotel management, which merely stated that Mr Grant and his friend had occupied separate rooms. Susie Rogol, a spokeswoman for Fabergé U.K., said, "She may have been one of the free-lance ladies we use from time to time. Obviously, we look after him." By then, after his weekend in Bristol, Grant had flown on to Paris in order to launch a new perfume for Fabergé. There, he was tracked down to his hotel, but he refused to reveal the identity of the woman in Bristol. "The lady is a public relations consultant with the company," he explained. "That is all. There is certainly no romantic attachment. I am not prepared to say who she is."

Others in the 'seventies were less reticent – sometimes the ladies themselves. In October of the same year, Sarah Marquis, a personable blonde working in public relations in Florida, claimed that she had had a secret romance with Grant lasting six months. (Public relations? Secret? Those who cared, especially if six months might be stretched to eight, could make what they liked of that.) Another name linked to Grant's was that of the young Victoria Morgan, about whom even less appeared to be known.

Grant's preferences retained strong hints of his English origins. In the summer of 1974, he had attended Fabergé's International Trade Show at the Royal Lancaster Hotel in London. There he met Barbara Harris, another blonde, in her early twenties, who was Press-officer for the hotel. (Public relations, yet again.) Her father had been a colonial officer in Tanganyika, where she had been born, and one of the sobering statistics of what was to become an extended relationship was that Grant, at seventy, was fifteen years older than Mr Harris, who was to die in 1979. One British newspaper referred to Barbara as "an English rose".

Right up to the present, Grant has maintained his alliance with her. After four broken marriages, he appears to have no matrimonial plans, but in 1978 Barbara joined him in California and is seen as his constant companion. He had spent months wooing her by transatlantic telephone, and when the two of them were seen dining with thirteen-year-old Jennifer, there were inevitable but so far inaccurate rumours of marriage. "Cary is an old-fashioned man," a friend was reported as saying. "He wanted Jennifer to meet Barbara so he could get his daughter's approval." Whether he did or he didn't, Grant is still single.

Throughout the decade, the kaleidoscope of his activities continued to shift, its patterns diverting a world that showed no signs of forgetting him. In 1976, he was at a White House Bicentenary Dinner, at which the guest of honour was Queen Elizabeth II; in the spring, he underwent a hernia operation in Santa Monica, registering as 'Cary Robins'; later that year, he was 'dinner chairman' at a charity function in Beverly Hills for Prince Charles; later still, he visited the Fabergé factory at Iver, Buckinghamshire, England; in 1978, he attended a royal charity gala at the London Palladium; in April 1979, he presented Sir Laurence Olivier with a special Academy Award, calling him "the actor's most admired actor"; in the fall, he appeared in London for the Mountbatten funeral.

It was not all medical drama, pomp and circumstance.

He rattled around the world having fun – a fact that you could see in the many pictures taken of him. Of course, he looked older – broader in the face, white of hair, frequently wearing large horn-rimmed glasses. (As Gypsy Rose Lee once said, "I have everything I had twenty years ago only it's all a bit lower.") But he was recognizably the much loved Cary Grant, and he looked convincingly happy, even if he could be tetchy at times, not least with photographers who might accentuate what he occasionally called the "fatness" of his features.

There were still those who described him as a social-climber, quick to accept an invitation from the mighty and the rich. (He might have countered that since he was at the summit, how could he still be climbing?) Well, that was all right – after so many years. He had never *despised* either the rich or, in F. Scott Fitzgerald's words, the "money with which to share their mobility and the grace that some of them brought into their lives". (Grant would have placed the emphasis on "some of them".)

His influence continued to exert itself, not merely and predictably because he remained a model for other performers to emulate (if they could) but also owing to his life-style, which seemed to have lessons even for those not born when he was in his prime. Thus Raquel Welch, who had given some stormy interviews in her time, announced that she had changed her approach towards people she disliked. She said only nice things about them. "It sends them crazy," she observed. "It's a technique I learned from Cary Grant."

As a new decade approached, the most sustaining influence of his life was female — not that of a woman but that provided by his teenage daughter Jennifer. Friends who knew him well were far from surprised.

Before Jennifer's birth, there had been those who strongly suspected the frustrated impulse of the superstar who appeared to have everything. In 1964, Roderick Mann had visited Grant on location at Ocho Rios, Jamaica, during the making of *Father Goose*, in which, on screen, he protected Leslie Caron and her six schoolgirl charges. Mann saw the children swarming all over Grant on the set and when he visited the hotel in which they were staying. Mutual affection warmed the process of movie-making. "I don't mind telling you," Grant said to the journalist, "I'll miss them terribly when the film is over. It's like having a family. I will really miss them."[6]

Less than two years later, he had a child of his own. As Jennifer grew up, she was his absorbing interest, so that every aspect of her existence inspired enthusiasm, from his hopes that, with her lovely voice and a talent for writing tunes, she might develop her musical gifts, to his delight in the sets of plates she painted. When she was younger, during a period when he had lost custody of her and was unhappy about the life she was leading with her mother, he had, it was said, considered marrying Maureen Donaldson in order to get Jennifer back. Coming to parenthood late, he had brought to it if not obsession then predictably dedicated feelings. The father who would allow no pictures of his daughter, fearing the warping effect of publicity as much as he feared kidnapping, was determined to give Jennifer the chance of an ordinary, domestic life ("I'll advise her to love one man and be loved."), though if she wanted to be an actress, he would not discourage her. The worst that could have been said about his attitude was that it was old-fashioned, poorly suited to the rearing of a girl during an era in which women's roles were departing from traditional stereotype.

Jennifer was his family – the one he had yearned for during the making of *Father Goose*. Four daughters would have been better, as he himself suggested, but one was enough. "The miracle of having given life to someone," he said, "is quite fantastic. I regard Jennifer as my ticket to immortality. I die off. She continues. All I want for her is to grow up happy. She'll have a better chance than I did, I should think. She's prettier."[7]

Immortality is an overrated and uncertain quality. Fame, however, is simpler and easier to assess, since it is contemporary with the lifetime of those who acquire it. Cary Grant was and is famous. What he does, thinks or says makes news, and people remember him – not with the knowing leer with which they recall Errol Flynn or the moralistic shaking of the head with which they speak of John Barrymore or even with the resigned respect they grant to the memory of John Wayne; but rather with the affection they reserve for James Cagney or James Stewart or even Grant's old rival Gary Cooper. Grant's admirers associate him affectionately with good times – occasionally the remembered belly-laugh of broad comedy, more often the happy smile of polished wit, sometimes the unexpected lump in the throat. He is a nostalgic figure – not in a bogus, sentimental way, but because he was a glamorous star of what is sometimes called the golden age of movies. He was one of a kind.

It cannot be said, either, that the good memories are vague and passive – predicated on idealized notions of what he did rather than on actual and recent viewing of his movies. Whenever they are shown on television, they command huge audiences. In 1980, the Los Angeles County Museum of Art devoted two months to screening more than forty of Grant's pictures – a retrospective tribute that confirmed the truth of the legend. "Acting is smoke," said Charlton Heston. Yet film captures the impermanent craft, and audiences at the County Museum witnessed an artist creating performances that were fluent and spontaneous, whoever the director and whatever the script.

"I often think my life has been a failure," Cary Grant said once in a moment of sceptical self-appraisal. "But whenever I drop into a theatre and hear women laughing at one of my films, I think, well, if I brightened their day before they went home and did the dishes, maybe my life wasn't wasted, after all." While the thought shows its age ("before they went home and did the dishes"), it was none the less apt, and if it was true for women, it was also true for men – whether they did the dishes or not.

If anybody doubted that the movie industry had a place for a seventy-six-year-old star, the 'eighties began with a choice news item. Cary Grant was being offered over a million dollars to make a film rejoicing in the title *One Thousand Cups of Crazy German Coffee*. There was an ironic twist in the tale: Grant had once owned the rights to the script, which he had sold at a handsome profit.

In 1975, Cary Grant was elected to the board of MGM, for which, according to the studio's Press-release, he was well qualified by virtue of his "credits as an actor and as an astute businessman". For however long, the world at large, it seems safe to add, will remember him as the first rather than the second.

Notes

Chapter 1
[1] Ernest Kingdon in conversation with the author.
[2] Bob Bennett in conversation with the author.
[3] Dora Morley (Mrs D.G. Hanney) in a letter to the author.
[4] Ernest Kingdon.
[5] Mrs Vera R. Bryant in a letter to the author.
[6] Ernest Kingdon.
[7] Ibid.

Chapter 2
[1] Ernest Kingdon in conversation with the author.
[2] Mrs Lillian Pearce in conversation with the author.
[3] Doris Guest (Mrs Doris Davis) in conversation with the author.
[4] Ibid.
[5] Mrs Lillian Pearce in conversation with the author.
[6] Doris Guest.
[7] Ibid.
[8] Ibid.
[9] Captain Eddie L. Plunkett in a letter to the author.
[10] Mr L.E. Grogan in a letter to the author.
[11] Bob Bennett in conversation with the author.
[12] Ibid.

Chapter 3
[1] An anecdote related to the author in several forms, notably by Bob Bennett in conversation and Miss Alice Davis in a letter.
[2] Mrs Lillian Pearce in conversation with the author.
[3] G.H. Calvert in a letter to the author.
[4] Mrs Lillian Pearce.
[5] L.E. Grogan in a letter to the author.
[6] Dora Morley (Mrs D.G. Hanney) in a letter to the author.

Chapter 4
[1] *The Hollywood Exiles* by John Baxter, p. 120.

Chapter 6
[1] Ernest Kingdon in conversation with the author.
[2] Ibid.
[3] Leonard C. Leslie in conversation with the author.
[4] *Sunday Express*, 2nd May 1976.

Chapter 7
[1] Interview with John Coe, *Bristol Evening Post*, 22nd July 1963.

Chapter 8
[1] Ernest Kingdon in conversation with the author.
[2] Ibid.
[3] Doris Guest (Mrs Doris Davis) in conversation with the author.
[4] Mrs Joan Stone in conversation with the author.
[5] *The Real F. Scott Fitzgerald* by Sheilah Graham, p. 154.

Chapter 9
[1] Related by Frederick Brisson in the preface to *Life is a Banquet* by Rosalind Russell.

Chapter 10
[1] John Russell Taylor in his introduction to *50 Superstars* by John Kobal, p. 5.

Chapter 11
[1] Leonard C. Leslie in a letter to the author.

Chapter 13
[1] Deborah Kerr in a letter to the author.

Chapter 14
[1] Article by Peter Shield in the *Sunday Graphic*, 19th October 1958.
[2] Deborah Kerr in a letter to the author.

Chapter 15
[1] Deborah Kerr in a letter to the author.
[2] Ibid.
[3] Ibid.

Chapter 16
[1] Deborah Kerr in a letter to the author.

Chapter 17
[1] Bob Bennett in conversation with the author.
[2] Ernest Kingdon in conversation with the author.
[3] Bob Bennett.
[4] Eddie Tinker in conversation with the author.
[5] Jack Garland in conversation with the author.
[6] Bob Bennett.
[7] H.R.C. Buston in a letter to the author.
[8] Eve Kellett in conversation with the author.

Chapter 18
[1] Jack Garland in conversation with the author.
[2] To Mary Kaye, *Bristol Evening Post*, 16th June 1972.
[3] Geraldine Ward in a letter to the author.
[4] Ernest Kingdon in conversation with the author.
[5] Michael Hobbs in conversation with the author.
[6] Roderick Mann, *Sunday Express*, 7th June 1964.
[7] To Mary Kaye, *Bristol Evening Post*, 1972.

Bibliography

Baxter, John, *Hollywood in the Thirties* (A.S. Barnes and Company, Inc., New York, 1968; The Tantivy Press, London, 1968)

Baxter, John, *The Hollywood Exiles* (Macdonald and Jane's Ltd, London, 1976)

Bayer, William, *The Great Movies* (Hamlyn, London and New York, 1973)

Bogdanovich, Peter, *Picture Shows* (George Allen and Unwin Ltd, London, 1975)

Brown Curtis F., *Ingrid Bergman: A Pyramid Illustrated History of the Movies* (Pyramid Publications, New York, 1973)

Canham, Kingsley, *The Hollywood Professionals* – Vol. I (A.S. Barnes and Company, Inc., New York, 1973; The Tantivy Press, London, 1973)

Coffee, Lenore, *Storyline: Reflections of a Hollywood Screenwriter* (Cassell, London, 1973)

Corliss, Richard, *Talking Pictures* (David and Charles, London, 1975)

Dardis, Tom, *Some Time in the Sun* (André Deutsch, London, 1976)

Deschner, Donald, *The Films of Cary Grant* (The Citadel Press, Secaucus, New Jersey, 1973)

Eels, George, *Cole Porter: The Life that Late he Led* (G.P. Putnam's Sons, New York, 1967; W.H. Allen and Company, London, 1967)

Eyles, Allen, *Cary Grant Film Album* (Ian Allen, London, 1971)

Farmer, Frances, *Will There Really be a Morning?* (G.P. Putnam's Sons, New York, 1972)

Govoni, Albert, *Cary Grant: An Unauthorised Biography* (Henry Regnery Company, Chicago, 1971; Robert Hale Ltd, London, 1971)

Graham, Sheilah, *The Real F. Scott Fitzgerald* (Grosset and Dunlap, Inc., New York, 1976; W.H. Allen and Company, London, 1976)

Graham, Sheilah. *Scratch an Actor* (W.H. Allen and Co. Ltd, London, 1969)

Grant, Cary, "Archie Leach", *Ladies' Home Journal*, Winter, March, April, 1963

Kael, Pauline, *I Lost It at the Movies* (Bantam Books, New York, 1966; Jonathan Cape, London, 1966)

Kael, Pauline, *Kiss Kiss Bang Bang* (Little, Brown, Boston, 1968; Calder and Boyars Ltd, London, 1970)

Kael, Pauline, *The Citizen Kane Book* (Bantam Books, New York, 1971; Martin Secker and Warburg, London, 1971)

Kobal, John, *50 Superstars* (Hamlyn, London, 1974)

Mercer, Jane, *Great Lovers of the Movies* (Hamlyn, London, 1975)

Niven, David, *The Moon's a Balloon* (Hamish Hamilton Ltd, London, 1971; G.P. Putnam's Sons, New York, 1972)

Niven, David, *Bring on the Empty Horses* (Hamish Hamilton, London, 1975; G.P. Putnam's Sons, New York, 1976)

Marx, Arthur, *Goldwyn: The Man Behind the Myth* (The Bodley Head, London, 1976)

Minnelli, Vincente, *I Remember it Well* (Doubleday and Company, Inc., New York, 1974; Angus and Robertson Limited, London, 1975)

Parish, James Robert *The Paramount Pretties* (Arlington House, New Rochelle, New York, 1972)

Parish, James Robert and Stanke, Don. E., *The Debonairs* (Arlington House, New Rochelle, New York, 1975)

Roeburt, John, *Get Me Giesler* (Belmont Books, New York, 1962)

Roman, Robert C., "Cary Grant" *Films In Review*, December 1961

Scherle, Vincent and Levy, William Turner, *The Films of Frank Capra* (The Citadel Press, Secaucus, New Jersey, 1977)

Sennett, Ted, *Warner Brothers Presents* (Arlington House, New York, 1971)

Shipman, David, *The Great Movie Stars: The Golden Years* (Hamlyn, London, 1970)

Stallings, Peggy, *Flesh and Fantasy* (St Martin's Press, New York, 1978)

Thomas, Bob, *King Cohn* (G.P. Putnam's Sons, New York, 1967; Barrie and Rockliff, London, 1967)

Thomas, Tony, *The Great Adventure Films* (The Citadel Press, Secaucus, New Jersey, 1976)

Thomson, David, *A Biographical Dictionary of the Cinema* (Secker and Warburg, London, 1975)

Tressider, Jack, *Heart-Throbs* (Marshall Cavendish, London, 1974)

Truffaut, François, *Hitchcock* (Simon and Schuster, New York, 1971)

Vermilye, Jerry, *Cary Grant: A Pyramid Illustrated History of the Movies* (Pyramid Publications, New York, 1973)

West, Mae, *Goodness Had Nothing To Do With It* (Prentice-Hall, New York, 1960; W.H. Allen and Company, London, 1960)

Zolotow, Maurice, *Billy Wilder in Hollywood* (W.H. Allen Ltd, London, 1977)

Filmography

Abbreviations: d. – director; sc. – screenplay; l. p. – leading players. As is customary, the dates given are release dates. Where no colour process is indicated, it may be taken that the film was made in black and white.

1 *This is the Night*, Paramount Publix, 1932; d. Frank Tuttle; sc. Avery Hopwood from *Pouche* by Rene Peter and Henri Falk; l. p. Lili Damita, Charlie Ruggles, Roland Young, Thelma Todd, Cary Grant.

2 *Sinners in the Sun*, Paramount Publix, 1932; d. Alexander Hall; sc. Vincent Lawrence, Waldemar Young, Samuel Hoffenstein from story "Beachcomber" by Mildred Cram; l. p. Carole Lombard, Chester Morris, Adrienne Ames, Alison Skipworth, Walter Byron, Reginald Barlow, Zita Moulton, Cary Grant.

3 *Merrily we go to Hell*, Paramount Publix, 1932; d. Dorothy Arzner; sc. Edwin Justus Mayer from play *I, Jerry, Take Thee* by Cleo Lucas; l. p. Sylvia Sidney, Fredrick March, Adrianne Allen, Skeets Gallagher; Florence Britton, Esther Howard, Kent Taylor, Cary Grant.

4 *The Devil and the Deep*, Paramount Publix, 1932; d. Marion Gering; sc. Benn Levy from story by Harry Hervey; l. p. Tallulah Bankhead, Gary Cooper, Charles Laughton, Cary Grant.

5 *Blonde Venus*, Paramount Publix, 1932; d. Josef von Sternberg; sc. Jules Furthman and S.K. Lauren from story by Sternberg; l. p. Marlene Dietrich, Herbert Marshall, Cary Grant, Dickie Moore, Sidney Toler.

6 *Hot Saturday*, Paramount Publix, 1932; d. William A. Seiter; sc. Seton I. Miller from novel by Harvey Ferguson; l. p. Nancy Carroll, Cary Grant, Randolph Scott, Edward Woods.

7 *Madame Butterfly*, Paramount Publix, 1932; d. Marion Gering; sc. Josephine Lovett and Joseph Moncure from story by John Luther Long and play by David Belasco; l. p. Sylvia Sidney, Cary Grant, Charlie Ruggles.

8 *She Done Him Wrong*, Paramount Publix, 1933; d. Lowell Sherman; sc. Harvey Theu and John Bright from play by Mae West; l. p. Mae West, Cary Grant, Gilbert Roland, Noah Beery Sr.

9 *The Woman Accused*, Paramount Publix, 1933; d. Paul Sloane; sc. Bayard

Veiller from magazine serial by misc. authors; l. p. Nancy Carroll, Cary Grant, John Halliday, Irving Pichel, Louis Calhern, Jack La Rue.

10 *The Eagle and the Hawk*, Paramount Publix, 1933; d. Stuart Walker; sc. Bogart Rogers and Seton I. Miller from story by John Monk Saunders; l. p. Fredric March, Cary Grant, Jack Oakie, Carole Lombard.

11 *Gambling Ship*, Paramount Publix, 1933; d. Louis Gasnier and Max Marcin; sc. Max Marcin and Seton I. Miller from stories by Peter Ruric adapted by Claude Binyon; l. p. Cary Grant, Benita Hume, Roscoe Karns, Glenda Farrell, Jack La Rue.

12 *I'm No Angel*, Paramount Publix, 1933; d. Wesley Ruggles; sc. Mae West; l. p. Mae West, Cary Grant, Edward Arnold.

13 *Alice in Wonderland*, Paramount Publix, 1933; d. Norman Z. McLeod; sc. Joseph L. Mankiewicz and William Cameron Menzies from the book by Lewis Carroll; l. p. Charlotte Henry, Richard Arlen, Gary Cooper, Leon Errol, W.C. Fields, Cary Grant.

14 *Thirty-Day Princess*, Paramount Publix, 1934; d. Marion Gering; sc. Preston Sturges and Frank Partos from story by Clarence Buddington Kelland; l. p. Sylvia Sidney, Cary Grant, Edward Arnold, Henry Stephenson.

15 *Born to be Bad*, United Artists, 1934; d. Lowell Sherman; sc. Ralph Graves; l. p. Loretta Young, Jackie Kelk, Cary Grant, Henry Travers.

16 *Kiss and Make Up*, Paramount Publix, 1934; d. Harlan Thompson; sc. Harlan Thompson and George Marion Jr from play by Stephen Bekeff; l. p. Cary Grant, Helen Mack, Genevieve Tobin, Edward Everett Horton.

17 *Ladies Should Listen*, Paramount Publix, 1934; d. Frank Tuttle, sc. Claude Binyon and Frank Butler from play by Alfred Savoir and Guy Bolton; l. p. Cary Grant, Frances Drake, Edward Everett Horton, Rosita Moreno.

18 *Enter Madame*, Paramount Publix, 1935; d. Elliott Nugent; sc. Charles Brackett and Gladys Lehman from play by Gilda Varesi and Dorothea Donn-Byrne; l. p. Elissa Landi, Cary Grant, Lynne Overman, Sharon Lynne.

19 *Wings in the Dark*, Paramount, 1935; d. James Flood; sc. Jack Kirkland and Frank Partos from story by Nell Shipman and Philip D. Hurn; l. p. Myrna Loy, Cary Grant, Roscoe Karns, Hobart Cavanaugh, Dean Jagger.

20 *The Last Outpost*, Paramount, 1935; d. Charles Barton and Louis Gasnier; sc. Philip MacDonald from story by F. Britten Austin; l. p. Cary Grant, Claude Rains, Gertrude Michael, Kathleen Burke, Akim Tamiroff, Colin Tapley.

21 *Sylvia Scarlett*, RKO Radio, 1936; d. George Cukor; sc. Gladys Unger, John Collier and Mortimer Affner from novel by Compton Mackenzie; l. p. Katharine Hepburn, Cary Grant, Brian Aherne, Edmund Gwenn.

22 *Big Brown Eyes*, Paramount, 1936; d. Raoul Walsh; sc. Raoul Walsh and Bert Hanlon from story by James Edward Grant; l. p. Cary Grant, Joan Bennett, Walter Pidgeon, Lloyd Nolan, Alan Baxter.

23 *Suzy*, MGM, 1936; d. George Fitzmaurice; sc. Dorothy Parker, Alan

Campbell, Horace Jackson and Lenore Coffee from novel by Herbert Gorman; l. p. Jean Harlow, Franchot Tone, Cary Grant, Lewis Stone, Benita Hume.

24 *Wedding Present*, Paramount, 1936; d. Richard Wallace; sc. Joseph Anthony from story by Paul Gallico; l. p. Joan Bennett, Cary Grant, George Bancroft, Conrad Nagel, Gene Lockhart, William Demarest.

25 *The Amazing Quest of Ernest Bliss*, Grand National, 1936 (released in the US in 1937); d. Alfred Zeisler; sc. John L. Balderston from story by E. Phillips Oppenheim; l. p. Cary Grant, Mary Brian, Peter Gawthorne.

26 *When You're in Love*, Columbia, 1937; d. Robert Riskin; sc. Robert Riskin from story by Ethel Hill and Cedric Worth; l. p. Grace Moore, Cary Grant, Aline MacMahon, Henry Stephenson, Thomas Mitchell.

27 *Topper*, MGM, 1937; d. Norman Z. McLeod; sc. Jack Jerne, Eric Hatch and Eddie Moran from novel by Thorne Smith; l. p. Constance Bennett, Cary Grant, Roland Young, Billie Burke, Alan Mowbray, Eugene Pallette, Hedda Hopper.

28 *The Toast of New York*, RKO, 1937; d. Rowland V. Lee; sc. Dudley Nichols, John Twist and Joel Sayre from books by Bouck White and Matthew Josephson; l. p. Edward Arnold, Cary Grant, Frances Farmer, Jack Oakie, Donald Meek.

29 *The Awful Truth*, Columbia, 1937; d. Leo McCarey; sc. Vina Delmar from play by Arthur Richman; l. p. Irene Dunne, Cary Grant, Ralph Bellamy, Alexander D'Arcy, Cecil Cunningham, Marguerite Churchill.

30 *Bringing up Baby*, RKO, 1938; d. Howard Hawks; sc. Dudley Nichols and Hagar Wilde from Wilde's story; l. p. Katharine Hepburn, Cary Grant, Charlie Ruggles, Walter Catlett, Barry Fitzgerald, May Robson, Fritz Feld.

31 *Holiday*, Columbia, 1938; d. George Cukor; sc. Donald Ogden Stewart and Sidney Buchman from play by Philip Barry; l. p. Katharine Hepburn, Cary Grant, Doris Nolan, Lew Ayres, Edward Everett Horton, Binnie Barnes.

32 *Gunga Din*, RKO, 1939; d. George Stevens; sc. Joel Sayre and Fred Guiol from story by Ben Hecht and Charles MacArthur suggested by Rudyard Kipling's poem; l. p. Cary Grant, Victor McLaglen, Douglas Fairbanks Jr, Sam Jaffe, Eduardo Ciannelli, Joan Fontaine.

33 *Only Angels Have Wings*, Columbia, 1939; d. Howard Hawks; sc. Jules Furthman from Hawks' story; l. p. Cary Grant, Jean Arthur, Richard Barthelmess, Rita Hayworth, Thomas Mitchell, Sig Ruman, John Carroll, Allyn Joslyn.

34 *In Name Only*, RKO, 1939; d. John Cromwell; sc. Richard Sherman from novel by Bessie Brewer; l. p. Carole Lombard, Cary Grant, Kay Francis, Charles Coburn, Helen Vinson.

35 *His Girl Friday*, Columbia, 1940; d. Howard Hawks; sc. Charles Lederer from play by Ben Hecht and Charles MacArthur; l. p. Cary Grant, Rosalind Russell, Ralph Bellamy, Gene Lockhart, Porter Hall, Ernest Truex.

36 *My Favourite Wife*, RKO, 1940; d. Garson Kanin; sc. Samuel and Bella Spewack from story by Leo McCarey and the Spewacks; l. p. Irene Dunne, Cary Grant, Randolph Scott, Gail Patrick.

37 *The Howards of Virginia*, Columbia, 1940; d. Frank Lloyd; sc. Sidney Buchman from novel by Elizabeth Page; l. p. Cary Grant, Martha Scott, Sir Cedric Hardwicke, Alan Marshal, Richard Carlson, Paul Kelly.

38 *The Philadelphia Story*, MGM, 1941; d. George Cukor; sc. Donald Ogden Stewart from play by Philip Barry; l. p. Cary Grant, Katharine Hepburn, James Stewart, Ruth Hussey, John Howard, Roland Young, John Halliday.

39 *Penny Serenade*, Columbia, 1941; d. George Stevens; sc. Morrie Ryskind from story by Martha Cheavens; l. p. Irene Dunne, Cary Grant, Beulah Bondi, Edgar Buchanan, Ann Doran.

40 *Suspicion*, RKO, 1941; d. Alfred Hitchcock; sc. Samson Raphaelson, Joan Harrison and Alma Reville from novel by Francis Iles; l. p. Cary Grant, Joan Fontaine, Sir Cedric Hardwicke, Nigel Bruce, Dame May Whitty.

41 *The Talk of the Town*, Columbia, 1942; d. George Stevens; sc. Irwin Shaw and Sidney Buchman from story by Sidney Harmon; l. p. Cary Grant, Jean Arthur, Ronald Colman, Edgar Buchanan, Glenda Farrell.

42 *Once Upon a Honeymoon*, RKO, 1942; d. Leo McCarey; sc. Sheridan Gibney from McCarey's story; l. p. Ginger Rogers, Cary Grant, Walter Slezak, Albert Dekker, Albert Bassermann.

43 *Mr Lucky*, RKO, 1943; d. H.C. Potter; sc. Milton Holmes and Adrian Scott from Holmes' story; l. p. Cary Grant, Laraine Day, Charles Bickford, Gladys Cooper, Henry Stephenson, Paul Stewart.

44 *Destination Tokyo*, Warners, 1944; d. Delmer Daves; sc. Delmer Daves and Albert Maltz from story by Steve Fisher; l. p. Cary Grant, John Garfield, Alan Hale, Dane Clark, John Ridgely, Warner Anderson.

45 *Once Upon a Time*, Columbia, 1944; d. Alexander Hall; sc. Lewis Meltzer and Oscar Paul from radio play by Norman Corwin and Lucille F. Herrmann; l. p. Cary Grant, Janet Blair, James Gleason, Ted Donaldson, Howard Freeman.

46 *None but the Lonely Heart*, RKO, 1944; d. Clifford Odets; sc. Odets from novel by Richard Llewelyn; l. p. Cary Grant, Ethel Barrymore, Jane Wyatt, June Duprez, Barry Fitzgerald, George Coulouris, Roman Bohnen.

47 *Arsenic and Old Lace*, Warners, 1944; d. Frank Capra; sc. Julius J. and Philip G. Epstein from play by Joseph Kesselring; l. p. Cary Grant, Raymond Massey, Priscilla Lane, Josephine Hull, Jean Adair, Jack Carson.

48 *Night and Day*, Warners, 1946; d. Michael Curtiz; sc. Charles Hoffman, Leo Townsend and William Bowers; l. p. Cary Grant, Alexis Smith, Monty Woolley, Jane Wyman, Eve Arden, Ginny Simms, Victor Francen. (Colour: Technicolor)

49 *Notorious*, RKO, 1946; d. Alfred Hitchcock; sc. Ben Hecht; l. p. Cary Grant, Ingrid Bergman, Louis Calhern, Madame Leopoldine Konstantin,

Claude Rains, Ivan Triesault, Moroni Olsen.

50 *The Bachelor and the Bobbysoxer*, RKO, 1947; d. Irving Reis; sc. Sidney Sheldon; l. p. Cary Grant, Myrna Loy, Shirley Temple, Rudy Vallee, Ray Collins.

51 *The Bishop's Wife*, RKO, 1947; d. Henry Koster; sc. Robert E. Sherwood and Eric Bercovici from novel by Robert Nathan; l. p. Cary Grant, Loretta Young, David Niven, Monty Woolley, James Gleason, Gladys Cooper.

52 *Mr Blandings Builds His Dream-House*, RKO, 1948; d. H.C. Potter; sc. Norman Panama and Melvin Frank from novel by Eric Hodgins; l. p. Cary Grant, Myrna Loy, Melvyn Douglas, Reginald Denny.

53 *Every Girl Should be Married*, RKO, 1948; d. Don Hartman; sc. Hartman and Stephen Morehouse Avery from story by Eleanor Harris; l. p. Cary Grant, Franchot Tone, Diana Lynn, Betsy Drake, Alan Mowbray.

54 *I Was a Male War-bride*, 20th Century-Fox, 1949; d. Howard Hawks; sc. Charles Lederer, Leonard Spigelgass and Hagar Wilde from story by Henri Rochard; l. p. Cary Grant, Ann Sheridan, Kenneth Tobey, Robert Stevenson.

55 *Crisis*, MGM, 1950; d. Richard Brooks; sc. Brooks from story by George Tabori; l. p. Cary Grant, Jose Ferrer, Paula Raymond, Signe Hasso.

56 *People Will Talk*, 20th Century-Fox, 1951; d. Joseph L. Mankiewicz; sc. Mankiewicz from play by Curt Goetz; l. p. Cary Grant, Jeanne Crain, Finlay Currie, Hume Cronyn, Walter Slezak, Sidney Blackmer, Will Wright.

57 *Room For One More*, Warners, 1952; d. Norman Taurog; sc. Jack Rose and Melville Shavelson from book by Anna Perrott Rose; l. p. Cary Grant, Betsy Drake, Lurene Tuttle, Randy Stuart.

58 *Monkey Business*, 20th Century-Fox, 1952; d. Howard Hawks; sc. Ben Hecht, I.A.L. Diamond and Charles Lederer; l. p. Cary Grant, Ginger Rogers, Charles Coburn, Marilyn Monroe, Huge Marlowe.

59 *Dream Wife*, MGM, 1953; d. Sidney Sheldon; sc. Sidney Sheldon, Herbert Baker and Alfred Levitt; l. p. Cary Grant, Deborah Kerr, Betta St John, Walter Pidgeon, Eduard Franz.

60 *To Catch a Thief*, Paramount, 1955; d. Alfred Hitchcock; sc. John Michael Hayes from novel by David Dodge; l. p. Cary Grant, Jessie Royce Landis, John Williams, Charles Vanel. (Colour: Technicolor)

61 *The Pride and the Passion*, United Artists, 1957; d. Stanley Kramer; sc. Edna and Edward Anhalt from novel by C.S. Forester; l. p. Cary Grant, Frank Sinatra, Sophia Loren, Theodore Bikel, John Wengraf. (Colour: Technicolor)

62 *An Affair to Remember*, 20th Century-Fox, 1957; d. Leo McCarey; sc. Delmer Daves and McCarey from story by McCarey and Mildred Cram; l. p. Cary Grant, Deborah Kerr, Richard Denning, Cathleen Nesbitt. (Colour: De Luxe)

63 *Kiss Them For me*, 20th Century-Fox, 1957; d. Stanley Donen; sc. Julius

J. Epstein from play by Luther Davis and novel by Frederic Wakeman; l. p. Cary Grant, Jayne Mansfield, Suzy Parker, Leif Erickson, Ray Walston. (Colour: De Luxe)

64 *Indiscreet*, Warners, 1958; d. Stanley Donen; sc. Norman Krasna from his play; l. p. Cary Grant, Ingrid Bergman, Cecil Parker, Phyllis Calvert (Colour: Technicolor)

65 *Houseboat*, Paramount, 1958; d. Melville Shavelson; sc. Melville Shavelson and Jack Rose; l. p. Cary Grant, Sophia Loren, Martha Hyer, Harry Guardino. (Colour: Technicolor)

66 *North by Northwest*, MGM, 1959; d. Alfred Hitchcock; sc. Ernest Lehman; l. p. Cary Grant, Eva Marie Saint, James Mason, Jessie Royce Landis, Leo G. Carroll, Martin Landau. (Colour: Technicolor)

67 *Operation Petticoat*, Universal, 1959; d. Blake Edwards; sc. Stanley Shapiro and Maurice Richlin from story by Paul King and Joseph Stone; l. p. Cary Grant, Tony Curtis, Joan O'Brien, Dina Merrill. (Colour: Eastman Color)

68 *The Grass is Greener*, Universal, 1961; d. Stanley Donen; sc. Hugh and Margaret Williams from their play; l. p. Cary Grant, Deborah Kerr, Robert Mitchum, Jean Simmons. (Colour: Technicolor)

69 *That Touch of Mink*, Universal, 1962; d. Delbert Mann; sc. Stanley Shapiro and Nate Monaster; l. p. Cary Grant, Doris Day, Gig Young, Alan Hewitt. (Colour: Eastman Color)

70 *Charade*, Universal, 1963; d. Stanley Donen; Peter Stone from story by Stone and Marc Behm; l. p. Cary Grant, Audrey Hepburn, Walter Matthau, James Coburn, George Kennedy, Ned Glass. (Colour: Technicolor)

71 *Father Goose*, Universal, 1964; d. Ralph Nelson; sc. Peter Stone and Frank Tarloff from story by S.H. Barnett; l. p. Cary Grant, Leslie Caron, Trevor Howard. (Colour: Technicolor)

72 *Walk, Don't Run*, Columbia, 1966; d. Charles Walters; sc. Sol Saks from story by Robert Russell and Frank Ross; l. p. Cary Grant, Samantha Eggar, Jim Hutton. (Colour: Technicolor)

Short Films and Guest Appearances

1 *Singapore Sue*, Paramount, 1932. (This short film, written and directed by Casey Robinson, starred Anna Chang, but Grant and Millard Mitchell had supporting roles.)

2 *Hollywood on Parade*, Paramount, 1932-4. (A series of ten-minute shorts giving glimpses of the stars, including Grant.)

3 *Pirate Party on Catalina Island*, MGM, 1936. (Twenty-minute colour film with miscellaneous star appearances.)

4 *Topper Takes a Trip*, United Artists, 1939; d. Norman Z. McLeod. (Grant appears by way of a clip from the original *Topper*.)

5 *The Road to Victory*, Warners, 1944. (A ten-minute film with miscellaneous star appearances.)

6 *Without Reservations*, RKO, 1946; d. Mervyn LeRoy; l. p. Claudette Colbert, John Wayne. (The film includes a brief, uncredited appearance from Grant.)

B

Index

Index